The Life Fantastic

The Life Fantastic

Myth, History, Pop and Folklore in the Making of Western Culture

Noa Menhaim

WATKINS
Sharing Wisdom Since 1893

The Life Fantastic
Noa Menhaim

Translated by Mirjam Meerschwam Hadar
Research assistant: Tamar Neugarten Folger

First published in the UK and USA in 2022 by
Watkins, an imprint of Watkins Media Limited
Unit 11, Shepperton House, 83–93 Shepperton Road
London N1 3DF

enquiries@watkinspublishing.com

A CIP record for this book is available from the British Library

ISBN: 978-1-78678-647-0 (Hardback)
ISBN: 978-1-78678-669-2 (eBook)

10 9 8 7 6 5 4 3 2 1

Typeset by JCS Publishing Services Ltd
Printed in the United Kingdom

www.watkinspublishing.com

CONTENT

PREFACE

Once upon a time, there were only stories. They were here before us, sleeping in darkness and silence, awaiting us. They were here before we learned to point at a snake slithering in the grass; to gesture at the tempting fruit up in the tree; before the first word was uttered. We made them our own, moulded them in clay and drew them in ochre on the walls of caves. Stories of nymphs and fairies, gods and monsters, dragons and the saints who fought them, unicorns and the virgins who tamed them, angel and devil and everything in between. We tried to drive them out, to believe in them, to pray to them and use them. We feared and adored them; in their names we killed and by their grace we lived. Some slumbered for ages, resting between a book's covers under the ruins of a lost city, the desert sands or the deep seas – until they were discovered and restored to life. Others have been with us throughout the ages, adjusting, spreading and shrinking, taking a myriad of forms.

Plato thought of them as ideas – pure forms – casting their shadows on the walls of our cave. For Carl Gustav Jung they were archetypes, images buried deep in our collective unconscious, blooming in a dizzying variety of expressions in the thicket of human culture. Richard Dawkins chose to call them memes, along the lines of genes – units of cultural meaning that use us as replication machines for their single, egotistical purpose, which is the endless proliferation of more cats, fascism, Kardashians, veganism, conspiracy theories and more, always more. And like the biological gene the meme, too, tends to join others of its kind, turning into something more complex. It's like a virus carried by the zeitgeist or transmitted by the genius loci to infect us with cultural diseases, which might take the form of catastrophic plagues such as racism, totalitarianism, xenophobia. Like genes, memes have no will of their own other than the drive to reproduce, to prevail. They multiply, morph into strange mutations, evolve.

And evolve stories must. Time and oblivion are their most formidable enemies, and their rivals are alternative narratives out

An ability, it seems, for which we must thank the snakes themselves (Here Be Dragons, page 79).

Like the one in the "Trois Frères" cave in France (The Human Animal, page 189).

Don't eat or drink anything they give you (Paper Fairies, page 161).

Using their bare breasts (The Lady and the Unicorn, page 179).

Where the oldest library lies (Ex Libris, page 9).

Allowing us to define the absolute *Other* (Blood Lust, page 93).

As a way to realize a utopian vision (Best of All Possible Worlds, page 247).

Which is behind one of the most persistent conspiracy theories (We Come in Peace, page 123).

Seeing their temples turn into churches (Number of the Beast, page 79).

Which were rumored beauties (Valley of the Dolls, page 205).

As they are forever wont to do (Ex Machina, page 213; The Body Electric, page 221).

to destroy and overpower them. Only those that can adapt and transform may survive the ravages of time. This is how pagan deities survive the impact of monotheism's meteor – by growing fangs and horns and resigning themselves to becoming hollowed rather than being hallowed. And this is why Atlantis bides its time, submerged under the waters, waiting until tectonic shifts in our collective psyche alter its aspect so it can rise and usher in a new age. This is also where progress forges a new heart and a new spirit for Hephaestus' automatons, who will rise up against their enslavers.

To shake off their predators, stories hide in fairy tales, lurk in the minds of poets and madmen, stay buried in the recesses of history or camouflage themselves in the most secure hideaway of all, where no one will look for them – the crowded, chaotic hubbub of downtown popular culture.

This collection of essays seeks to trace the sprawling and branching roads and the tangled web these stories, ideas, archetypes and memes weave through the ages, as they interact and intersect each other's orbits. Because every time they cross paths they affect each other, creating new mutations, acquiring additional layers of meaning. Where do they meet? How do they connect? Why do they change in the way that they do? These are some of the questions this book seeks to answer. To that end, I have woven its essays into a cultural network, a web of references – sidenotes – connecting them and allowing readers to plot their own course through the book. Each reference sends you to a different chapter, another adventure, a crossroads where the stories meet, expanding the narrative. You can read the chapters in the order they appear or choose your own path by selecting a particular story you wish to follow, while hopping between references as if they were stepping-stones – for example, from mermaids frolicking in the margins of maps, through bold, fearless Amazons, directly to witches, wicked or otherwise.

The perfect women (Heads or Tails, page 183).

Both real and imaginary (The Territory and the Map, page 47).

Who may or may not have existed (Wonder Women, page 37).

Former goddesses (Weird Sisterhood, page 25).

This book wishes to explore the network, to offer a glimpse into the evolution of stories, illuminate episodes in their past and the path they had to take to get here, revealing the complex relationships they have with each other and with us.

These are the stories we think we are telling.

In fact, they're telling us.

Noa Menhaim

The Life Fantastic

I

A FAUSTIAN BARGAIN

On 15 April 1912, in the cold and dismal waters of the northern Atlantic, 1,517 people drowned. Lost with them in the depths was a special edition of the *Rubáiyát* by the Persian poet Omar Khayyám. Produced in London by the famed bookbinders Sangorski and Sutcliffe, it was known as *The Great Omar* and is one of history's unluckiest tomes. "It has to be the greatest example of bookbinding in the world … Put what you like into the binding, charge what you like for it; the greater the price, the more I shall be pleased, provided only that it is understood that what you do and what you charge will be justified by the result,"[1] instructed the owner of Sotheran's Rare Books and Prints in London, who commissioned this splendid edition. With this carte blanche, Sangorski set to work, throwing himself into the task like a man possessed. He bribed a guard at London Zoo to let him observe a snake swallowing a mouse, to enable him to describe precisely how it opened its maw. He pleaded with a friend who was a medical student to get him a human skull so he could draw it in the finest detail. He worked on the book for two years, in the course of which he used 600 sheets of 22-carat gold leaf and 4,967 leather inlays, as well as ivory, ebony and silver. The binding was embossed with 1,051 precious and semi-precious stones: ruby and emerald, topaz and garnet, turquoise and amethyst. The book in all its splendour was sold to an American collector, carefully packaged and dispatched, only to encounter obtuse tax officials who demanded over twice its value to release the book from customs. Sotheran's refused to pay the exorbitant sum, and so the book was returned to Britain and put into an auction. It only fetched half the price Sangorski and Sutcliffe had hoped to get. Grudgingly, they sent the book to its new owner in New York on board a ship that was famously unsinkable.

About a month after the sinking of the *Titanic*, Sangorski leapt into the water to rescue a drowning woman. He could not swim. The depths claimed him, just as they had swallowed up his creation, *The Great Omar*.

Six years later a second edition was made by Stanley Bray, based on Sangorski's original drawings. When it was completed, it was placed in a safe at a London bank for security. In 1941, during the Blitz when the German Luftwaffe bombed London, this safe, with the book inside it, went up in flames, ironically reflecting Omar Khayyam's own wise words, "The worldly hope men set their hearts upon turns [to] ashes."[2]

Books burned in that very same war were the inspiration for one of the great dystopias of the twentieth century (Best of All Possible Worlds, page 247).

But while the worldly glory of these two volumes of *The Great Omar* was lost to water and fire, the poet's words were preserved, thanks to the most brilliant and revolutionary invention ever, a simple time machine, a capsule of immortality, an object of desire.

"When our genes could not store all the information necessary for survival, we slowly invented brains," wrote Carl Sagan, "but then the time came, perhaps ten thousand years ago, when we needed to know more than could conveniently be contained in brains. So, we learned to stockpile enormous quantities of information outside our bodies. We are the only species on the planet, so far as we know, to have invented a communal memory stored neither in our genes nor in our brains."[3] This external memory is the book.

Despite doomsday prophecies of the book's impending demise and periodic laments about its waning glories, rumours concerning its death are highly exaggerated. Books are the building blocks of our culture, the paper engines of the first information revolution and one of the most marvellous synergies of technological progress driving our civilization.

The person responsible for this sea change was a failed businessman. He was a serial inventor who often found himself knee deep in debt, a man whose promises were not worth the paper they were written on, as Ennelin, a woman from Strasbourg to whom he proposed, soon found out. In 1439, the city of Aachen was preparing to display its holy relics. Among them were the Virgin Mary's immaculately white delivery robe; Jesus's swaddling clothes; the sponge that wetted His lips on the Cross; a piece of the Cross encased in gold, known as the Talisman of Charlemagne; part of the skull belonging to the first holy Roman emperor himself; and many more.

Johannes Gensfleisch, scion of a family of goldsmiths, could smell an opportunity in the stifling, ill-reeking air of the thriving medieval city. In Aachen Cathedral, these famous relics were put on public display every seven years. They drew tens of thousands of pilgrims daily, all hoping to sneak a peek at the richly decorated golden reliquaries. The sheer number of pilgrims was so vast that those standing at the back had no hope of redemption. As medieval Catholicism was a visual religion, the pilgrims had to be able to see the relics, feasting their eyes on saintly remains such as St Thomas the Apostle's finger, to benefit from their miraculous properties. This gave Gensfleisch an idea. He polished some small metal mirrors to sell to the pilgrims, to hold up and catch a glimpse of the marvellous rays emanating from the relics. But the relic display was delayed by heavy flooding, and Gensfleisch's investment tanked. He fled to Strasbourg in an apparent attempt to escape his creditors and changed his name into something that sounded more respectable than Gensfleisch, which means "goose flesh". He chose his mother's maiden name: Gutenberg.

When he had his next big idea, he happened to be in the right place at the right time. Paper makers had refined their production methods and were coming up with smoother and more evenly textured sheets; metal refining processes enabled Gutenberg to produce an alloy of lead, tin and antimony that could be made into the casts needed for the 297 letters, punctuation marks and special characters making up movable type. Meanwhile, he was able to adapt wine presses, which had become smaller and more transportable, to press the raised type surfaces onto the paper.

Strictly speaking, printing was not invented by Gutenberg. Some 400 years earlier, on the other side of the globe in China, the artisan Bi Sheng had attempted to stamp ink onto paper using ceramic type surfaces, but due to the many thousands of characters Chinese script required and the fragility of the material used to make them, his invention was only marginally successful. Gutenberg had both the inspiration and the ability to bring everything together into a working mechanism, but he needed financial support for his start-up. His angel investor was named Faust, Johann Faust. The 800 guilders seed money Faust gave Gutenberg is the current equivalent of about $275,000 (£200,000). Gutenberg set to work. He wanted to demonstrate the beauty and legibility of his press by printing what was considered the greatest work bestowed on humankind: the Bible. But in the fifteenth century, creating a copy of the holy book took more than just inspiration – Gutenberg needed to obtain the Church's permission. So, the first printed sheets that came off

Pilgrims who wished to use shortcuts could avail themselves of mazes (A Rat in a Maze, page 147).

There is at least one synthetic religion in which emanating rays signal a mortal threat (Remember to Forget, page 139).

his printing press were aimed at currying favour with the clerics. To enable them to exploit the Holy See's most lucrative source of income, absolution, Gutenberg made handsome and astonishingly identical copies of indulgences.

In her book *The March of Folly*, Barbara Tuchman quotes Johann Tetzel, God's sales representative in Germany, who displayed his wares at town gates announcing, "I have here the passports ... to lead the human soul to the celestial joys of Paradise." And when penance for a mortal sin came to seven years of atonement, not many people hesitated to spend a quarter of a guilder on an indulgence, which could also be used for others, post-mortem "... as soon as a coin in the bowl rings, a soul from purgatory springs."[4] Still, someone had to produce all the indulgences in the first place, and this exhausting task generally fell to monks. Well, no longer: Gutenberg's press was a licence to print money for the Church. Gutenberg was given permission to print the Bible and on 23 February 1455 the print-run began. The first edition consisted of between 158 and 180 copies.

But power-drunk with the new possibilities of the printing press, the Church forgot that once Gutenberg's revolutionary invention was widely known and copied, everyone would be able to use it. Meanwhile, the lifestyle of the pope and the princes of the Church grew more and more extravagant, though no one went as far as Pope Leo X, Johann Tetzel's direct employer. He had gratefully accepted a gift from the King of Portugal of a white elephant that carried "under a jewelled howdah a chest decorated with silver towers and battlements and contained rich vestments, gold chalices and books in fine bindings for Leo's delight,"[5] as Tuchman recounts. To fund such displays of riches, the Church created a lively trade in indulgences, which resulted in a vertiginous rise in their spread. This provoked the ire of a monk and priest in Wittenberg, who was also a doctor of theology – a certain Martin Luther. Responding to Tetzel's undertakings with a (probably apocryphal) act of defiance that bordered on the heretical, Luther nailed his "Ninety-five Theses" to the door of a church. Though this particular pamphlet was handwritten, a shrewd entrepreneur had the theses quickly printed and distributed widely. And so, Protestant protest took off.

Gutenberg's movable-type printing press may not have been much more than a small step for the man who invented it, but it

Like any good travel agent, he neglected to mention the place was probably boring (Moving Heaven and Hell, page 71).

Since it was forbidden to light a fire in the scriptorium, many of them were built near the kitchen so the monks could enjoy some warmth (Ex Libris, page 9).

was a giant leap for humankind. A new type of human emerged, no longer just *homo sapiens* or thinking man, but *homo legens*, reading man. Books published before 1500 now became known as *incunabula* (from the Latin for swaddling clothes). Wrapped in them, humanity crawled out of its cradle. The hand that rocked it – Gutenberg's – was stilled only a dozen years after his movable type set a new era in motion. Gutenberg had had to borrow more and more money and was forced to sell increasingly more of his business to repay his debts. His reward was devastation rather than indulgence, as the Faustian bargain he signed left him destitute. He lost all rights to his invention and the revenue it made, and in his later years lived on a stipend awarded by Archbishop von Nassau, along with tax exemptions on wheat and wine. Gutenberg died in 1468 and was buried at the Franciscan church in Mainz. In August 1942, RAF Bomber Command launched 158 bombers to attack the city. When they returned to England, all that remained of the Franciscan church was a scorched shell. Like *The Great Omar* the year before, Gutenberg's grave went up in flames.

As the scholar who sold his soul for knowledge found out in a story that emerged in Germany only a few years later, one should never bargain with the Devil. (Number of the Beast, page 79)

The fate of other cultural treasures during this war was more fortunate (Flame and Moth, page 17).

The Old and New Testaments, which had habitually been chained to the shelves in monasteries and churches, were now set free from their intellectual bondage. Until the printing press revolution, reading was the privilege of the few, while owning books was enjoyed by even fewer. Within 50 years, the number of printed books in Europe rose from a few hundred to about nine million. Books were now held in the calloused hands of the working classes, written in local vernacular, and could be bought at a (relatively) reasonable price. Literacy became all the rage among the aristocracy and knights set aside their swords for the mighty pen. Books paved the way for those who wished to improve their social status, and created new classes composed of men of words and letters. Henry VIII, concerned that women and apprentices would get unholy ideas, forbade them to read the Bible. The English Civil War produced a slew of pamphlets and posters, bolstering religious fervour. Before the French Revolution was written in blood on the cobblestones of Paris, it was composed in ink on Rousseau's pages. His popular works, which were printed and reprinted, had such an extensive readership and explosive content that they were burned in Geneva and banned in Paris.

Who also had other dangerous ideas (Paradise Lost, page 171).

The Communist Manifesto, a modest 23-page pamphlet written in the Reading Rooms of the British Library (which, coincidentally, still holds the third and final copy of *The Great Omar* completed by Bray in 1989), had the historic fortune to leave the printing press less than two weeks before the outbreak of the 1848 revolution in Berlin.

But the printing press did not only spell blood, sweat and tears. From its cradle, childhood itself emerged: dividing those who didn't yet know how to read from those who had mastered that coveted skill. Women, too, achieved liberation, first as readers then as writers, producing some of the greatest bestsellers of the nineteenth century. The popularity of books was such that respectable ladies were sternly advised to abstain from excessive reading, to avoid a descent into promiscuity and other infirmities of the body and soul.

Although sometimes they themselves remain anonymous (The Body Electric, page 221).

If only Emma Bovary had heeded this warning (The Pleasure Principle, page 195).

One more revolution, maybe the most important of all, entered under the paper wings of the printing press: privacy. At first, high book prices and low literacy rates meant that gathering around someone else reading aloud was the norm. Even after book prices dropped and literacy rates rose, dramatic readings, whether with 3,000 other people in a crowded hall listening to Charles Dickens or in the company of friends and family in a private parlour, remained a popular and inexpensive form of entertainment.

But eventually reading became an intimate act between reader and book, whether in bed or in a crowded train compartment. Privacy is what allows the reader to burst out laughing alone in a café, to dissolve in tears on a street bench or to sink into profound reflection while waiting for their doctor's appointment. No wonder then that throughout history, dictators have censored books. The individual is a dangerous creature once it becomes aware of its own existence.

They did more than just censoring them (Best of All Possible Worlds, page 247).

The library, the second-hand or antiquarian bookshop – these are book lovers' meeting places. They have their communities, imagined or physical. They recognize each other by special marks and signs. The dog-ear community, the community of marginal notes, used books aficionados, bestseller fans, rare book hunters, slow and fast readers, those who go for polyamorous relations with three or five books at once, or the monogamous – faithful to one book until the end do them part – cookbook gluttons, travelogue tourists and, of course, bibliophiles, lovers of the book for its own sake. As Michel Montaigne wrote in the sixteenth century, there are "more books upon books than upon any other subject".[6]

Books have been dedicated to the history of the book, like *A History of Reading* by Alberto Manguel; the pleasures it gives: *Ex Libris* by Anne Fadiman; about how we may enter a book, as in Jasper Fforde's *The Eyre Affair* or Michael Ende's *The Neverending Story;* there are books about bookshops, like Helene Hanff's *84 Charing Cross Road*, including mobile ones, as in *The Uncommon Reader* by Alan Bennett or *Parnassus on Wheels* by Christopher Morley. And more books – about books' mysterious and mystical powers – for example, Arturo Pérez-Reverte's *The Club Dumas*, Scarlett Thomas' *The End of Mr Y*, Carlos Ruiz Zafón's *The Shadow of the Wind* or Umberto Eco's *The Name of the Rose*.

Some books are better left unopened, or at least returned (Ex Libris, page 9; Fear Itself, page 237)

Bibliophilia is all about sensual and fetishistic pleasure: you take your book to bed. With trembling fingers, you stroke the smooth binding, the rough cloth, the spine; you open the hard cover to reveal the virginal white pages inside or fold back the soft cover enclosing much handled yellowing ones; you sniff, take a deep breath and immerse yourself.

Print has the power to transform and stir us, to transport us elsewhere and take us inside ourselves to other places of delight, wonder, terror, awe and illumination.

A book is a monument. A memorial. Whether it is the priceless Gutenberg Bible or the online Gutenberg Project preserving the literature of the past; whether we read it printed on actual paper or digitally on a screen. It is a hallowed space, a place of refuge and a destination.

2
EX LIBRIS

It was 27 December 2012 when Mrs Shannon Benoit opened her front door to face police officer Daniel P Dowd. In front of her appalled five-year-old daughter Hailey, the police officer explained to Mrs Benoit that he was there because the family had failed to return two books to the local library. Hailey asked her mom if the police were going to arrest her, then burst into tears. "Sending the police around was like pounding a ten-penny [small] nail with a sledgehammer",[1] Shannon Benoit said, when she explained why she turned to the local media in Massachusetts. "I'm getting email from all over the country," stated Cheryl Hansen, Charlton Library Director. "I've been called a f—ing moron, an idiot, a Nazi, a Communist."[2] In a TV interview, Hansen clarified that the police visit hadn't been about returning Hailey's book, which was two years overdue, but concerned an audio book by Stephen King, which her father Tony had taken out in 2009 and forgotten to take back. The Benoit household was one of 13 to receive a visit of this kind that day, in an attempt to recover a total value of $2,634 (£1,918) in fines for the municipal library. The Benoits' share came to $133 (£97).

It's better not to get in his way (Fear Itself, page 237).

The audio collection of horror stories Tony Benoit had borrowed from the library was called *Just After Sunset*. He might well have been more prompt in returning the item if it had been King's *Four Past Midnight*. The hero of one of the stories in that collection, "The Library Policeman", encounters the ghost of a monstrous librarian, who feeds off the fear of children she confronts with a trauma from their past, while warning them to be sharp about returning their books.

Other librarians used a less subtle approach, as shown in this inscription from a Bible enshrined in the hallowed halls of the British Library: "A book of [the Abbey of] SS Mary and Nicholas of Arnstein: if anyone steals it, may he die [the death], may he be roasted in a frying pan, may the falling sickness [i.e. epilepsy] and fever attack him and may he be rotated [on the breaking wheel] and hanged. Amen."[3]

An implement of punishment also used on werewolves (Lupus Est, page 93).

In 1172, those were the words a monk in Germany in charge of copying manuscripts scribbled into the colophon – the page that shows a book's publishing details. In addition to the illustrations in the book's margins (the marginalia), the colophon was the one space where the scribe could leave his own mark. "In the scriptorium there were rules within rules," writes Stephen Greenblatt in *The Swerve: How the World Became Modern*. "Absolute silence reigned. Scribes were not allowed to choose the particular books that they copied or to break the dead silence by requesting aloud from the librarian such books as they might wish to consult."[4] The harsh discipline of the scriptorium was imposed because of the high value of the objects being copied by the scribes, who worked from dawn till dusk (use of candles was strictly prohibited) as an act of humility and obedience. "Books were scarce and valuable. They conferred prestige on the monastery that possessed them …. On occasion monasteries tried to secure their possession by freighting [loading] their precious manuscripts with curses,"[5] writes Greenblatt. However, the colophon curses of the German scribe pale into insignificance compared to the words King Ashurbanipal ordered to be inscribed in cuneiform on the clay tablets in his library: "Whosoever shall carry off this tablet, or shall inscribe his name on it side by side with mine own, may Ashur and Belit overthrow him in wrath and anger, and may they destroy his name and posterity in the land." [6]

History shows such warnings are not enough (Remember to Forget, page 139).

Containing the first account of a zombie apocalypse (Head Hunters, page 231).

The library kept by Ashurbanipal, last of the great Assyrian kings, had been passed down to him by his grandfather, the famous Sennacherib, who had established it in his palace in 689 BC. Among other items the library held the most ancient known literature: the *Epic of Gilgamesh*, which includes the first written account of the myth of the Great Flood, and *Enuma Elish*, the Babylonian creation narrative. Unlike most rulers of his time, Ashurbanipal was literate and personally devised a system to organize his library. He also told his warriors to bring him any book they found on their military exploits so that he could add it to his library. In this same collection, British archeologist Austen Henry Layard also uncovered remnants of the kingdom's bureaucracy: contracts, ordinances, grants and royal correspondence, which were all carefully copied and preserved for posterity. But when the Median–Babylonian–Scythian alliance invaded the city and destroyed it in 614 BC they set no store by souvenirs. Nineveh, as the prophet Jonah had foretold, was turned upside down. Many of the texts it held were made of inflammable materials, such as parchments or papyrus scrolls, and these were consumed by the fires, lost forever. But maybe thanks to the ruler's mighty curses, the clay tablets were preserved by the flames. As opposed to paper, which burns at 451° Fahrenheit (232.8° Celsius), the unbaked clay tablets of the Nineveh library solidified in the fire, and were buried under the smouldering ruins and the desert sands.

The natural enemy of books (Flame and Moth, page 17).

As Ray Bradbury illustrated effectively (Best of All Possible Worlds, page 247).

According to legend it was when facing these ruins – which by then had cooled down considerably – that Alexander the Great conceived of his megalomaniac idea of building a library to outdo Ashurbanipal's. In the city named after him, his heirs took up the challenge to realize this grand vision.

Ptolemy I, a general in the great conqueror's army, became the ruler of a city that started as a small fishing village and within 50 years had grown into the largest metropolis of its time. Ptolemaic Alexandria was a lively trading hub, a polyglot, cosmopolitan and bustling capital that was waging a military and cultural war for supremacy against other inheritor-kingdoms after Alexander the Great's death. The construction of the library, which was attached to the *mouseion* – the hall of the muses, an adjacent research institute – was an important step in both establishing the city's identity and imposing its language and values on its surroundings. If Alexander, a follower of Aristotle, had sought to rule the entire world, then the library erected in the city named after him came to annex the knowledge of that world. The city's rulers and librarians had infallible methods for enriching their collection. They used money: the library's envoys were sent to scout for books throughout the land (the fruits of their labour included forgeries made by clever businessmen that were only revealed to be fakes centuries later). They used force: all papyrus scrolls they could find on ships anchored in the city's port were impounded and copied (with the owners receiving back the copies). They used stealth: as did Ptolemy when he paid the city of Athens a huge surety in return for a glimpse of the authorized version of the great tragedies, which was kept under lock and key in that cradle of Western civilization. (The Athenians were eventually persuaded to let Ptolemy see the texts and he never returned them.) And finally, they used words: the library initiated several translation projects that made knowledge

An act with diabolical consequences (Number of the Beast, page 79).

from other cultures available to its Greek-reading scholars. This was how Persian texts were translated, introducing them to Zoroastrianism, and also how the Septuagint, the first Greek translation of the Hebrew Bible, was produced. The library drew in people, too: philosophers and mathematicians, poets and engineers. The greatest minds of the times gathered there to wander through its wide corridors and exchange ideas with other great thinkers while enjoying a very generous reception, courtesy of the city.

Estimates of the number of books the library held range between half a million and 70,000. Even the most modest estimates would still make any abbot turn green with envy and drive the blind venerable Jorge, the ancient monk in Umberto Eco's *The Name of the Rose*, to reach for his cask of poison. But it wasn't the Christians who were responsible for the destruction of the great library of Alexandria and its large collection of pagan writings. Nor can Julius Caesar be blamed for burning the library during Rome's imperialist wars, even if the flames apparently reached parts of the collection and damaged it when he set fire to the ships anchored in Alexandria's harbour. Fittingly for a library that became legendary, the stories circulating about its destruction took on mythical proportions. It was attributed not only to the Christians and the Romans, but also to the Muslims led by Caliph Umar ibn Al-Khattab, even though they occupied the city almost a thousand years after the library was built. Contemporary historians believe that the real enemy behind the destruction of the Great Library was the most fearful of all – the enemy no wall holds out against and who vanquishes even the most experienced warlords – time itself.

Don't believe everything you hear about him (Flame and Moth, page 17).

As the fourth-century Roman historian Ammianus Marcellinus wrote, "And the libraries closed for ever, like so many graves."[7] By AD 350 Rome had erected 29 public libraries for its citizens throughout the city, including some in the bathhouses – inventing, it seems, the habit of reading in the toilet. But eventually even the eternal city fell and, along with it, Western culture declined. Its central storehouse of memories – the library – sank into the oblivion of the Dark Ages. The one spark of light that survived in this gloom was that the monks, usually Benedictines, preserved what remained of this knowledge in their painstaking work, as well as recording the wisdom of their own times.

Still, as long as these books had to be copied by hand and were accessible to only a very limited literate readership in a largely illiterate Europe (while literacy was blossoming and libraries abounded in the Muslim world), they were few and far between, and vulnerable to religious reformations and political upheavals. All this took an unexpected turn in 1440 when a hapless goldsmith converted a wine press into the first movable type printing press and changed the world forever.

Who never cashed in a penny from this invention (A Faustian Bargain, page 1).

What would have happened if the Great Library of Alexandria had survived? This is the question behind a series of books by Rachel Caine called *The Great Library*. Her alternative history imagines that the library continued into present times, turning into the world's most powerful institution. Because, if "Ignorance Is Strength", as the Party ruling the life of Winston Smith, the hero of George Orwell's *1984*, dictates, then the force of knowledge is even more immense. That is why Big Brother and his collaborators do everything to destroy it through the actions of the Ministry of Truth where Winston Smith works. Terry Pratchett used a similar principle when he formulated the equation: knowledge = power = energy = mass. He argues that since general relativity theory teaches us that mass distorts time and space, a book store is but a "genteel Black Hole that knows how to read",[8] to say nothing of a library. By this illogic, which underlies his series of *Discworld* books, the larger the library, the greater the distortion in space–time. And the greatest library of all, of course, is the Library of Babel, created by Jorge Luis Borges, whose name Umberto Eco used for his blind monk, Jorge de Burgos.

A dystopia pretending to be a utopia (Best of All Possible Worlds, page 247).

Borges' fictional library holds the largest possible number of volumes, covering all variations of what can be generated by the 52 upper-and-lower-case letters of the Latin alphabet, the 14 customary punctuation marks and the space. This comes to about $67^{1,312,000}$ (67 to the power of one million, three hundred and twelve thousand). Of necessity, among these must appear all the classics of literature, past, present and future, but one could search the library for an entire lifetime without finding anything. The protagonist of Borges' story, who was born in this near infinite library, has witnessed the misery of those who scour it for meaning but only find books that make no sense. They know that all knowledge, everything secret and all answers are within their grasp, but are condemned to spend their lives looking for them in vain. This library has its own history, religions, a god even – or rather a librarian who has managed to lay his hand on the library's catalogue. This is the key of keys to everything including "the detailed history of the future, the autobiographies of the archangels … thousands and thousands of false catalogs, the proof of the falsity of those false catalogs, a proof of the falsity of the true catalog … the true story of your death, the translation of every book into every language, the interpolations of every book into all books, the treatise Bede could have written (but did not) on the mythology of the Saxon people, the lost books of Tacitus".[9]

At least the one in which he immortalized Boudica survived (Wonder Women, page 37).

Borges based his library on, and even lent some of the books in it from, "The Universal Library", a short story by Kurd Lasswitz, a little-known early-twentieth-century German writer of science fiction. This story is essentially a scholarly thought-experiment in dialogue form, exploring "all the variations of wording nobody has thought up yet. You'll find the lost works of Tacitus and their translations into all living and dead languages. Furthermore … all forgotten and still undelivered speeches in all parliaments, the official version of the Universal Declaration of Peace, the history of the subsequent wars, all the compositions all of us wrote in school and college".[10] In Garth Nix's series *The Old Kingdom*, only armed and well-trained librarians can find their way into the lower tiers of the library of everything. Pratchett's Unseen University's library swarms with voracious thesauruses, and research students lost in its thickets have organized themselves into tribes, preying on each other among the shelves. The library in Patrick Rothfuss's *The Name of the Wind* is an enormous labyrinth, with secret passages and dubious under-catalogued zones, which are best avoided after dark. In the *Dr Who* episode entitled "Silence in the Library", the great library of everything is the size of a planet, infested by a race of flesh-eating shadows, lurking – well, in the shadows.

That maybe – and maybe not – a Minotaur resides in (A Rat in a Maze, page 147).

For Borges, libraries were something else altogether, "I have always imagined Paradise as a kind of library."[11]

Most representations of paradise have no books (Moving Heaven and Hell, page 71).

It fell to Borges to become a ministering angel in this paradise. In 1937, he was employed as an assistant librarian in the municipal library in his hometown of Buenos Aires. In the beginning, not unlike Milton's Satan, he felt he might be better off reigning over hell. His job consisted mainly of the classification and cataloguing of the library's substantial collection, a tedious job, which he described in retrospect as years of misery. His colleagues, who tended to be more interested in fast horses and loose women than literature, were irritated by his efficiency and asked him to slow down so they did not look bad by comparison. Borges learned how to make the best of his predicament and made a habit of finishing all of his daily duties as soon as he arrived, which gave him plenty of time to translate William Faulkner and Virginia Woolf, as well as work on his own stories such as "The Library of Babel", which was written in this limbo and reflects his sense of occupational ennui. The years of misery ground to a halt with the rise to power of Juan Perón in 1946 who, like other fellow dictators throughout history, had a special dislike of intellectuals, books and libraries. Borges the anti-Peronist was "promoted" to oversee the sale of chickens and rabbits at the local markets, and resigned from this lofty position almost immediately. Three years later he wrote "The Wall and the Books", which was about the iniquities of another absolute and cruel ruler, Shih Huang Ti, who united China and had the Great Wall constructed. This same emperor also ordered the "burning of books and burying of scholars", resulting in hundreds of Confucians being buried alive and a huge number of philosophical tracts, books of poetry and scientific publications being burned. "That the two gigantic operations … issued from one person and were in a certain sense his attributes, inexplicably satisfied me and, at the same time, disturbed me," wrote Borges. And, "Perhaps Shih Huang Ti walled in the empire because he knew it was fragile and he destroyed the books because he understood they were sacred books, or rather books that taught that which the entire universe teaches or the consciousness of every man."[12] In one of those about-turns befitting the Fates' macabre sense of humour, when Perón was removed from office in 1955 Borges was appointed director of Argentina's national library, by which time he had gone totally blind due to a hereditary disease. "Of God; who with such splendid irony, granted me books and night at one touch,"[13] he wrote.

Those who accused the library director of Charlton, Massachusetts, of Communism had a point. Perón and his ilk disliked books and the places where they are kept – "palaces for the people" as Andrew Carnegie, the industrialist and patron of libraries, called them – because of their power to democratize. This is probably why President Trump's administration cancelled the federal

Both real and imagined (Best of All Possible Worlds, page 247).

They have to maintain their sense of humour after everything they have had to endure (Weird Sisterhood, page 25).

budget for public libraries in the years 2018, 2019 and 2020 and why Shih Huang Ti punished book collectors by dispatching them to toil on his great construction project. Public libraries have the power to break down walls. Eric Klinenberg, in his *Palaces for the People*, writes that they are "places where people from different backgrounds not only share space but seek each other's presence, and occasionally forge relationships as well".[14] That was what Andrew Carnegie believed when he contributed $550,000,000 (£400,000,000) for the establishment of 2,509 libraries worldwide, more than half of which were in the United States. "It was from my own early experience that I decided there was no use to which money could be applied so productive of good to girls and boys who have good within them and ability and ambition to develop it, as the founding of a public library," said Carnegie, "I am sure that the future of those libraries I have been privileged to found will prove the correctness of this opinion."[15]

For the poet Maya Angelou, the library "is a rainbow in the clouds". As she declared during an event at the New York Public Library celebrating her work, "No bad thing can happen to you in the library." She recounted how she felt when she first visited a library, looked at all the thousands of books and wondered if she could ever read them all: "Will I live long enough?"[16] she asked herself.

From the first Flood, documented in cuneiform on the clay tablets kept in Ashurbanipal's library at Nineveh, all the way to Maya Angelou's rainbow – no matter what universe libraries inhabit, they will always be redolent of dust and paper. Their halls will always be filled with a murmuring silence and they will be home to more books than we will be able to read in a lifetime, for libraries are the gateway to eternity.

3

FLAME AND MOTH

In the huge archives of the British Library, a bunch of yellowing pages lingered for around two centuries. They carried the text of a play written in the early seventeenth century. Even in that same century attempts had been made to identify the author of what was known as *The Second Maiden's Tragedy*. An anonymous hand had added three possible names to the title page: Thomas Goffe, a minor Jacobean playwright; George Chapman, the Elizabethan translator and poet; and William Shakespeare, the most famous playwright of all time. When Charles Hamilton, an expert on manuscripts, came across the text in the early 1990s, he became convinced that this was *Cardenio*, Shakespeare's so-called lost play. The most prevalent assumption is that this play, if it ever existed, proves the link between two great authors who happened to die only a day apart: Shakespeare and Miguel de Cervantes. Cardenio, a man who loses his mind because of his unrequited love for a young lady by the name of Luscinda, is one of the figures whom Don Quixote, "the knight of the sorry face", keeps meeting on his travels. As the first part of Cervantes' novel was translated into English in 1612, it would have been available to Shakespeare at the time *Cardenio* might have been composed.

Hamilton's argument drew criticism. The quality of *The Second Maiden's Tragedy* left many experts and other readers in doubt. The fact that there was another claimant to the title "the real Cardenio" didn't help either. In 1727, a playwright called Lewis Theobald published *Double Falsehood*, suggesting it was based on three lost manuscripts by Shakespeare and constituted an adaptation of the original play, an argument that has the support of many contemporary researchers. The quest for the holy grail of the stage continues to fascinate specialists and laypeople alike, providing the plot for Jasper Fforde's amusing *Lost in a Good Book*, in which inferior forgeries of *Cardenio* are part of a worldwide literary conspiracy.

Quite a few conspiracies were involved in the search for it, too (King of Cups, page 153).

Literature has many enemies – humanmade and God-sent alike. Masterpieces were lost in the vicissitudes of time and fell prey to fire and moths. The long history of burning books branded

Predecessors of Winston Smith and his colleagues at the Ministry of Truth (Best of All Possible Worlds, page 247).

In spite of its pagan tendencies (Twilight of the Gods, page 65; Lupus Est, page 93).

Scientist and poet, like many of his contemporaries (The Body Electric, page 221).

After all, he clerked for Oliver Cromwell (Number of the Beast, page 79).

Who was used to being persecuted for his opinions (Moving Heaven and Hell, page 71).

In his case, at least, they may have had good reasons (The Pleasure Principle, page 195).

This quote is, apparently, apocryphal. It was already attributed by some to the Caliph in the context of the burning of the Library of Alexandria, but as early as the eighteenth century the historian Edward Gibbon doubted its veracity and it has since been repeatedly refuted (Ex Libris, page 9).

Which was undoubtedly beautifully printed (A Faustian Bargain, page 1).

as harmful is seared into the annals of civilization. Jehoiakim, King of Judah and the prophet Jeremiah's great rival, cast the prophecy that spelled his fate "into the fire that was on the hearth, until all the roll was consumed".[1] Less flamboyant methods of dealing with this burning problem were available as well. No need to set fire to books if all it takes is to ban them and put them under lock and key. This is the insight behind the *Index Librorum Prohibitorum*, the Catholic Church's most unwanted list, first published in 1529. The people with the best job in the Vatican, those who got to gawk at all that forbidden material, were the members of the Sacred Congregation of the Index, established in 1571. The most recent change to the Index was made in 1948. While it omits *Mein Kampf*, the blacklist includes authors like Laurence Sterne, Erasmus Darwin, Germaine de Staël, Daniel Defoe, John Milton, Dante Alighieri, the Marquis de Sade, George Sand, Simone de Beauvoir and Nobel laureates such as André Gide and Jean-Paul Sartre.

From Jehoiakim's days, the Jews themselves were responsible for a few book burnings of their own because of internal antagonisms – Maimonides' writings, like later Hasidic texts, landed on the pyre. Fervent religious faith fanned the flames kindled by Umar ibn Al-Khattab, the second caliph of the Rashidun Caliphate, in the seventh century. This was the brilliant syllogism he used when telling his army to set fire to the books of the vanquished Persians, "If these writings agree with the book of God, they are useless and need not be preserved; if they disagree, they are pernicious and ought to be destroyed."[2] Which did not prevent his own holy book, the Qur'an, from eventually being thrown into the flames by the inquisitor Torquemada, along with the Jews' sacred texts.

Christians were not fire resistant either – in 1520 Martin Luther burned Pope Leo X's papal bull *Exsurge Domine*, which threatened him with expulsion if he did not recant his heresy. Leo X's own writings were cast into the fire by Charles V following the Diet of Worms a year later, as well as by Henry VIII and Luther himself. In 1817, Wartburg Castle, where Luther had translated the Bible into German, was the site where books considered "anti-German" were committed to the flames. This was the event that led Heinrich Heine to write *Almansor*, a tragedy set in Granada, Spain in 1492, depicting the burning of the Qur'an by the Christian conquerors. It includes his famous prophecy, "That was but a prelude; where they burn books, they will ultimately burn people also."[3] Heine's hot potato was consigned to the bonfire on 10 May 1933, where it burned together with 20,000 other books, including works by Thomas Mann, Karl Marx, Sigmund Freud, Stefan Zweig, Erich Kästner and many others. And as Heine foresaw, this was just a prelude. The epilogue is Micha Ullman's artistic response, sunk into Berlin's Bebel Square, formerly Opernplatz, precisely at the spot where Goebbels' pyre burned. "The Empty Library", unveiled in 1995, is marked by a copper plate carrying Heine's above quoted words and consists of an underground room with a glass ceiling window, set into the square's pavement. Looking down into this space you see empty white shelves going down to a depth of five metres (16 feet), representing shelves robbed of the 20,000 books taken from the world and sent up in smoke.

One of the casualties of the war that Ullman's memorial eternalizes is the library at Monte Cassino, the first monastery Benedict of Nursia erected around AD 530. It is situated on a high hill overlooking the road between Naples and Rome. Because of its strategic location, his acolytes, the Benedictines, were forced to counter repeated raids that started with the Lombards in the fifth century and continued down through the ages to Napoleon's soldiers in the eighteenth century. The site also survived natural disasters, such as a severe earthquake in 1349 that completely destabilized it. The monastery was destroyed and rebuilt. Demolished yet enduring, its library had assumed a place of honour and renown in the annals of Western culture and learning by the early twentieth century, as it contained rare ancient manuscripts, including works by Virgil, Horace and Ovid. These had been collected, kept and copied on the site throughout the centuries. But neither stone walls, paper barricades nor faith's fortifications were of any avail on 15 February 1944. War was raging and amid the devastation there was a struggle for preservation. The hurly-burly of battle was almost hushed by the voices of those who sought to protect what Lord Cosmo Lang of Lambeth called – during a heated debate in the House of Lords – "objects of historic or cultural value within the theatres of war". Not everyone agreed, of course. "There are those who ask impatiently, and rather contemptuously, 'What is the worth of these dead stones and dead pictures in comparison with the life of one single soldier?'" admitted Lord Lang. "But," he continued, "these things are not dead. They are always alive;

> On the foundations of an ancient pagan Temple for Apollo, which was still active when St Benedict arrived at the site and, as was customary, smashed the statues and appropriated it (Number of the Beast, page 79).

they have … the quality of enhancing life, of giving fresh vitality to the mind and spirit of successive generations."

He was referring, among other things, to repositories of knowledge such as the monastery of Monte Cassino, "renowned through all these centuries for its scholarship and devotion. It contains priceless manuscripts and books."[4]

This sentiment was echoed across the ocean in the words of US President Dwight D Eisenhower, who in a memo to army commanders dated 26 May 1944, wrote, "Shortly we will be fighting our way across the countries of Europe in a battle designed to preserve our civilization. Inevitably in the path of our advance will be found historical monuments and cultural centers that symbolize to the world all that we are fighting to preserve. It is the responsibility of every commander to protect and respect those symbols wherever possible."[5] American Army General George Marshall sought to address the Italian population, "by the use of radio, leaflets and any other means available" and advised them "to remove all movable works of art from cities and locations subject to damage by military operations".[6]

These concerns did not fall on deaf ears among the nation that produced Thomas Mann, Karl Marx, Sigmund Freud, Stefan Zweig, Erich Kästner and Heinrich Heine. In October 1943, the Germans reached an arrangement with the abbot of Monte Cassino that the abbey's literary and cultural treasures would be evacuated.

The collection consisted of around 70,000 volumes and 80,000 documents, in addition to priceless works of art by da Vinci, Raphael, Titian and others, as well as ancient sculptures, tapestries, reliquaries and more. All these items were packed by the monks, residents of the area and German soldiers into 700 crates and transported in 100 trucks to where the ravages of war could no longer hurt them.

But all this took time. And in war time equals life. So, when the library treasures had been removed and secured but the Germans remained on the mountain, the Allied forces decided to attack the stronghold. A cluster of bomber planes was sent to drop 1,400 tons of high explosives on the monastery and its surroundings. All that remained of it was a heap of rubble. The Battle of Monte Cassino claimed the lives of 55,000 Allied soldiers, 20,000 German soldiers and thousands of innocent local civilians.

Inside one of the B-25 bombers that day sat a young American tail-gunner by the name of Walter M Miller Jr. What he witnessed from his small window changed him forever. As his colleague the science fiction writer John Haldeman said about him in an interview with the *Washington Post*, "Walt was deeply depressed by post-traumatic stress disorder and had been for half a century. I don't know how many people he felt responsible for killing, but it was a lot."[7] The horrific bombardment left its indelible marks on Miller and is inscribed on each and every page of the single, full-length novel he published in his lifetime – the epic *A Canticle for Leibowitz*. In this post-apocalyptic work Miller, who had become a Roman Catholic after his release from the army, tells the history of a monastery built following a nuclear war. The monastery carries the name of Leibowitz, a technician who died a martyr's death in the effort to preserve what was left of human knowledge for the generations to come. Published in 1951, the novel spans centuries as it accompanies the holy order of Saint Leibowitz, which seeks to decipher and save the archive left behind by its founder through the post-nuclear Middle Ages, the New Renaissance and up to the second, inevitable collapse. The knowledge the monks secure from the smouldering embers of one holocaust helps to create the conditions for another.

It might have been better just to bury it (Remember to Forget, page 139).

Sometimes though, rather than an external enemy, it is the author himself who declares war on his work and seeks to have it incinerated, as in the famous case of Franz Kafka's request to his friend Max Brod. Mikhail Bulgakov set fire to a novel he wrote about the life of Jesus – an act that reverberates in his late monumental work, *The Master and Margarita*. Nikolai Gogol even went as far as spending most of his money to obtain the rights to buy back and burn all the copies of a poem he wrote in 1829 under the pen name Hans Küchelgarten. Years later he burned the second part of his novel *Dead Souls*. When exiled in poverty in Kazakhstan, the philosopher, literary critic and scholar Mikhail Bakhtin was forced to use the original manuscript of a book on the *Bildungsroman* and its significance in the history of realism as rolling paper for cigarettes during the wartime shortage. Presumably, he did this only after first using the pages of his Bible, which also went up in holy smoke.

A bitter lesson learned by many of his colleagues, including Yevgeny Zamyatin (Best of All Possible Worlds, page 247).

Besides the plays, texts on science and philosophy, literary prose and poetry we only know about from secondary or even tertiary sources, such as references, quotes and notes in margins, some books seem to have miraculously survived the whims of history. Three of Archimedes' texts were erased in 1229, so the parchment on which they were written could be reused for a prayer book. Its sanctity must have protected them because in 1906 they were revealed by the Danish scholar Johan Ludvig Heiberg, who managed to decipher the palimpsest and restore the ancient writings. Muhammed edh-Dhib, a Bedouin shepherd, inadvertently uncovered a parchment that turned out to be a fragment of the hidden Qumran scrolls; and a jar an Egyptian farmer stumbled upon happened to hold the library of Nag Hammadi, which included unique Gnostic-Christian texts. In 1417, the scholar Poggio Bracciolini discovered the manuscript *De Rerum Natura*, or *On the Nature of Things*, a long poem by Roman poet and philosopher Lucretius. Bracciolino was so struck by its beauty that its revolutionary, scandalous subject matter did not prevent him from copying the forgotten manuscript, thus reinjecting it into the cultural bloodstream. It included references to the atomistic nature of the universe and what we might call a proto-evolutionary theory. The literary scholar Stephen Greenblatt mentions the major impact this had on the development of Western thought, through its influence on personalities like Galileo and Newton, Darwin and Einstein.

Greenblatt is not alone in being captivated by the huge potential of forsaken books, whether real or invented. Many writers have been fascinated by the possibilities entombed in books lost and found, books banned and burned. The story Margaret Atwood recounts in *The Handmaid's Tale* is based on a supposedly lost document revealed many years later, while there is a report by scientists deciphering subversive messages left by a rebel ant in Ursula Le Guinn's story "The Author of the Acacia Seeds and Other Extracts from the Journal of the Association of Therolinguistics". William of Baskerville, the Franciscan monk inspired by Sherlock Holmes and William of Oakham in Umberto Eco's *The Name of the Rose*, fails to prevent the destruction of Aristotle's book on comedy by the blind monk Jorge, who is attempting to protect Christianity from having to face its revolutionary contents. Many of these lost books somehow unleash great occult and sinister powers, and those who read them expose themselves to terrible catastrophes. This is the

A very heady combination (Number of the Beast, page 79; Force Majeure, page 135).

A feminist dystopia (Best of All Possible Worlds, page 247) dedicated to a witch (Weird Sisterhood, page 25).

Especially if you're using a real spell book (Weird Sisterhood, page 25).

case with the *Necronomikon* by horror fiction writer H P Lovecraft because anyone who reads it loses their mind; or with *The Nine Gates of the Kingdom of Shadows,* the book that summons Lucifer in Arturo Pérez-Reverte's novel *The Club Dumas.*

Whether we're out to destroy them or dying to read them, lost books have the power to reconstruct our reality. "A random fire, an act of vandalism, a decision to snuff out the last trace of views judged to be heretical, and the course of modernity would have been different,"[8] writes Greenblatt about Lucretius' *De Rerum.* When we discover alternative narratives, stories that add to or remove something from our assumptions, we may come to read our cultural, political or religious history differently. This challenges our understanding and beliefs, introduces cracks of doubt where we had concrete truths.

Every archeologist or book hunter is driven by the hope of one day coming across the vault or volume holding one of those mysterious word-capsules. "The lost book ... becomes infinitely more alluring simply because it can be perfect only in the imagination,"[9] writes Stuart Kelly in *The Book of Lost Books: An Incomplete History of All the Great Books You'll Never Read,* a tragicomic bibliography encompassing extinct works from cuneiform times down to the present. Or are we looking at a process of natural selection, like the one Lucretius speculated about? Might it be that these books are better off in oblivion? And perhaps they were lost in the first place because they didn't measure up? The one thing that would be worse than never discovering *Cardenio* at all would be to identify it beyond any doubt, then to realize that it's actually a mediocre or embarrassing play. Could it be then, that history has simply been doing us a favour by sparing us bad writing or dangerous books that upend our truths and discredit our conventions? Faith in such an evolutionary theory of books, in the idea that only those that successfully adapt endure, while inferior ones find themselves in the ash heap of history, is comforting to an extent.

It is a hopeful thought that truths will in the end find their way to us one way or another, reveal themselves anew, emerge from other works, get rewritten, copied. The story, though, is not a simple one. "The entire history of literature was also the history of the loss of literature,"[10] writes Kelly. History is a graveyard of books and we can only see some of the tombstones – hidden

There was at least one occasion when it is suggested that the Devil himself helped someone complete his book (Number of the Beast, page 79).

everywhere there are many more we are not even aware existed. How many geniuses, brilliant inventions, narratives that could have changed hearts and minds never made it? The past is a confusion of struggle and flight, and those who survive it do so by sheer luck.

4

WEIRD SISTERHOOD

Do you have more (or fewer) than two nipples? Do you own a broom? Do you float on water? And above all: are you a woman? If you have answered "yes" to at least one of these questions and your neighbours covet one of your cows, or they are infuriated because a woman you helped died during childbirth or are looking for someone to blame for the current drought, then you must be a witch and your destiny is sealed.

More than anybody else, the Moirai, the three great ancient Greek goddesses who held the thread of life in their very hands, knew how useless it was to try and avoid a date with destiny. Clotho, who spun it, Lachesis, who determined its length and Atropos, who cut the thread, decided how and when a human life would end. Even the gods were tied by fate and entirely bound by the verdict of these goddesses. And the Erinyes – the Roman Furies – were their enforcers. Virgil named them in his *Aeneid*: Allecto, goddess of endless anger; Tisiphone, goddess of vengeful destruction; and Megaera, goddess of jealous rage. According to Hesiod's *Theogony*, these three terrifying deities "that under earth take vengeance on men"[1] came into being during a primal scene when castration anxiety and the Oedipus complex joined forces. They materialized from the blood of Uranus after his son Chronos hacked off his genitals because he had caught him having sex with his mother–wife, Gaia.

In Norse mythology, too, three deities are busy weaving and watering the roots of Yggdrasil, the World Tree. They are Urðr, Verðandi and Skuld, who represent "what was", "what is" and "what will be". The Celts had their own trio, the three Morrígna or Morrigan: Badb, Macha and Nemain, war goddesses who appear as a raven or a wolf as they announce the fate of battles and foretell the future of kings.

Robert Graves, the poet and writer, believed all these female triumvirates were reflections of the one White Goddess whose traces he was seeking through ancient mythologies. This is the monomyth of the female who is the maiden, the mother and the

Metamorphoses that emphasize our primal connection to the natural world (The Human Animal, page 189).

A term originally related to a hero's journey and not to a goddess or goddesses (Force Majeure, page 135).

crone all at once; the bride, mother and slayer of the hero or the king who married her and the land in a holy union lasting one year, at the end of which he was sacrificed in supplication. She was the heavens and all its host, ruler of the earth and all that was upon it, mistress of the netherworld below. Three that are one, like three-faced Hecate, goddess of crossroads and boundaries, sorcery and poison, who ages throughout the day to be reborn at night.

However, when the devotees of these goddesses were defeated by the almighty and awesome God of monotheism, their fate was worse than death. There was a new trio in town, impeccably masculine, purely patriarchal; and the Father, the Son and the Holy Ghost did not like competition. "The archetypal projection of the Masculine experiences, not without justice, the Earth as the unconscious-making, instinct-entangling, and therefore dangerous Feminine … the Masculine principle identifies itself with the world of Heaven and projects the evil world of Earth outwards on the alien Feminine principle," writes Erich Neumann, one of Jung's most prominent students, about the rise of one of the most destructive archetypes. "That is why the religious fanaticism of the representatives of the patriarchal World of Heaven reached its climax in the Inquisition and the witch trials, at the very moment when the influence of the archetype of Heaven, which had ruled the Middle Ages and the previous period, began to wane, and the opposite image of the Feminine Earth archetype began to emerge."[2]

As many more Pagan deities had the opportunity to experience (Number of the Beast, page 79).

Whose depictions are very often non-corporeal (Moving Heaven and Hell, page 71).

Clotho, Lachesis and Atropos, now diminished and the object of contempt, take the form of the three wayward sisters, predicting changes in the political tides, "All hail, Macbeth, thou shalt be king hereafter!"[3] and mumbling over their boiling pot, "Double, double toil and trouble; Fire burn, and cauldron bubble."[4] It has been claimed that Shakespeare took these incantations from a book of spells that somehow fell into his hands and that the ghosts of these purloined witches, enraged by this breach of copyright, haunt the pages of the accursed play. But if *Macbeth* is really under the spell of ill-treated restless spirits, then they must be those of the women (and the few men) of North Berwick in Scotland, who were put on trial in 1590, accused of having cast a spell on a ship carrying King James I and his young bride Queen Anne of Denmark to make it sink. It's an accusation that, with the aid of torture, turned into well-founded guilt. James attended the trials, cross-examined the accused and in the wake the events even wrote *Demonologie*, a learned treatise on witchcraft, which might have been one of Shakespeare's sources. Agnes Sampson, Euphame MacCalzean, Barbara Napier, Geillis Duncan and many more ended their lives at the stake. Between 1560 and 1707 around 4,000 women in Scotland alone were accused of witchcraft and were executed in this fashion. It may just be that presenting a play about a Scottish king who murders his way to the throne, to King James – another Scottish king who was the son of one of the former's victims and had just risen to power after mercilessly persecuting witches – was meant to appease him.

The three witches or Weird Sisters as they are also known, are not the only women in *Macbeth* invoking dark powers. "The raven himself is hoarse," says Lady Macbeth, as the spectre of the Morrigan looms. "Come, you spirits that tend on mortal thoughts," she beckons as if summoning the ancient goddesses, "unsex me here ... Come, thick night, and pall thee in the dunnest smoke of hell."[5] she pleads, as if calling on Hecate, daughter of the night, and on the ruler of pandemonium, to give her the power to carry out the deed that will enable her husband to lay claim to the throne. She pays for this unholy covenant with her sanity, "Out, damned spot! Out, I say!"[6] – and eventually with her life.

Joan of Arc, too, was accused of the two-fold sin of gender-bending and siding with Satan (Wonder Women, page 37).

The witch trials were a lose–lose situation for women. If the accused managed to change shape and rise like a phoenix from the ashes, she was a witch. If she burned, maybe she wasn't. Should she float on the water, she was in thrall to the fallen angel; should she drown, she was collateral damage. The history of Europe's witch-hunt in the sixteenth and seventeenth centuries is a history of mass hysteria. "The witch-craze is an important study in human evil, comparable to Nazism and Stalinism."[7] write Jeffrey Russell and Brooks Alexander in their *A History of Witchcraft: Sorcerers, Heretics and Pagans*. In the 200 years during which this collective madness raged in Europe, something of the order of 40,000–60,000 people – 80 per cent of whom were women – were persecuted, tortured and executed in an unprecedented "gendercide". The first witch trials were held in the middle of the fifteenth century near Lake Geneva and spread like wildfire across Europe. In the Holy Roman Empire, especially in areas belonging to present-day Germany, the local folk approached this grim endeavour in typically thorough and efficient style. It is estimated that over 40

Ideologies that wanted to create a heaven on earth (Best of All Possible Worlds, page 247)

Not to worry – men had their own problems to deal with (Lupus Est, page 93)

The nineteenth-century birthplace of two of the most terrifying monsters to ever haunt the human imagination (Blood Lust, page 93; The Body Electric, page 221).

per cent of all European witchcraft executions took place in these territories. According to some sources, in the small province of St Maximin 500 women – a quarter of the overall population – were executed over a period of only 18 years. There were two small villages in the Catholic diocese of Trier that were left with only one female resident each. Accounts from the Würzburg witch trials of 1625–31 list the victims. In the first burning, there were four people described as: the wife of Liebler, old Ancker's widow, the wife of Gutbrodt and the wife of Hooker. In the second burning, four people: the old wife of Beutler, two strange women and the old woman who kept the pot-house.

They didn't even have names of their own.

The roots of this evil were many, various and contested: the Little Ice Age which led to frosts, floods and plagues, and to people looking for scapegoats; the Renaissance's renewed interest in ancient Greek sources that confirmed Christian misogyny; the increasing prestige of medical doctors, which had the effect of sidelining midwives and other wise women; and the meteoric developments in science, which spurred a paranoid response.

Consider the story of Katharina, the mother of Johannes Kepler the astronomer, who took him at age six to observe the Great Comet of 1577 and was also accused of witchcraft. Katharina Kepler's case was textbook: an elderly widow (she was 68 at the time), who had some knowledge of traditional medicine, which she used to help members of her community, she was accused of witchcraft by a sick neighbour who claimed Kepler poisoned her. Then came the usual accusations of animal mutilation and transformation, in this case, into a cat. Charged in 1615, she was incarcerated in late 1619 and shackled to the floor of her cell. Her fate, like that of so many others, would have been sealed were it not for her son's intervention. In 1620, Kepler, already a famed astronomer, came to his mother's defence and used his scientific analytical ability, a little basic knowledge of medicine and a lot of common sense, to get his mother released. It took a year. Just six months after the trial ended, Katharina Kepler died.

Did Kepler's excommunication, only a few years earlier, contribute to the accusations levelled against his mother? It was certainly not easy to be the "heretic's mother" in the small Lutheran town where Katharina lived. But the intra-Protestant rivalry to which Kepler fell prey was a mere skirmish in the larger

Who speculated there were demons on the moon (Man in the Moon, page 115).

The very same one that Tycho Brahe, his future employer, observed and from which he deduced that comets did not originate in the earthly sphere as Aristotle believed, but from beyond the moon (We Come in Peace, page 123).

battle being waged elsewhere at the same time: the violent flare-ups of the religious war between Catholics and Protestants, a battle for souls, a fight for religious resources and spiritual supremacy. Whether they worshipped a Protestant Satan or a Catholic Lucifer, witches were the ideal human sacrifice to assuage the wrath of God. The one book that both sides could agree on was a raving bestseller, written by an inquisitor named Heinrich Kramer. The *Malleus Maleficarum* – *The Hammer of Witches* – was first published in 1486. By 1600 it had undergone 28 editions, had a blurb by Pope Innocent VIII and could boast an incredibly wide distribution. Its roaring success can be ascribed to Gutenberg's invention, which helped to make it one of the first books to reach a broad readership. Like the internet, the printing revolution caused a growth spurt of knowledge, but it was accompanied by some unforeseen side-effects, such as the chance to gawk at exposed female body parts and bizarre sexual spectacles.

> Who got his name from the planet Venus (Number of the Beast, page 79).

> From the moment it came into existence, it was used for dubious purposes (A Faustian Bargain, page 1).

The *Malleus* included juicy descriptions and titillating woodcuts of witches throwing ecstatic and wildly sensual orgies during which they swear allegiance to the Devil, kiss his backside and greedily devour the babies they have stolen from their innocent neighbours. The author reaches a poetic climax in describing why women occupy the centre of these Satanic activities, quoting St John Chrysostom, "What else is a woman but a foe to friendship, an unescapable punishment, a necessary evil, a natural temptation, a desirable calamity, a domestic danger, a delectable detriment, an evil of nature, painted with fair colours!" and adding, "sin introduced by woman kills the soul as well as the body by depriving it of Grace as a penalty for sin."[8] Ergo, women are a fate worse than death.

And sometimes it was simply their most feminine of organs that was their downfall.

On a cold, damp November morning in 1589 in the small village of Warboys in England, ten-year-old Jane Throckmorton, daughter of a local squire, fell ill and began suffering from bizarre fits. She pointed a finger at an old local woman, Mother Alice Samuel, who, she said, had put a curse on her. After one of England's most momentous witch trials, Samuel and her family were executed.

The postmortem, carried out by the prison guard and his wife, was unequivocal. They identified on Samuel's corpse "a little lump of flesh, in manner sticking out as if it had been a teat, to the length of half an inch". The two hesitated about whether to disclose this, "because it was adjoining so secret a place which was not decent to be seen". But eventually, "not willing to conceal so strange a matter, and decently covering that privy place ... they made open show thereof unto diverse that stood by." But that did not end the disgrace of the dead. The jailer's wife reached for the body's nether region and "took the same teat in her hand, and seeming to strain it, there issued ... a mixture of yellow milk and water".[9]

Poor Mother Samuel was not the only one whose witch's mark manifested itself in such a manner, of course. In 1619, a herbal healer, Margaret Flowers, and her two daughters were accused of witchcraft and the killing of two young nobles. Under torture she confessed that a black rat sucked upon a teat on the "inward parts of her secrets".[10] In the 1652 case of Joan Peterson from Wapping, the inquisitors identified a "teat of flesh in her secret parts, more than other women usually had".[11]

These were not isolated incidents. After all, it was the great Kramer himself, who in the witch-finders bible, stated, "All witchcraft comes from carnal lust, which is in women insatiable" clarifying that the "mouth of the womb"[12] is never satisfied. In his *Demonologie*, King James I expanded on how a woman might acquire such an abomination, "the Devil does lick them with his tongue in some private part of their body, before he does receive them to be his servants, which mark commonly is given them under the hair in some part of their body."[13]

Not only men held these views, as Thérèse Philosophe discovered (The Pleasure Principle, page 195).

One hopes that old Mother Samuel and her fellow sufferers at least derived some pleasure from their "witch's teat" in their lifetime, as the description leaves not much room for doubt about the true nature of this "little lump of flesh".

The genesis of this gender bias toward women being witches could be traced back to Judaism, the mother of Christianity. The Jewish prohibition on sorcery was taken extremely seriously. In the second century BC, Shimon ben Shetah, a scholar and president of the Jewish Court of Law, dispensed with 80 witches in one day in the city of Ashkelon. He and his followers were convinced that "most witchcraft is in women", and that he who "takes on many wives may encounter many spells". The basis for their belief derived directly from holy writ, "Thou shalt not suffer a witch to live",[14] as it is decreed in the Book of Exodus. This didn't prevent

A hotspot for supernatural activity (Here Be Dragons, page 79; Heads or Tails, page 183).

King Saul from seeking "a woman that hath a familiar spirit"[15] – the witch of Endor – and asking her to conjure up the spirit of the prophet Samuel to advise him.

But the prophet's namesake, the Reverend Samuel Parris, who had acquired a house slave by the name of Tituba in Barbados in 1680, had no idea he was bringing a witch with him to the small town in Massachusetts that entrusted him, nine years later, with its spiritual welfare. The town's name was Salem.

We don't have much reliable information about Tituba. She seems to have been of South American descent and it is assumed she married another slave owned by Reverend Parris, a Native American man called John; she looked after the family's children and devoted herself to her housekeeping chores. In the winter of 1692, all this came to an abrupt end. First the Reverend's daughter Betty fell ill, then her cousin Abigail Williams. They had convulsions, spasms and hallucinations. Next, two other girls, Ann Putnam and Elizabeth Hubbard, started to suffer from strange symptoms. One of them admitted that she had been dabbling with prognostication – wishing to know which boy in their Puritan town might take a fancy to her – and since the doctors could not find any worldly or physical explanation for these seizures, the good people of Salem began to suspect evil might be at work. Today historians tend to believe that the real cause of the girls' affliction was *Claviceps purpurea*, a fungus that infects grains, especially rye, which was an important staple in the community. The fungus can cause neurotropic symptoms such as delirium, irrational behaviour, convulsions and even death. In the absence of the necessary mycological knowledge, though, the three most unusual women around were accused. These were: Sarah Osburne, an old and wayward widow with whom the Parris family had a longstanding dispute as neighbours; Sarah Good, a beggar woman who may well have been cognitively disabled; and Tituba from Barbados. The former two denied any involvement in witchcraft and pleaded innocent. Then Tituba was brought into the courtroom. "The Devil came to me and bid me serve him," said the enslaved woman. She went on to describe him as a tall man with white hair, wearing a black robe; he came from Boston, she said, and he forced her under pain of death to hurt the girls. The man's associates were a red cat and a black cat, a great black dog, a hog, a strange, hairy two-legged animal and a winged creature with a woman's face who was Sarah Good, one of the other suspects, in disguise. "I rode upon a stick or pole and Good and Osburne behind me,"[16] she said. The Devil had a book that contained the names of other servants of his, she confessed. She signed her name in the book and the letters looked like blood. The cross examiner asked her 84 questions and she answered all of them in detail. Hers was the longest, most substantial account.

Not just one (Flame and Moth, page 17).

Tituba's confessions went viral and everybody became infected with this fatal fever. It was estimated that somewhere between a 144 and 160 people stood accused. Most were jailed and many were deprived of legal rights. Nineteen were hanged. Giles Corey, an old farmer who refused to answer his examiners, objecting that as far as he was concerned the entire trial was baseless, was subjected to death by pressing: he was stripped naked and boulders were heaped upon his prone body. There was no escape. Not even for dogs, two of which were put to death because they were believed to have consorted with the Devil. One of them was pardoned posthumously by the Puritan minister, Cotton Mather, who declared the dog innocent. Had the dog been the Devil in disguise, it would not have been possible to kill it, he argued. But the dog had died, so it was not bewitched.

And what of Tituba herself? Perhaps she did have formidable supernatural powers, for she – the only person who confessed her pact with the Devil outright – was eventually released from jail unscathed, after an unidentified person bailed her out for seven pounds. Or was it 30 pieces of silver?

Though she vanished from the pages of history, Tituba continued to feature in the annals of culture. In the years to follow she changed skin colour. While she is referred to as an "Indian" during her trial, it is also mentioned that she hailed from the West Indies and practised hoodoo, the art of sorcery we now call voodoo. The fact that the trial protocols confused these two allowed those who wrote about her to mould and shape her racial identity as they saw fit. First, she was turned into half-Indian, half-white; then to half-black, half-white; eventually becoming completely black. Native Americans were the great enemies of the white inhabitants of Massachusetts, who not only changed the name of the tribal people – the Massachusett – whose land they appropriated, but also fought them in a series of bloody battles. But when, in 1868, Henry Wadsworth Longfellow came to write his play about the

Which has a close connection to colonialism (Head Hunters, page 231).

stubborn farmer Giles Corey, the United States of America was still licking its wounds left by a greater trauma than this struggle against the expropriated natives: the Civil War. Under its influence, Longfellow turned Tituba into the daughter of a wild black man, who was responsible for her unholy powers. In his *Crucible*, Arthur Miller had her singing in Creole, using the blood of a black rooster and presented her as an unambiguously black slave. Maryse Condé, the Guadeloupean writer, in her book *I Tituba: Black Witch of Salem*, not only invented a biography full of passion and sexual violence for Tituba, but also added an imaginary encounter with Hester Prynne, the heroine of *The Scarlet Letter* by Nathanael Hawthorne, whose grandfather had been one of the judges during the Salem trials. However, in *Calligraphy of the Witch*, a novel by Alicia Gaspar de Alba, she features as an Arawak Native American.

Tituba's changing racial identity, depending on local circumstances and the Other culture most perceived as a threat by those under her spell, is merely one aspect of how the image of the witch evolved. Once people stopped believing in witches, their fate turned. "Fair is foul, and foul is fair",[17] as Shakespeare's sisters chant. Released from her traumatic historical shackles, shedding her status of victim of religious and misogynic persecution, the witch transformed into an icon of female power, a role model, an artistic inspiration. As is often the case with people's frenzied fantasies, the witch captured artists' imagination through the ages variously as a cunning slave or a vengeful queen, a cruel beauty or a crooked, blasphemous old woman.

In the Grimm brothers' tales, witches now featured as evil stepmothers, and their threefold aspect was streamlined into two: a polished and polite public side and a cruel and corrupt inner self. This simplistic dualism was very convenient for Disney's animators who used it spectacularly in early works such as *Snow White and the Seven Dwarfs* and *Sleeping Beauty*. The Romantic movement, drawn into the worship of nature and idolizing the idolatrous, transformed these hellraisers into heavenly creatures. Once the smoke had lifted, the witch-hunt could be used as a metaphor for McCarthyism, as done by Arthur Miller, and the colour of Tituba's skin could serve as a blank page onto which America's bloody past – its treatment of those whose skin was black or red – could be written. Margaret Murray, the archeologist and anthropologist, argued in her 1926 book *The Witch Cult in*

Which left its mark on the walls of caves (The Human Animal, page 189).

Western Europe that witchcraft had been a major, important pre-monotheistic, pagan religion. Even though Murray's research was discredited, she became known as the "Grandmother of Wicca", in which witches are worshipped as priestesses of the Moon Goddess and latter-day pin ups of a neo-pagan fertility cult. Now it became possible to reinvent legendary witches like Morgana le Fay, King Arthur's half-sister, as a disciple of the White Goddess, starring in the books of Marion Zimmer Bradley as a mouthpiece of anachronistic feminist views. Another possibility was to offer reparation for the cultural injustice witches had had to suffer by rewriting the Grimm brothers' tales and *Macbeth*, as did Terry Pratchett with his bunch of wonderful witches.

Who first appeared as a historical figure in Geoffrey of Monmouth's *Historia Regum Britanniae* (King of Cups, page 153).

In the twentieth century witches once again stirred the cauldron of politics to their heart's delight, just as they had done in the distant past when they decided the fates of men on the battlefield. And in the 1960s, the war was in full swing. The Women's International Terrorist Conspiracy from Hell, or WITCH, was an independent feminist group and a loosely jointed part of the women's liberation movement, established in New York in 1968 on All Hallows Eve. Dressed in capes and pointy black hats and wielding brooms, they announced they were putting a hex on New York's financial district. Attributing the oppression of women to capitalism, they occupied Wall Street chanting, "Double, bubble, war and rubble, when you mess with women, you'll be in trouble."[18] It has been said that the next morning the Dow dropped 13 points.

When deposed deities walk the earth (Number of the Beast, page 79).

Their manifesto states that "WITCH is a theater, revolution, magic, terror, joy, garlic flowers, spells. It's an awareness that witches … were the original guerrillas and resistance fighters against oppression … down through the ages. Witches have always been women who dared to be groovy, courageous, aggressive, intelligent, nonconformist … before the death-dealing sexual, economic, and spiritual repression of the Imperialist Phallic Society took over and began to destroy nature and human society."[19]

When 55,000 people took to the streets of Warsaw, Poland, in March 2018 to protest against the right-wing government's attempt to criminalize abortion, photographer Marlena Kuczko captured the image of a young woman carrying a placard stating, "We are the granddaughters of the witches you couldn't burn."

And all over the world women protesting against the attempt to control their bodies and their freedom of choice took to the streets wearing red robes and white hats, drawing creative inspiration from Margaret Atwood's *The Handmaid's Tale*. Mary Webster, also known as Half-Hanged Mary, to whom Atwood dedicated the novel, was accused of practising witchcraft in 1685, seven years before the Salem trials. She was hanged and left for dead, but she survived.

A work that takes place in the future and is based entirely on the past (Best of All Possible Worlds, page 247).

Witches survive. They endure. Admired, humiliated, persecuted, tortured and ridiculed and finally, hailed and hallowed once more.

Sooner or later they always take their fate into their own hands.

5

WONDER WOMEN

In Concord, Massachusetts on 19 April 1775 "the shot heard around the world" started the first of the great revolutions of the eighteenth century. Its repercussions reached Europe, where people were anxiously following the fortunes of the British colony that had just declared independence. Adventurers, freedom fighters, idle aristocrats and other trigger-happy gentleman made their way to the North American coast to get in on the action. Many of these foreign recruits brought what was in short supply among Virginia's tobacco farmers, Georgia's cotton growers and Boston's businessmen – experience. The Prussian Baron Friedrich Wilhelm von Steuben wrote his *Regulations for the Order and Discipline of the Troops of the United States* for them, and it served as the standard military guide until 1812. The Marquis de Lafayette escaped prison to join their ranks and Polish Count Casimir Pulaski wrote in a letter to Washington, "I came here, where freedom is being defended, to serve it, and to live or die for it."[1] And so he did: he died for it. During the siege of Savannah, the "father of the United States cavalry" was severely wounded and died two days later, aged 34. His bones were only identified in 2019 through the mitochondrial DNA analysis of a second-degree niece. The researchers not only unveiled his identity, but also found that "The skeleton looked very female,"[2] as the anthropologist who examined the results put it. Had Pulaski actually been born an intersex, equipped with both sword and sheath – male and female sex characteristics? Or was he, perhaps, a she? We have no conclusive answer, but if the Polish gentlewoman decided to dress up in men's clothes to finally see some action, she would surely not have been the first to do so.

"I take off my battle cloak, And put on my old-time clothes," says Hua Mulan in the ballad that was written about her in the sixth century. "I adjust my wispy hair at the window sill, And apply my bisque makeup by the mirror," she recounts, according to the anonymous author writing about the legendary female warrior from China, who joined the emperor's army in order to save her old father from compulsory military service, "I step out to see my comrades-in-arms, They are all surprised and astounded: 'We travelled twelve years together, Yet didn't realise Mulan was a lady!'"[3] But while this historically unconfirmed narrative was eventually put to use by Disney's princess-industry in the film *Mulan*, there were plenty of actual women who donned men's clothes in order to join wars. Phoebe Hessel enlisted for love. She got herself conscripted to the British army in the mid-eighteenth century because she wanted to stay close to her husband, and her identity was only revealed when she had to strip for a flogging after committing a misdemeanor. Throwing a look over her shoulder at the stunned sergeant, she hissed, "Strike and be damned!" For others, like Nadezhda Durova, life in the army offered a way out of the bonds of family, and she left her husband and her young son to join the Russian forces in 1806. Later Pushkin encouraged her to publish her memoirs under the title *The Cavalry Maiden*. Some used the uniform to get a front seat in the theatre of war, like the journalist Dorothy Lawrence, who reported on the events of World War I. There were those who took the army's commitment to make a man out of them more literally, such as Catharina Margaretha Linck, who in the early eighteenth century enlisted in the Prussian army as a man. After being discharged from service she went on to marry a woman and it was never disclosed if the latter knew in advance that her husband was different. It was Linck's suspicious mother-in-law who revealed her biological sex and the couple was taken to court. During the trial, it turned out that Linck had "made a penis of stuffed leather with two stuffed testicles made from [a] pig's bladder attached to it and had tied it to her pubes with a leather strap. When she went to bed with her alleged wife, she put this leather object into the other's body and in this way had actually accomplished intercourse."[4] She was accused of sodomy and executed in 1721. She was by no means the only woman who paid with her life for having had the temerity to don a man's attire.

When she was 13 years old, the daughter of a well-to-do farmer heard the voices of Archangel Michael (he of the flaming sword), Saint Catherine of the Wheel and Margaret of Antioch – the one who emerged perfectly unharmed from a dragon's belly – with all three of them informing her that God had chosen her to set her country free from English domination and restore the Dauphin, the crown prince, to the throne of France. Aged 17 and having vowed never to marry but to dedicate herself to the service

Which he used to defeat Lucifer (Number of the Beast, page 79).

Whose sanctity was so great that this instrument of torture and execution, used only in cases requiring cruel and unusual punishment, was broken when it touched her flesh (Lupus Est, page 93).

After all, virgins were the preferred food of his kind until their nutritional requirements changed (Here Be Dragons, page 79).

of God, she marched to Charles IV's court, demanded armour, a sword and a horse, and then proceeded to lead the army to Orléans. The soldiers under her command had probably never heard of Thomas Aquinas, who wrote the following comment on the verse from Deuteronomy, "The woman shall not wear that which pertaineth unto a man"[5]: "Nevertheless this may be done sometimes without sin on account of some necessity, either in order to hide oneself from enemies, or through lack of other clothes, or for some similar motive."[6] But they would have been familiar with the hagiographies of the "holy transvestites", female saints who put on their pious brothers' habits to live as monks, and they would have seen Joan of Arc as these women's heir, a holy virgin warrior. But unlike those who tried to completely efface all signs of their sex, Joan did not hide the more salient features of her femininity. The fact that she fought and prevailed as a female and did not pretend to be a man, made her a woman who unsettled the patriarchal social order rather than simply a mentally unstable girl prone to hearing voices. As the English inquisitor put it at the beginning of her trial, she was a woman "wholly forgetful of womanly honesty, and having thrown off the bonds of shame, careless of all the modesty of womankind, she wore with an astonishing and monstrous brazenness, immodest garments belonging to the male sex."[7]

During the trial, Joan stated that wearing hose was the chaste solution when fighting alongside men, but her actions suggest a more profound element to her preference, as she was willing to die and not give up her power suit and the self-expression she found in it. She broke down eventually. Joan admitted she was guilty of witchcraft, conspiracy to put a heretical king on the throne and wearing men's clothes. On 24 May 1431, she signed her full confession, wearing a gown. However, when her judges visited her some days later in her cell, they found her in tears – and in hose. "For nothing in the world will I swear not to arm myself and put on a man's dress,"[8] she said. Reneging on her word and resuming her old habit in this way sealed her fate. Joan of Arc was burned at the stake on 30 May, only six years after she heard God's voice commanding her.

About 160 years later, the woman in armour who rode her horse to speak to her troops on Tilbury beach was heir to the men who had persecuted Joan of Arc. Elizabeth I was 55 years of age when the

At least according to one literary genre, what happened in these monasteries was far from pious (The Pleasure Principle, page 195).

The Inquisitor also tried to accuse her of associating with fairies: "Did your Godmother, who saw the fairies, pass as a wise woman?" he asked her, "She was held and considered a good and honest woman, neither divineress nor sorceress,"[a] she replied (Paper Fairies, page 161).

invincible Spanish Armada threatened the green pastures of Albion and the national morale had sunk to an all-time low. Mounted on a grey gelding she appeared on top of a hill, the sun was glittering on her shining helmet with its single feather, gleaming on her polished breastplate and sparkling in her radiant red hair, which cascaded down her white velvet robe like a fiery waterfall. Raising her sceptre in front of her awe-struck subjects, she delivered the speech of a lifetime, "[I am] ... resolved, in the midst and heat of the battle, to live and die amongst you all; to lay down for my God, and for my kingdom, and my people, my honour and my blood, even in the dust. I know I have the body of a weak and feeble woman; but I have the heart and stomach of a king, and of a king of England too."[9] Cheered by her adoring soldiers, to whom she was a holy virgin like Joan of Arc before her, she deftly turned her mount and rode back to the safety of her court. The heavenly host fought on her side – a great storm broke out aborting the Spanish effort and the Armada never reached the shore. Elizabeth had delivered a great performance, a perfectly calculated show. She, who prohibited the unlicensed circulation of her likeness, was fully aware of the power of images. The carefully staged event aimed to evoke Pallas Athene, the Greek goddess of wisdom and war, who was traditionally depicted wearing armour and a helmet. Her flowing red hair was meant to refer to another queen born on the British Isles, who was a fierce warrior against invading forces – Boudica.

In her own version of the Tilbury speech – rendered by Tacitus, the Roman historian – Boudica tells her tribe, "On this spot we must either conquer, or die with glory. There is no alternative. Though a woman, my resolution is fixed: the men, if they please, may survive with infamy, and live in bondage."[10] Cassius Dio describes Boudica as "possessed of greater intelligence than often belongs to women". According to him she was "in stature ... very tall, in appearance most terrifying, in the glance of her eye most fierce, and her voice was harsh; a great mass of the tawniest hair fell to her hips". He writes about the horrors her army inflicted on Londinium, Camelodunum and Verolaminum (present day London, Colchester and St Albans). "They hung up naked the noblest and most distinguished women and then cut off their breasts and sewed them to their mouths, in order to make the victims appear to be eating them; afterwards they impaled the women on sharp skewers run lengthwise through the

One of the most ardent defenders of Christianity would adopt this barbaric method of execution, which would give him his nickname (Blood Lust, page 93).

entire body. All this they did to the accompaniment of sacrifices, banquets and wanton behaviour." These gruesome descriptions might have been propaganda. It was required, to an extent, to cover up the local authorities' own responsibility for the uprising, as until the death of her husband Prasutagus, Boudica's family had been loyal to the foreign regime. However, when the imperial tax collector requisitioned the widow's estate on behalf of his employer, Nero, whom she later described as an effeminate "lyre-player, and a poor one too", [11] the queen of the Iceni wouldn't have it. The emperor's representative then ordered her to be stripped and flogged and her two daughters to be raped – as a warning to the people. Boudica gave as good as she got, leading a revolt against the Romans to repay them for what they had done to her.

Was Boudica buried under what is now King's Cross station in London, between platforms 9 and 10 where J K Rowling's Hogwarts Express departs from? Probably not. But the opening of other burial sites in England long attributed to hulking Viking invaders entombed with their swords and armour, have revealed skeletons suggesting they are the final resting place of warrior women. Before these discoveries, stories about ferocious Norse female warriors were considered wild speculation. Freydis Eyriksdottir, half-sister of the Norse Columbus, Leif Erikson, assailed the inhabitants of Vinland bare-breasted, wielding her sword high above her pregnant belly; Lagertha, wife of Ragnar Lodbrok, led a military attack and saved her husband from defeat; and 300 shield maidens fought for the Danes in the battle of Bravellir, with Sextus Grammaticus commenting, "On these captains who had the bodies of women, nature bestowed the souls of men." [12] Norse religion gave a place of honour to the women who participated in battle, from the Valkyries who selected Odin's top warriors and accompanied them on their way to Valhalla after death, to Eowyn, the "wild shieldmaiden of the North", [13] one of the heroines in J R R Tolkien's fantasy epic *Lord of the Rings*; Tolkein was greatly influenced by its mythology. She is a noblewoman of Rohan, who dresses up as a man and defeats her enemy – the lord of the Nazgûl, one of Sauron's dreaded Ringwraiths – who had boasted that "no living man may hinder me." [14]

Another burial mound, among those discovered in the area stretching from the north coast of the Black Sea to Siberia, contained the skeleton of a young woman whose legs had grown

As women who were involved in warfare and politics, and able to change form, their fate was also to become witches (Weird Sisterhood, page 25).

bowed from a life spent on horseback; to her left lay an iron dagger and to her right a quiver containing 40 bronze arrowheads. These finds may well point to the physical existence of the greatest women-warriors of all – the Amazons. The Babylonian Talmud recounts how Alexander the Great came across these women of valour, and Isidorus of Seville claimed they removed their own right breast so it wouldn't hamper them when drawing their bows. Garci Rodriguez de Montalvo wrote in the late fifteenth century that they lived on the legendary island of California, their skin was black and they rode on the backs of giraffes. Columbus was convinced he had caught sight of them; Boccaccio mentions them in his *Decameron*; Geoffrey Chaucer has some fun at their expense in the *Canterbury Tales*; and in Rick Riordan's series *The Heroes of Olympus,* they are the true power behind the online shopping empire, Amazon. But long before all these, the mythic Amazons formed a community of women warriors who had no need of men except for procreation – the absolute antithesis of the patriarchal Greco-Roman society, which despised women as inferior beings. A kind of upside-down Sparta, their matriarchy existed on the conceptual and geographical margins of antiquity, liminal in every sense. From that position the Amazons' existence allowed male heroes to define their own limits and exercise their power. Hercules and Theseus snatch Hippolyta, the queen of the Amazons; Achilles fights her sister, Penthesilea, and falls in love with her as she lies dying. Love and death were constant companions of the Amazons, as befitted the daughters of Ares, the god of war (according to Apollonius of Rhodes) and Harmonia the nymph. Thus, in many of these stories, the real challenge was to get them to surrender in the bedroom rather than to defeat them on the battlefield, with war serving as nothing but foreplay.

A man who tried to force himself upon the "black Amazons of Sparta", as the traveller Richard F Burton enthusiastically called them, was bound to lose body parts, which the French who fought them in 1890 discovered. Burton, who was intimately familiar with more than a few women, wrote, "Such ... was the size of the female skeleton, and the muscular development of the frame, that in many cases femininity could be detected only by the bosom."[15] The 6,000 female warriors of Dahomey (Benin, these days) were married to the king in a symbolic ceremony, remained chaste until they left the military, underwent gruelling training from the age of

He had, overall, a strange affinity to female breasts (The Lady and the Unicorn, page 179).

No one took the trouble to circumnavigate it, which would have revealed it as part of a continent (The Territory and the Map, page 47).

But he was also adamant he had seen mermaids (Heads or Tails, page 183).

In at least one feminist utopia, women have solved this problem as well (Best of All Possible Worlds, page 247).

Who gave his Roman name to the angry red planet (We Come in Peace, page 123).

The man who was willing to go to great lengths to penetrate forbidden places and circumcised himself to pass as a Muslim, also introduced the West to the *Kama Sutra* in the nineteenth century (The Pleasure Principle, page 195).

eight and specialized in decapitation with a machete. Their fellow Dahomeyans called them *mino*, "our mothers". But according to their own battle prayer they saw themselves differently, "As the blacksmith takes an iron bar and by fire changes its fashion, so we have changed our nature. We are no longer women, we are men." The scholar Maeve Adams argues that the woman warrior of Dahomey not only "inverted gender roles. She has literally and figuratively redrawn the boundaries separating men from women. The pre-eminently powerful female body has effaced the male body and usurped its place on the battlefield."[16]

Many of these boundaries were redrawn in popular culture: from TV series such as *Warrior Queen*, in which the unforgettable Sian Phillips portrays Boudica, through Merida, the red-haired, passionate Celtic heroine in Disney's *Brave*, who challenges her suitors for the right to her hand, down to the warrior princess Xena enacted by Lucy Lawless, who fought alongside gods (Ares), heroes (Hercules) and emperors (Julius) throughout six seasons. Some of these women were following their destiny, like Buffy the Vampire Slayer; others were modelled on the perfect Dahomey women warriors, such as the guardswomen of the "Black Panther" in the Marvel cinematic universe. Carol Danvers, one of the last characters to join the ever-expanding cosmos of the comics, is a brave former test pilot who uses her supernatural fighting powers to protect the galaxy. She made her first appearance in comic books in 1968. Her "father" was Dr Walter Lawson, who officiated as Captain Marvel from 1967 until he handed her the baton. Her "mother" was an incarnation of all the Amazons who came before her. "Wonder Woman" was created in 1941, by the psychologist and inventor of the polygraph, William Moulton Marston, whose wife inspired him to create a new kind of superhero. "Not even girls want to be girls so long as our feminine archetype lacks force, strength, power. Not wanting to be girls they don't want to be tender, submissive, peace-loving as good women are. Women's strong qualities have become despised because of their weak ones," he said, "the obvious remedy is to create a feminine character with all the strength of a Superman plus all the allure of a good and beautiful woman."[17] Marston himself had two wonder women in his life: Elizabeth Holloway, an attorney and psychologist, and Olive Byrne, an ex-research assistant and the niece of the feminist activist Margaret Sanger, who in 1916 opened the first birth-control clinic in the United States with Ethel, Olive's mother. Byrne became a third party in their triad, and while William and Elizabeth looked after their careers, Olive looked after their home and the four children she and Elizabeth bore. Unable to legally marry Olive, Marston gave her a couple of bracelets in lieu of a wedding ring, which can be seen gracing Wonder Woman's arm. Similarly, Wonder Woman's physical appearance was modelled after Olive's tall stature and statuesque figure, while her lasso of truth pays homage to Marston's experimental work on the lie detector. More elements of their unique lifestyle trickled through into the comics, such as the private and professional research Marston conducted into bondage with the aid of Olive and Marjorie Huntley, another activist with whom he had a relationship. These inspired myriad situations when Wonder Woman finds herself tied up or entangled, but always manages to free herself. "Give men an alluring woman stronger than themselves to submit to and they'll be proud to become her willing slaves!"[18] claimed Marston.

In her book *The Secret History of Wonder Woman*, the historian and New Yorker contributor Jill Lepore writes that the Amazon princess inspired the second wave of feminists, including Gloria Steinem and many others. Steinem chose Wonder Woman to feature on the cover of the first issue of her magazine *Ms* with the caption, "Wonder Woman for President". She argued that "Wonder Woman symbolizes many of the values of women's culture that feminists are now trying to introduce into the mainstream: strength and self-reliance for women; sisterhood and mutual support among women; peacefulness and esteem for human life; a diminishment both of 'masculine' aggression and of the belief that violence is the only way of solving conflicts."[19] But neither the popularity of the comics, the beloved TV series featuring Linda Carter nor the success of the movies starring Gal Gadot contrived to solve the crisis Wonder Woman experienced at the UN General Assembly. The organization, having decided to appoint the fictional character ambassador for gender equality and female empowerment in the presence of Carter and Gadot, had to endure a demonstration outside the building by employees who carried placards saying, "real women deserve a real ambassador." They formulated a petition that argues choosing "a large breasted, white woman of impossible proportions, scantily clad in a shimmery, thigh-baring body suit with an American flag motif and knee-high boots" equals choosing a pin-up girl, and that the UN's decision to recruit for this role "a sexualized fake"[20] was horrifying. The 45,000 signatures on the petition brought the UN to its knees and the appointment was cancelled two months later.

Even though the battlefields may change, it turns out that women must always be prepared to struggle – and not only against real flesh-and-blood adversaries. "Pretending there's only one way a woman lives or has ever lived – in relation to the men that surround her – is not a single act of erasure, but a political erasure,"[21] writes Kameron Hurley in her Hugo-award-winning essay, "We Have Always Fought". We don't know enough about these women, she argues, nor do we write about them, and so we don't ensure their cultural presence. When they are not portrayed, they become invisible. Hurley's essay strongly resonated within the spheres of science fiction and fantasy, calling for both male and female writers to struggle for more female representation. These genres have long since been in the vanguard, seeking to introduce greater diversity in the way women are portrayed in general, and strong women in particular.

Hurley is right, of course. We have always fought. There seems always to have been a need to protest or rise up in arms, not only for freedom against oppression or injustice or in defence of land, but for peace itself. Women fight because people fight. They go to battle for the same reasons men do. But unlike her brother in arms, the warrior woman is in constant conflict with her gender roles, the cultural structures she lives within and for which she sometimes gives her life. And when women lose, they often lose more than men. In a global patriarchal society in which men and masculinity constitute the default setting, a woman is expected to win on all fronts. Anything less will be her downfall and not hers alone because it will have implications for others of her sex. The mythical Amazons embodied this bitter lesson. For it was not enough for the Greeks to measure their strength against them, they also had to subdue them. And if the mightiest of us have fallen, what may befall the rest?

6

THE TERRITORY AND THE MAP

The research team attempting to anchor on Sandy Island in the vicinity of Vanuatu hit a snag. The island was not where it was supposed to be according to their map and the Google navigation app. The team, headed by the chief scientist Maria Seton, did the necessary deep-sea exploration and came up with nothing: there was no trace of an island and it had probably never existed in the first place. The sea floor, which they studied using magnetic resonance tests, was about one kilometre (more than half a mile) deep in all directions, without obstructions. Once they returned to land with their non-findings, Seton tried to solve the enigma of the island that wasn't there. Eventually the error was traced back to the logs of the whaling vessel *Velocity*, which had sailed in the area in 1876. The mistake – if indeed it was one – was repeated and copied down through the years. What was it then that the sailors on the *Velocity* had seen? Was it a coral atoll that had later broken up and disappeared without a trace? Could it have been a pumice field – volcanic rock that can resemble a "carpet" several kilometres wide – floating in the ocean? We will probably never know.

Those who insisted over the span of two centuries that California was separate from the mainland, didn't even have that pretext. Human nature, rather than some rare natural phenomenon, was behind the faulty maps produced by the Spanish cartographers of the sixteenth century. The "Island of California" was mentioned in written texts at the end of the fifteenth century, long before it was put on a map and, as befits a fictional island, its name originated in a novel. In 1533, a renegade conquistador landed on what is known now as the Baja California Peninsula. Its elongated shape led him to mistake it for an island and he believed he had reached a place featured in a contemporary chivalric romance called *Las Sergas de Esplandian*, by Castilian writer Garci Rodríguez de Montalvo. He was one of the scores of authors who regaled

Of the kind that established the legends of King Arthur (King of Cups, page 153).

audiences with the valiant exploits of Amadís de Gaula, a shining example of knighthood. Garci Rodríguez waxed poetic about the magical island with its dark-skinned Amazons and their weapons of pure gold, so it may not be surprising the conquistador saw exactly what he expected to see, in the same way that Don Quixote – an admirer of Amadís – was convinced he was looking at giants, not windmills. The first map to include the island appeared in 1622, and once something is recorded on a map, it tends to stay there. In spite of repeated, failed attempts to circumnavigate California, including one by renowned cartographer Gerardus Mercator, the island continued to be immortalized on maps until 1776 when Juan Bautista de Anza proved once and for all that it was part of the North American continent.

There were such women – but not there and not then (Wonder Women, page 37).

Which may or may not have influenced William Shakespeare's lost play (Flame and Moth, page 17).

Smaller cartographic mishaps could have fateful outcomes, like the one on a map Napoleon used during the Battle of Waterloo. As Belgian historian Bernard Coppens noticed, there appears to be a discrepancy of about one kilometre (about two-thirds of a mile) between the hand-drawn map and the printed one showing the location of the farm of Mont-Saint-Jean, where the Duke of Wellington's forces camped. As a result, the French aimed their artillery in the wrong direction and the British remained unscathed. We may never gauge the impact of this mistake on the outcome of the battle, but it couldn't have helped Napoleon.

Certain errors were of a size to fit the ego of those who generated them: for example, "New South Greenland" or "Morrell's Land" – places that Captain Benjamin Morrell claimed to have discovered in 1820 but which only existed on his maps. As a result, he went down in history as the biggest liar in the Pacific.

Another mistake of this kind was documented by the eighteenth-century geographer James Rennell, who mapped a huge mountain range stretching across the western part of Africa between the Gulf of Guinea and the Niger River. The "Mountains of Kong" appeared on almost every commercial map of the continent. The rock-hard certainty of their existence – it came from maps, the best authorities – led to at least one guidebook describing not only these towering mountains but also the city of Kong, "unvisited by any European, but reported by natives to be the biggest market town of the region, and the origin of cotton sought after throughout the entire Soudan".[1] In 2017, artist Jim Naughten created stereoscopic images of this fictitious mountain range, populating these Victorian illusions with a host of creatures, from the notorious King Kong to pygmy hippopotamuses, all painted in bright, luminescent and other-worldly colours. "It's a sort of Shangri-La ruled by the animals,"[2] Naughten says.

Explorer Richard Burton wrote the book about the Mountains of Kong and went in search of another legendary mountain range in his quest for the source of the Nile: the famed Mountains of the Moon, which presumably cut a swath through the entire width of Africa. John Hanning Speke, who followed in his footsteps, prepared to cross this enormous continental barrier only to find it was a figment of the collective imagination. The mere thought that these unpassable land formations existed left many parts of Africa unexplored for years and led to Jonathan Swift's famous sarcastic quatrain:

> "So Geographers in Afric-Maps
> With Savage-Pictures fill their Gaps;
> And o'er unhabitable Downs
> Place Elephants for want of Towns."[3]

Swift himself knew only too well how convincing maps could be, with their easily gained appearance of authority, especially in the eighteenth century, in the wake of Europe's age of discovery and colonialism. In his *Gulliver's Travels* he included detailed maps showing his imaginary islands nestled among well-known, actual places: Brobdingnag, his kingdom of giants, is located near the west coast of North America, not far from the legendary island of California. Swift knew in his cynical heart that the more real places these maps depicted, the easier it would be to convince readers of the existence of the made-up locations.

Henceforth, the map became almost obligatory for anyone who wished to create a fantastic realm. The first thing a traveller should do, writes Diana Wynne Jones in her satirical travel book, *The Tough Guide to Fantasyland*, is to "Find the map. It will be there. No Tour of Fantasyland is complete without one."[4] Even though he had some eminent predecessors, such as L Frank Baum in *The Wizard of Oz*, J R R Tolkien was the greatest mapmaker in this genre, creating his imaginary Middle Earth equipped not only with languages and a mythology but with climatological zones and detailed territorial outlines, all hand drawn. "I wisely

The Victorians were so fascinated by photography that they were willing to accept other illusions as truth (Paper Fairies, page 161).

A literary invention by the British author James Hilton in his 1933 novel *Lost Horizon*, possibly modelled after the legendary Himalayan city of Shambhala. The nineteenth-century Theosophist Helena Blavatsky mentioned it as the domain of the Masters of the Ancient Wisdom, who gave her knowledge of humanity's root races (No Man's Island, page 57).

The kind of book that might have helped children trapped in these lands (Paradise Lost, page 171).

Whose fictional landscape owes much to Norse mythologies (Twilight of the Gods, page 65).

started with the map, and made the story fit," wrote Tolkien to Mrs Mitchison, his editor, "the other way about lands one in confusions and impossibilities."[5] Ever since, no epic fantasy has been complete without its map, which miraculously tends to fit a double spread, and which no less miraculously happens to include all the locations – and only them – which the fearless protagonists visit on their quest to save the world from the forces of darkness. Fantasy maps take no interest in the dragons outside their scope, in *terra incognita*. They care only for the ones within their own borders, like those who follow Khaleesi, threatening the Seven Kingdoms of Westeros, in George R R Martin's book series, *A Song of Ice and Fire*. The detailed maps he made were put into a magnificent three-dimensional version in the opening credits of the TV series *Game of Thrones*, based on his novels. These maps themselves become part of the story, unveiling new life-forms and civilizations. Isaac Stewart, cartographer of the imagined, who is responsible for the art and mapping of Brandon Sanderson's bestselling *Cosmere* novels, claims maps are to fantasy literature what science is to science fiction – they give it a sense of credibility, anchoring it in physical reality.

Maps were not always expected to be an accurate depiction of reality. The Imago Mundi, the oldest surviving map of the world, which dates back to the sixth century BC, zooms in on the Euphrates River and its surrounding kingdoms, where it was unearthed. This map is carved in the shape of a star, suggesting that rather than serving for navigation, it was a symbolic representation of the world known to the mapmaker. It was only in the Hellenistic era when a common effort to produce detailed descriptions of the world got underway, a time that coincides with the waning of the assumption the world was flat. Now circular-shaped maps began to proliferate, including some of the most impressive achievements of antiquity, such as Strabo's *Geographica*.

All this cartographic progress was undone in the Middle Ages with maps like the Hereford Mappa Mundi, when practical maps were relegated to the geographers and navigators. Rather than charting the physical space, the job of mapmakers such as Brother Richard of Haldingham and his team of illuminators, who created the most intact surviving map of the world of their time, was to depict the spiritual domain. His map was drawn on parchment in England in 1300 and shows Jerusalem at the centre of a world inhabited by cannibals and griffins, featuring Noah's Ark, the

Which was also located in the centre of certain labyrinths (A Rat in a Maze, page 147).

Tower of Babel, unicorns and the Golden Fleece. Even though Brother Richard's map reveals the site of paradise and carries a marginal reference to the Day of Judgment, God help the weary traveller who wishes to follow it.

Richard of Haldingham's vellum map was a piece of Christian propaganda in sheep's clothing. He used the same means as those who later realized the power of maps for creating an imaginary reality. "Suggestive cartography" or "cartographic rhetoric", based on allegorical mapping, was also used in Nazi Germany, where maps showed the Allied Forces shaped like the tentacles of the Jewish octopus; British maps represented Germany as a black spider carrying Hitler's face; and Chinese maps simply dropped the name of Taiwan. Propaganda maps were deliberately misleading. For example, those produced under the Soviet regime omitted certain villages, towns and roads, which were then razed in earnest. Such maps convey a message, something they are perfectly suited for because mapping mechanisms constitute a central component in the formation of our social, cultural and political existence. They singularly suggest themselves as objective sources of information while in essence they are selective abstractions of reality.

Even maps like Mercator's projection map, which pride themselves on their objectivity, are likely to perpetuate an imperialist, Eurocentric world view. Thus, for example, the upper part of the map represents the northern hemisphere and the lower, the southern. This is an arbitrary perspective that we in the West tend to take for granted or as natural, and in adopting it we take a superior-versus-inferior approach. The German filmmaker and historian Arno Peters claimed in 1974 that he devised a more trustworthy alternative. After researching synchronoptic world history, Peters developed an equal-area projection very similar to the one suggested more than a century earlier by the Scottish clergyman, Reverend James Gall. Many cartographers dispute Peters' claims about the neutrality and accuracy of his map, asserting that no rectangular depiction of a globe can faithfully represent it. The Gall–Peters projection map is frequently used today, promoted by international bodies such as UNESCO, though Peters' vision of one map for one world has proved polarizing in itself.

But what if we could see our globe in its entirety or at least rise above the petty squabbles? In 1785 Thomas Baldwin became

Spotted near Mount Sinai in 1486 (The Lady and the Unicorn, page 179).

While other maps depicted it as a vampire (Blood Lust, page 93).

the first man to draw aerial maps from the relative safety of a flying circus, and the experience changed him forever. Vincenzo Lunardi had made his maiden voyage in England a year earlier, accompanied by a cat, a dog and a caged pigeon. A crowd of 200,000 people had gawked at his ascent in the presence of the Prince of Wales. After his trip with Lunardi, Baldwin, a balloon-crazy clergyman's son, wrote and illustrated a book he named *Airopaidia*, "But what Scenes of Grandeur and Beauty! A Tear of pure Delight flaſhed in his Eye! Of pure and exquiſite Delight and Rapture; to look down on the unexpected Change already wrought in the Works of Art and Nature, contracted to a Span by the NEW PERSPECTIVE, diminiſhed almoſt beyond the Bounds of Credibility ... Their Beauty was unparalleled. The Imagination itſelf was more than gratified; it was overwhelmed."[6]

From the moment our feet left the ground, we humans tried to describe what we saw for the benefit of those left behind. Panoramas, invented in the late eighteenth century, helped recreate this experience and during the American Civil War depicted scenes of various battlegrounds inspired by the Union Army's use of balloons for scouting and surveillance.

And this point of view gave one airman a very broad perspective on the future (Flame and Moth, page 17).

The world looks a lot smaller from a bird's eye – or fighter plane's – view, and humanmade borders blur into insignificance. According to the historian Alan K Henrikson, after World War II this changed outlook helped "to promote a new world outlook among Americans, termed 'Air-Age Globalism', which profoundly shaped the conduct of the war and the planning of the peace".[7] By the same logic we might have expected that nowadays, when satellites enable us to observe the earth from beyond our atmosphere, we should be able to come up with even more precise maps, freer from human prejudices.

This is not so. The sequence of blunders around the launch of Apple's map application did away with the belief that satellite-guided navigation is less vulnerable to error: Jerusalem failed to appear on the map of Israel and travellers on their way to the Australian town of Mildura found themselves in a remote nature reserve, stuck without food or water for 48 hours.

But these mistakes can also be invaluable insurance certificates, watermarks where there are none. In the days before satellite maps, good, detailed maps were a precious commodity, but they were vulnerable to copyright infringement. Because if your map is accurate, meaning it documents physical reality perfectly (or as perfectly as possible), how can you prove that someone has stolen it from you? To combat such theft, cartographers set up a snare and waited to see who would be caught in it. To protect reality from being stolen you need imagination. Mapmakers used lies to reveal the truth, charting trap streets to get stuck in, paper towns where thieves could get lost and hidden errors that copyists would inadvertently duplicate, thereby incriminating themselves.

These fictional and subversive territories beckoned science fiction writer Fred Saberhagen. In his 1979 short story *The Annihilation of Angkor Apeiron*, a space-travelling salesman of the "Encyclopedia Galactica" lets a copy containing a phantom planet designed as a copyright trap, fall into the hands of an alien war machine, thereby deflecting its attack. He was not the only one. Science fiction writer China Miéville designed trap streets as safe havens for the magically inclined population of his alternate London in his 2010 novel *Kraken*, and author John Green wove the plot around such traps in his novel *Paper Towns* and its film adaptation. His heroine finds shelter in the most famous one of all – Agloe.

Dreamed up in the 1930s, Agloe was constructed out of thin air somewhere in the US Catskill Mountains by General Drafting founder Otto G Lindberg and his assistant Ernest Alpers. The name was an anagram of their initials. Their fantasy turned into reality though, when someone opened the "Agloe General Store" in the same location as the fictitious town.

No one actually built The Crown and Ferret pub in the phantom settlement of Argleton in Lancashire, England, which appeared one day on the Google Maps app. But someone did erect a site virtually, albeit only a website showing generic images of the British countryside. The mysterious town builder took the trouble to narrate Argleton's history dating back to the year 788, when "It is believed to have been first inhabited by a tough and independent Viking clan called the Argles who originated from the Baltic island of Bornholm," which, by the way, does exist. He added that "Argleton is mentioned in the Doomsday Book as 'Argleston'"[8] and has a longstanding animosity with the neighbouring village of Lydiate (also real).

Each historical era gets the map it deserves, reflecting its zeitgeist. Medieval maps had a distinctly theological bias, the age

A compendium of all knowledge, first conceived by science fiction writer Isaac Asimov in his 1942 short story "Foundation", as a repository of information that will allow the human race to recover after the decline and fall of the Galactic Empire (Remember to Forget, page 139).

They did leave an indelible mark on other, real parts of Britain (Twilight of the Gods, page 65).

of discoveries preferred maps that justified imperialist tendencies and early-twentieth-century maps had their own ideological purposes. It now falls to us to have capitalistically inclined maps. GPS systems have an inbuilt commercial hierarchy: the huge amount of information they contain is not there simply for us to avoid traffic jams, but also to enable it to offer us a nice cool drink, to point out a good restaurant or an attractive hotel – all, as it happens, right along the route we're following.

Maps are an answer to one of the oldest questions we humans have been asking ourselves – a question that is both geographical and existential: where am I? If the Mappa Mundi responds, "On the way to Jerusalem on high, the spiritual centre of the universe", and Mercator's projection's answer is "up" or "down", the satellite has a much simpler reply. You yourself are at the centre. You are, in fact, the centre itself and everything is shown in relation to you – the main point of reference on the contemporary map. On applications mapping the heavens, the whole world and cosmos, not just the earth on which you tread, revolve around you.

Alfred Korzybski, the founder of general semantics, is known for the dictum: "the map is not the territory." The map of reality is not reality. It is a reduction of what it represents.

Differentiating between map and territory is sometimes possible under ridiculous conditions, such as the map made in Professor Mein Herr's country in Lewis Carroll's *Sylvie and Bruno*, whose scale is one mile to one mile. "It has never been spread out, yet," he explains, "the farmers objected ... so we now use the country itself, as its own map, and I assure you it does nearly as well."[9] These are the same absurd realms Jorge Luis Borges evokes in his story "On Exactitude in Science", in which "the Cartographers Guilds struck a Map of the Empire whose size was that of the Empire, and which coincided point to point with it."[10]

Whether the territory comes before the map or the other way around – "the map makes the territory", as Baudrillard put it – maps always have been and seemingly will go on being an aesthetic-scientific illustration of the narrative through which we perceive the world and our own place in it. The map is not a truth but a story; it includes gaps and blank spaces. And as with a story we can decide whether we believe in it enough to use it as we set out in search of the Mountains of the Moon, the kingdom of the giants or California. As with other stories, every

Oscar Wilde remarked about another imaginary spot saying "a map of the world that does not include Utopia is not worth even glancing at, for it leaves out the one country at which Humanity is always landing. And when Humanity lands there, it looks out, and, seeing a better country, sets sail. Progress is the realisation of Utopias."[a] (Best of All Possible Worlds, page 247).

map will include plot twists that run into dead ends or empty spaces clamouring to be filled; sometimes, too, it will include deliberate mistakes and outright exaggerations. Like stories, maps may have an agenda and when we look for the world in them, sometimes we find ourselves.

7

NO MAN'S ISLAND

Hi-tech company Merlin Burrows proudly announces, "We find anything that has been lost, forgotten or hidden with pin-point accuracy."[1] This location and recovery firm employs historians, archeologists, security guards and salvaging experts who use satellite-scanning technologies to trace shipwrecks, hidden treasures and ancient sites. One of their projects is the most famous lost city in the world – more celebrated than Shambala, more passionately desired than El Dorado and more mysterious than Shangri-La – the city of Atlantis, on the fabled island of the same name. Prosaically, the company believes it is located somewhere off the coast of Spain.

Indeed, it wasn't very far away from there that the city of Atlantis was conceived – in Athens, Greece. The first signs of its existence appear in *Timaeus* and *Critias*, two of Plato's dialogues. The philosopher mentions that knowledge of a huge island, "greater in extent than Libya and Asia",[2] had reached him from Solon, the great Athenian lawmaker, who had in turn heard about it from an Egyptian priest. The latter had told Solon about an incredibly advanced culture that had existed about 9,000 years before his time. However, the beginnings of Atlantis may have occurred at a much later event, closer in time to Plato himself. In the fifteenth century BC a volcano erupted on the Aegean island of Thera, causing one of the most violent and destructive events in 10,000 years. The result was a gigantic tsunami and a dense blanket of clouds that darkened the sky. The central part of the island became submerged in the sea, leaving behind only remnants, which we now know as the archipelago of Santorini.

Could this powerful catastrophe also help us solve the mystery surrounding the fate of the vanished Minoan culture? Did it imprint itself on the collective memory of the nations inhabiting the region, giving rise more than a millennium later to the narratives about Atlantis and its ruin? Plato has it that the people of Atlantis ruled the entire eastern Mediterranean and only the Athenians succeeded in defeating them – with the aid of Zeus

In Voltaire's satirical novella, *Candide*, which mocks Leibniz's optimistic philosophy, his titular protagonist arrives at El Dorado, which is an isolated utopia in whose streets children play with precious stones, and "the roads were covered, or rather adorned, with carriages of a glittering form and substance, in which were men and women of surprising beauty …"[a] (Best of All Possible Worlds, page 247).

The same happened around another eruption in 1815 (Blood Lust, page 93; The Body Electric, page 221).

who was enraged at the Atlanteans' arrogance, greed and lack of due sacrificial practices – and together they annihilated the island. Alberto Manguel and Gianni Guadalupi, in *The Dictionary of Imaginary Places* recount that: "After the cataclysm that brought destruction to Atlantis, two major sections of the island were miraculously preserved, one ... under the sea; the other ... in the Sahara desert." In the latter location the descendants of Atlantis are ruled by a queen and continue to observe and develop their esoteric practices, which include the embalming of male visitors: "First the skin is painted with silver salts; then the body is placed in a bath of *oricalcum sulphate*. An electrical exchange takes place and the body is transformed into a statue of solid metal."[3]

Even though most scholars agree that no Atlantis of any kind ever existed, the image of the decline and fall of a mighty civilization swallowed by the abyss proved to be persistently alluring to the human imagination – despite Plato himself mentioning it as a cautionary tale. "Atlantis is not a place to be honoured or emulated at all. Atlantis is not the perfect society... Quite to the contrary... Atlantis is the embodiment of a materially wealthy, technologically advanced, and militarily powerful nation that has become corrupted by its wealth, sophistication, and might,"[4] writes Kenneth Feder, the archeologist and an outspoken critic of pseudo-archeology, in his book *Encyclopedia of Dubious Archeology: From Atlantis to the Walam Olum*.

Some considered Atlantis an allegory and others did believe in its physical existence, including archeologists, cartographers and a Minnesota Member of Congress. In 1882, Ignatius Donnelly, a politician, fished Atlantis from where it had lingered for generations – deep below the surface in the murky depths of cultural memory – and presented it as not just a lost island but as the very cradle of humanity. The same earthquake that ruined Atlantis, he claimed, was civilization's big bang: the island's inhabitants and their arcane lore were dispersed across the world, becoming the Greek gods, the forebears of the Aztecs, the founders of Mesopotamian cities, the origin of all progress. Donnelly's book *Atlantis: The Antediluvian World* announced a new age of Atlantic renaissance and Helena Blavatsky, founder of the Theosophists in the late nineteenth century, jumped on the bandwagon. Blavatsky, who claimed she received her ancient knowledge directly from a number of spiritual teachers, thus learned about the existence of seven root races, the

The ancient Greeks liked to imagine mighty queens and all-female societies just so they could fight them – and win (Wonder Women, page 37).

In Charlotte Perkins Gilman's feminist utopia men were treated better (Best of All Possible Worlds, page 247).

Who often drew non-existing places into their maps (The Territory and the Map, page 47).

fourth of which originates in Atlantis. Like Donnelly, she believed that the wisdom of this race spread worldwide when Atlantis went under and she argued that its descendants still live among us, with the unique attributes of their fatherland still coursing through their blood. They were the Aryan race.

She believed in a great many things, not least among them, fairies (Paper Fairies, page 161).

The 1901 translation of Blavatsky's *The Secret Doctrine* profoundly affected pan-German thinkers who were preoccupied with gathering support for theories about their racial origins. Guido von List, the Austrian occultist, established a neo-pagan movement that sought to encourage Aryans to resume worshipping the Norse god Wotan, and to popularize Aryosophical teachings, the wisdom of the Aryan race. For the former monk Jörg Lanz von Liebesfels, the Aryans were none other than the sons of gods and they were able to use electromagnetic radiation to communicate telepathically. Followers of occultist, intelligence agent and political activist Rudolf von Sebottendorf believed that the Aryans were the offspring of a race of ice giants who lived in the mythical land of Hyperborea. Von Sebottendorf was the founder of the Thule Society, which took its name from Ultima Thule – the farthest north – a land mentioned in Virgil's *Aeneid*. Ian Kershaw, Hitler's biographer, observed that the Thule Society list of members included many prominent Nazi supporters and leaders including Alfred Rosenberg, who became the movement's ideologue, stating in his book *The Myth of the Twentieth Century*, "The old legends of Atlantis may appear in a new light. It seems far from impossible that in areas over which the Atlantic waves roll and giant icebergs float, a flourishing continent once rose above the waters, and upon it a creative race produced a far-reaching culture and sent its children out into the world as seafarers and warriors."[5] Another member of the Thule Society, Heinrich Himmler, eventually became head of the SS and the Gestapo, as well as interior minister of the Third Reich. He was also the executor of the Final Solution and the founder of Ahnenerbe, a Nazi research group dedicated to the study of German ancestral heritage. Himmler, as Heather Pringle in *The Master Plan* writes, "conceived of this research organization as an elite think tank, a place brimming with brilliant mavericks and brainy young upstarts – up-and-comers who would give traditional science a thorough cleansing".[6] Ahnenerbe sought to emphasize the scientific in "scientific racism" and make it a respectable substitute for "Jewish" sciences that would academically validate

Or Odin, the one-eyed All-Father of the Vikings (Twilight of the Gods, page 65).

As did the rulers of Francis Bacon's 1624 utopia, "The New Atlantis" (Best of All Possible Worlds, page 247).

Dante's tour guide (Moving Heaven and Hell, page 71).

the archaic beginnings and superiority of the Aryans. For this purpose the institute organized expeditions to the four corners of the earth: the members included musicologists, philologists and anthropologists who collected evidence and documentation from Iran to Tibet to Finland. One such expedition to Bolivia was headed by Edmund Kiss, an amateur archeologist and eventually SS *Obersturmführer* who argued that the monumental structures at Tiwanaku were built by Aryans who reached the region after the demise of their native Atlantis.

These were the explorations that sparked the imagination of the *Indiana Jones and the Raiders of the Lost Ark* and *Indiana Jones and the Last Crusade* screenwriters, the creators of the *Hellboy* comics and the computer game designers of *Wolfenstein 3D* (*Castle Wolfenstein*), who brought the "Hydra" plot line into the Marvel comic books and cinematic universe. They also inspired many others, including scholars who were fascinated by the connection between humankind's most efficient ever war machine and arcane powers. For Eric Kurlander, author of *Hitler's Monsters: A Supernatural History of the Third Reich*, what's so troubling about this type of imagery is that it makes us less capable of identifying real, similar threats. "By creating a caricature of Nazi occultism that is outside of all reality, we can't learn any lessons that might help us anticipate the same kinds of problems today," he explained in an interview he gave when his book came out. "In times of crisis, supernatural and faith-based thinking masquerading as 'scientific' solutions to real problems helps facilitate the worst kind of political and social outcomes."[7]

The historian Nicholas Goodrick-Clarke believed that the source of this issue lies in the work of "occult historiography" which, delighting in the more exotic elements of Nazi dabblings with occultism, go for a simplistic and somehow reassuring answer. In his book *The Occult Roots of Nazism: Secret Aryan Cults and Their Influence on Nazi Ideology*, he argues that "The occult historiography chooses to explain the Nazi phenomenon in terms of an ultimate and arcane power." This view allows the portrayal of National Socialism "as an uncanny interlude in modern history". And its appeal lies in the "intrusion of an extinct order, generally considered both monstrous and forbidden, upon the familiar world of liberal institutions ... The remarkable story of the rise of Nazism is implicitly linked to the power of the supernatural. According to this

Toward the end of the war, when it seemed that the master race was about to be overrun by Allied Forces, Minister of Propaganda Joseph Goebbels urged German citizens over the airwaves to join a guerrilla movement named after the Nazis' favourite monster, whose purpose was to bite the ankles of the enemy. One enthusiastic broadcaster announced: "I am so savage, I am filled with rage, Lily the Werewolf is my name. I bite, I eat, I am not tame. My werewolf teeth bite the enemy." (Lupus Est, page 93).

Which makes it very clear that the Grail reveals itself only to those who are truly pure (King of Cups, page 153).

Whose aesthetics and monsters are drawn from H P Lovecraft's nightmarish worlds (Fear Itself, page 237).

A word that has a deep and lasting connection to horror (Fear Itself, page 237) and especially to the perturbation that any deviation in what is familiar and known to us tends to evoke (Valley of the Dolls, page 205).

mythology Nazism cannot have been the mere product of socio-economic factors. No empirical or purely sociological thesis could account for its nefarious projects and continued success."[8] This approach, while it tickles our sense of sensation and delights our wildest fantasies about the intervention of mighty and mysterious powers in human life, exonerates and to some extent absolves the crimes committed by the Nazis. They were the result of conscious choice and the outcome of ideology, rather than imposed by some external and demonic force that corrupted the perpetrators' souls.

By no means did the entire party elite put their faith behind Atlantis, astrology, ice giants and archaic gods. It is doubtful that Hitler himself believed in these things, and attempts to advance these ideas often met with resistance. But the wish to ground racial and occult doctrines in scientific findings, to weld together the supernatural with the unnatural to construct a new *Übermensch* did not remain limited to a Platonic love of the sublime and esoteric exploits, the sort of thing that now causes more hilarity than anxiety. Documents presented during the Nuremberg trials refer to bodies of 112 Jews that were set aside to join August Hirt's anthropological collection of human skeletons at the Reichsuniversität Straßburg and include a telex from Wolfram Sievers, the Ahnenerbe's managing director, asking for instructions in the face of the Allied Forces' advance, for "He is able to carry out the maceration and thus render them irrecognizable [sic]. However ... the entire work would have been partly done in vain, and it would be a great scientific loss for this unique collection, because hominit [sic] casts could not be made afterwards. The skeleton collection as such is not conspicuous. Viscera could be declared as remnants of corpses, apparently left in the anatomical institute by the French, and ordered to be cremated." As the court records show, "Sievers knew from the first moment he received Hirt's report of 9 February 1942 that mass murder was planned for the procurement of the skeleton collection. Nevertheless, he actively collaborated in the project, sent an employee of the Ahnenerbe to make the preparatory selections in the concentration camp at Auschwitz, and provided for the transfer of the victims from Auschwitz to Natzweiler."[9]

The so-called scientific experiments carried out by the institute's staff to prove their theories were not a marginal phenomenon of World War II but one of its most horrific justifications. Harnessing magic in the service of science, and mythology to support ideology played an important role in the formation of what the historian Uriel Tal calls, in his collection of essays *Religion, Politics and Ideology in the Third Reich*, "political theology" that relied on a "total revaluation of all values; the apocalyptic condition according to which catastrophe must precede redemption; the struggle between the forces of light and those of darkness, between the Aryan and the Jew; ritual purification from defiled blood; personal cleansing of the new Germanic man from contamination by the anti-German, the Jew; social and economic deliverance from parasites; unmasking of all evil".[10]

The Nazis did not heed Plato's old warning. The thousand-year Reich they tried to create out of nothing – and into nothing – fell, like the legendary island, at the hands of those who received Athens' democratic heritage and neither their military power nor their technological advances were a match for the wrath of the Allied Forces. And while the latter were fighting the Reich on the seas and oceans, in the air and on the beaches, someone sought to defeat them on paper: Aquaman. Under the aegis of his creator Mort Weisinger, the son of Jewish immigrants from Austria, Aquaman first appeared in 1941 in the comic magazine *More Fun Comics* #73, where he rescued refugees from a German submarine. He was not the only hero created and recruited by a Jewish artist. Fighting shoulder to shoulder with him were superheroes invented by those branded *Untermenschen* by the Nazis, such as Superman (created by Jerry Siegel and Joe Shuster) and Captain America (by Jacob Kurtzberg and Stanley Martin Lieber, also known as Jack Kirby and Stan Lee) among others. However, Aquaman was neither a journalist nor a soldier – he was powered directly by Atlantis' secrets. In the 2018 film adaptation of his adventures, he is the heir of a submarine kingdom who has been exiled because of his mixed parentage; the Nuremberg laws would have called him a *Mischling*. His mission is to save the earth from the rage of the seven seas, which his half-brother and ruler of the city threatens to unleash upon humankind as punishment for the sins we committed in our ignorance, our greed and our contempt for the sea and all that is in it. Robert Silverberg, another Jew, crowned a different ethnic group also mercilessly persecuted by the Nazis as the rulers of Atlantis. In *Star of Gypsies* Atlantis is home to an advanced gypsy kingdom,

As expressed in Nazism's attraction to visions of Ragnarök (Twilight of the Gods, page 65).

Like the rats they were compared to in Nazi propaganda films (Blood Lust, page 93).

Like the Escapist, the superhero invented by the protagonists of *The Amazing Adventures of Kavalier & Clay* by Michael Chabon (The Body Electric, page 221).

As the ones committed against a multitude of narwhals, who found themselves featuring in one of history's biggest scams (The Lady and the Unicorn, page 179).

which evolved from an alien culture and, from the moment its people are expelled from their paradise, they wander the earth in time and space.

And must therefore conceal themselves from us xenophobic humans (We Come in Peace, page 123).

The claim for ownership of Atlantis by lovers of Nazi esoterica is not just a historical curiosity and great subject matter for genre literature and comics. Even those who did not believe the lost continent was their ancient fatherland harnessed its powers. For once politics and ideology yoke together mythos and ethos, using one as justification for the other, enabling bodies like the Ahnenerbe to go about unhindered, forcing themselves on the collective imagination.

If we ever lose sight of that, our fate too will be sealed in the depths of the sea.

8
TWILIGHT OF THE GODS

It was in August 1876 that the Vikings first grew horns. They did so specifically in honour of the first performance of Richard Wagner's *Ring* cycle, inspired by the history and mythology of the Norse invaders and the *Nibelungenlied*, a thirteenth-century German epic lost for generations that had resurfaced in the seventeenth century.

> This was not the only case in which a lost work had a profound cultural impact once it was discovered (Flame and Moth, page 17).

It took Wagner 26 years to complete the four works making up his prodigious Teutonic musical marathon: the story of a cursed ring that brings disaster upon its owners, gods fighting against each other and the doomed love of the brave Siegfried and beautiful Brünnhilde. While the world's dignitaries were settling their backsides into the unforgiving seats of the new opera house in the small town of Bayreuth, girding their loins for 15 hours of terrifying revenge and rivers of blood, the opera singers were donning the costume designer's senseless creations on their heads. Wagner's wife, Cosima, "politically incorrect to the end", writes Roberta Frank in *The Invention of the Viking Horned Helmet*, "lamented that Professor Carl Emil Doepler's costumes brought to mind '*Indianerhauptlinge*'"[1] – Indian chiefs.

However, the operatic image stuck and continues to headbutt culture, whether it is in Mel Brooks' Viking funeral, where the bearded invaders remove their helmets to reveal horns that grow straight out of their heads or in the logo of the Minnesota Vikings football club.

Nonetheless, there is evidence of early horned helmets. They were found on twelfth-century BC figurines in Crete; they adorn the lavishly decorated silver vessel known as the Gundestrup cauldron in its Celtic imagery; and they proudly protrude from protective head gear found near Veksø in Denmark, dating back to the Bronze Age. Like other helmets with horns, these were probably used merely for ceremonial purposes and there is no sign that they were ever used in battle.

Similarly, there is no archaeological evidence to support the possibility the Vikings wore helmets like the ones Herr Doepler gave them when they set out on their conquests. Nor indeed, is there any common sense in his design, as the Vikings sat crowded like sardines, cheek by jowl, in the longships that took them to Byzantium, North America, Britain and Russia, leaving no room to butt horns; not to mention the folly of such a helmet when you're fighting packed together.

And fight they did. From the late eighth to the late eleventh centuries the Vikings cut a wide swath through parts of Europe and beyond, raiding and trading, pillaging and raping, settling and ruling. They were not squeamish about fighting dirty. Ahmed Ibn Fahdlan, the famous envoy of the Abbasid caliph, described them as "the filthiest of God's creations".[2] And Alcuin of York said of the havoc they wreaked in the monasteries of Northumbria that "Never before has such terror appeared in Britain."[3]

However, in the late nineteenth century the ignorant, dirty berserkers received a romantic makeover. The Scandinavians, who coined the fantastical phrase "Viking Age", and even more so the Germans, who believed an infusion of ancient Norse blood would bolster their national origin story, retouched the Vikings' image, turning them into a symbol of the unadulterated Aryan – a noble savage.

While seeking to purify it from all outside influences (No Man's Island, page 57).

Were the Vikings in fact nothing but gentleman-adventurers, whose name was blackened by biased monotheists? Were they shrewd marine-based businessmen? Daring seafarers and explorers? Representatives of Norse culture and mythology, who enriched the West with some seminal literary works like the Eddas and the Völsunga saga? They were all these things and more.

Or lady-adventurers (Wonder Women, page 37).

It appears that wherever these brave and energetic seafarers reached, they mauled the men and molested the women. DNA sequencing of more than 400 Viking remains from archeological sites across Europe and Scandinavia suggests that not only is the image of the towering flaxen-haired Viking wrong, but so is the assumption that these pirates all looked similar. The sequencing conclusions indicate that many Vikings were brown-haired, of average height and of diverse genetic heritage – and that this genetic legacy lives on today, as 6 per cent of people in the UK have Viking DNA in their genes, compared to 10 per cent in Sweden.

However, complaints about their personal hygiene remain unresolved, as cleanliness is in the eye of the beholder. The undiplomatic diplomat, Ahmad Ibn Fadlahn, was shocked by the Vikings' tendency not to wash their hands after indulging in food or sex. The Brits, by contrast, were taken aback by the fact that these barbarians bathed once a week and spent much time combing their long hair.

The Vikings were a lot more polished than the islanders they brandished their swords against – so much so that the word for Saturday in Scandinavian languages still is *lördag*, or *laurdag*, derived from the old Norse word meaning "bath", as this was the day when Vikings traditionally conducted their ablutions. The Norse pantheon bequeathed Tuesday, Wednesday, Thursday and Friday to the Anglo-Saxons: Tuesday for Týr, the god of justice, equality, courage and war; Wednesday for Odin, all-father, god of wisdom, inspiration, poetry and also war; Thursday for Thor, god of thunder, lightning, rain – and yes, war as well; and finally Friday named for Frigg or Freyja, two deities sharing many similar traits, such as love, beauty, fertility – and war, of course.

In most Latin languages (Italian, French, Spanish, Catalan, Romanian and more) the day is named after Mars, god of war (We Come in Peace, page 123).

The exploits of these gods and their believers have gained renewed interest and more faithful representation in books such as Neil Gaiman's *Norse Mythology* and Carolyne Larrington's *The Norse Myths*, in television series such as *The Vikings*, which depicts the hair- (and horn-) raising experiences and bloody struggles of Ragnar Lodbrok. He is a historic figure who, with the help of his wife, former shield-maiden Ladgerda, becomes king of all Scandinavia. The fact that the programme abounds with generously endowed, fair-haired women and muscular, sword-wielding men is only part of its appeal. Its creators draw heavily on historical accounts and in-depth research, such as Saxo Grammaticus' twelfth-century *Gesta Danorum*, thirteenth-century sources like the *Saga of Ragnar Lodbrok* and the *Tale of Ragnar's Sons*, and even Ibn Fadlahn's snobbish reports, which imbue the show with blood-curdling realism. Contemporary Norwegians take their own history with a pinch of salt in the TV comedy *Norsemen*, which is more preoccupied with everyday Viking life and problems, such as how hard it is to get rid of blood stains on your clothes, how to dry fish in a rainy climate and how to navigate the internal politics of a small settlement dominated by stressed-out bearded men and strong-willed intelligent women. Cressida Cowell, the UK's Children's Laureate 2019 and author of the *How to Train Your Dragon* books (turned into successful animated films), also enjoys making fun of these historical

Who wore men's clothes to fight alongside him and only – according to Saxo Grammaticus – her long, lush locks betrayed her sex (Wonder Women, page 37).

fiends, and the same is true for the Monty Python team in their film *Erik the Viking*.

There were those who sought to summon these ancient gods and their followers into our midst, as did mythology enthusiast Rick Reardon in his *Magnus Chase* trilogy, master of the imagination Neil Gaiman in *American Gods* and Douglas Adams, the high priest of humour, in *The Long Dark Tea-Time of the Soul*, which all revolve around the dispossessed gods trying to restore their former glory.

Restoring former glory was also on the mind of Snorri Sturluson, Icelandic scholar, politician and womanizer. His work, the *Prose Edda*, compiled in the early twelfth century at the time Saxo Germanicus was writing his accounts, together with the unattributed *Poetic Edda*, a collection of Old Norse poems, form the earliest written sources about the exploits of the militant Norse pantheon. The works also tell of Yggdrasil, the mighty World Tree at the centre of the universe on whose branches hang, like cosmic fruits, the nine worlds, including Midgard where humans live; Jotunheim, the home of the giants; Helheim, the realm of the dead. Situated at the highest point of Bifrost, the burning rainbow bridge, is Asgard, the domain of the gods up in the heavens. This is where you will find the great hall of Valhalla – the warriors' paradise. From here, too, one-eyed Odin's handmaidens, the Valkyries, go on their mission to select the best slain warriors. This is also the tree that will shake during Ragnarök, the all-consuming war foretold to erupt between the gods of Asgard and the powers of chaos. This war will be led by the shapeshifting and vengeful trickster god Loki, and his son the great wolf Penryr, who is kept on a chain forged by the dwarves from impossible things such as the sounds of cat paws, the spittle of birds, the hairs of a woman's beard, the breath of fish and the roots of a mountain.

The aesthetic potential and tragic grandeur of gods on the brink of decreed oblivion, accompanied by the lament of a heavenly choir of crows and wolves, giant snakes and greedy dragons fascinated not only Wagner but other creative people and influenced their works throughout the centuries. They include J R R Tolkien, whose cursed golden ring and other elements derive their mythic power from these ancient sources; Viking-styled heavy metal bands roaring about the twilight of the gods; Fritz Lang's expressionist adaptations; and Stan Lee, who in 1951 introduced Thor as a secondary character in a comic

Who can transform into swans (The Human Animal, page 189).

Not their only mortal sin (Here Be Dragons, page 79).

devoted to the goddess Venus. Thor was then reinvented and made his debut in the anthology *Journey into Mystery #83*. With the help of his magic hammer Mjölnir, the hero slowly fought his way to a more prominent place, making the acquaintance of other divine entities such as Egyptian Seth and Greek Hercules, eventually becoming a regular member of Marvel's eclectic "Avengers". Lee also fell prey to Doepler's restyling: "I pictured Norse gods looking like Vikings of old," he said, "with the flowing beards, horned helmets, and battle clubs."[4]

Which never existed. Or did it? (No Man's Island, page 57).

Comics are the setting for contemporary polytheism, an abundant pantheon in which the gods of Asgard and Mount Olympus, the people of Atlantis and Krypton coexist happily or alternatively do merciless battle.

One of Christianity's most prominent holy relics (A Faustian Bargain, page 1).

But the appeal of the Viking and the Norse myths was not limited to entertainment. Rejecting the Christian kingdom of heaven, Nazism opted for Valhalla, preferring Odin, who hung from Yggdrasil for nine days with a self-inflicted wound in his side, to Jesus, nailed to his cross for six hours having been injured by the Lance of Longinus. Searching for the great German *Volksgeist* and seeking to forge the new Aryan race from a fabricated, quasi-ancient origin, Hitler saw a fitting antecedent for his fatherland in the splendour of the gods of Asgard.

He also found the images of his villains (Blood Lust, page 93) and role models (Lupus Est, page 93).

A utopian endeavour bound to turn into a dystopia (Best of All Possible Worlds, page 247).

Hitler was Wagner's foremost admirer and he considered the composer's anti-Semitic writings to be deeply congenial. For him, Wagner's visions of a bloody twilight offered a mirror image of his own apocalyptic revelations.

He was not the only one. Richard Schulze-Kossens, commander of the SS cadet school named Grenadier-Division 38 "Nibelungen", was another, although the helmet that was selected as their emblem accurately bore wings, not horns. And the thundering notes of the *Ring* were heard both at party conferences and in the death camps.

However, this fiery composer's music had already formed the soundtrack of another ideology. When Hitler was only seven years old, the journalist Theodor Herzl, a Wagner aficionado himself, drafted *Der Judenstaat (The Jewish State)* during a performance of *Tannhäuser*, "My one form of relaxation in the evenings was to listen to Wagnerian music ... Only on the evenings when there was no opera did I have doubts about the correctness of my ideas."[5] *Tannhäuser*'s overture opened the Second Zionist Congress in Basle dedicated to the idea of creating a Jewish state, the very state where his work is banned from being publicly performed till this day. "I can't listen to that much Wagner," said another Jew, Woody Allen, "I start getting the urge to conquer Poland."

This dichotomy of destruction and inspiration, carnage and renewal, has always been part and parcel of Norse mythology and continues to permeate everything its great tree has inspired, ever since the days of the Viking invaders. And it will continue to do so – until the fat lady sings.

9
MOVING HEAVEN AND HELL

Sharp-eyed visitors may well notice a detail in Michelangelo's huge fresco "The Last Judgment", which adorns the altar wall in the Sistine Chapel. In the far bottom-right corner, a man with donkey's ears is being dragged toward the underworld; he is nude and a snake is biting his own one-eyed snake. This is King Minos depicted with the face of Biagio da Cesena, the Papal Master of Ceremonies, who complained to the Holy See about the many naked figures rising up to heaven or being dragged down toward hell in the half-finished work he had sneaked in to observe. Such imagery, he argued, was more fitting for a bath house or a tavern. Having discovered that Buonarotti painted him among the damned, he begged the pope to intervene and have his image removed. The sixteenth-century writer Lodovico Domenichi claims that Pope Paul III replied: "Messer Biagio, you know that I have from God power in heaven and on earth; but my authority does not extend into hell, and you must have patience if I cannot free you from there."[1] In other words, if Michelangelo dispatched you there, you're doomed. That's how it is in the inferno: it's easy to get into and hard to get out of, as those who arrive at its gates discover – gates on which Dante, in one of the most formative works of Western culture, had engraved, "All hope abandon ye who enter here."[2]

John Cleland had about 50 such euphemisms in *Fanny Hill: Memoirs of a Woman of Pleasure*, published in 1748 (The Pleasure Principle, page 195).

His ancient Roman predecessors weren't shy about such frescoes but elected to open libraries in bath houses (Ex Libris, page 9).

Midway upon the journey of his life, at the age of 35 and in the wake of the bloody Guelph–Ghibelline conflict, Dante Alighieri was exiled from the city-state of Florence and found himself "within a forest dark, for the straightforward pathway had been lost".[3]

In medieval Italy the Guelphs, who supported the pope, and the Ghibellines, who sided with the Holy Roman emperor, were at each other's throats during the twelfth and thirteenth centuries, with their enmity persisting until the fifteenth century. After Dante's party the White Guelphs lost the battle for Florence, he travelled extensively and began working on his masterpiece.

As many exiles – such as Ovid – did (The Human Animal, page 189).

The morose sentiment in the opening lines of the first Canto of *Inferno* quoted above, speaks volumes. Dante felt like hell, and the only thing to do was to go down there. He is accompanied on his journey by the eminent Virgil, the poet who had managed to redeem his own epic hero Aeneas from Hades, the Greek underworld.

Inferno is the first book of the literary triptych *Comedia* (the adjective "Divine" was a later addition), which also includes *Purgatorio* and *Paradiso*. In this immensely influential work, Dante describes both the upper and the lower realms and seeks, as many of the Renaissance artists who followed in his footsteps did, to achieve a form of cultural syncretism in which the Greco-Roman tradition merges with Christian doctrine. His protagonist and namesake, the Catholic poet, journeys in the company of a pagan writer. In limbo – the anteroom for those who died before the Saviour's birth – he meets men like Socrates and Homer, women like Penthesilea and Electra, and even Muslims like Saladin and Avicenna – the Who's Who of antiquity, all waiting in vain for a redemption that will never come. "The poetry of Dante", writes Percy Bysshe Shelley in *A Defence of Poetry*, "may be considered as the bridge thrown over the stream of time, which unites the modern and ancient world."[4]

Queen of the Amazons (Wonder Women, page 37).

Shelley's wife, Mary, built her own bridge between present and future, and became the mother of what was to become known as the science fiction genre (The Body Electric, page 221).

Dante's *Inferno* is not just populated by notable ancients, but includes mythical dignitaries like the Fates, who found ample employment for themselves there, or Charon, the ferryman of Hades, who managed to hold on to his job despite changes in management. On lower levels, many of Dante's political adversaries are condemned to suffer eternity in inventive torment.

The fate that awaited them outside of *Inferno* was far more horrific (Wonder Women, page 37).

In all nine circles, the punishment fits the crime. So, "brown-nosers" flounder in pools of boiling excrement, and those who stirred discord, such as the Prophet Mohammed, are rewarded with having their bodies ripped to pieces.

At the bottom of the pit dwells Lucifer, the Fallen Angel, encased in ice up to his waist, "were he as fair once, as he now is foul".[5] His three mouths chew forever on traitors like Judas Iscariot. With this, Dante and Virgil have reached their final destination and after they climb on top of the bat-winged Devil, everything takes a turn for the better – what was up goes down, vice changes to virtue and they re-emerge from hell into the world.

Unsurprisingly perhaps, *Inferno* gained more attention than its successors, *Purgatorio* and *Paradiso*. Images of hell and its afflictions, rendered in art, were the horror films and porn movies of the Middle Ages. They were morality plays showing plenty of bare human flesh exposed to cruel and unusual torment. While the Church fathers and holy scriptures balked at any specific description of hell because it exceeds human understanding, Dante took this as a challenge and set to imagining the unimaginable. But even he, a man whose Tuscan dialect was to become the basis for standardized Italian, found himself at a loss for words, "Ask it not, Reader, for I write it not," he says of the ninth and final circle, "because all language would be insufficient."[6] In *The Body in Pain*, Elaine Scarry observes that "Physical pain does not simply resist language but actively destroys it,"[7] but when words fail the image prevails, and painters and sculptors – from Michelangelo, through Blake to Rodin – tried to render infernal suffering by nonverbal means.

The human animal loves to be terrified (Fear Itself, page 237).

And titillated (The Pleasure Principle, page 195).

When we take a close look at the nauseatingly inventive and invasive torments of the great depicter of hell, Hieronymus Bosch, in his triptych "Garden of Earthly Delights," we discover a dizzying variety of such visual attempts. Among other things Bosch presents us with a knife with a huge pair of ears pressing down on some unfortunates, people tied to enormous musical instruments and a man with a flute stuck up his behind. There is a monstrous owl seated on a toilet bowl as it eats and simultaneously excretes the sinners; a knight being gnawed by huge rats as the Eucharist drops from his hands and a tiny, armored demon dragging along a severed foot from which dangles a scroll confirming the marriage of a man to a pig in a nun's habit.

It was not only Bosch who expressed such sarcastic innuendo, aimed at the established Church. For over a millennium, ever since the aggressive and comprehensive soul-acquisition campaign that started off with Constantinus' conversion in the fourth century, Christianity dangled hell like a stick over the heads of believers, with indulgences, its promissory notes of reprieve, as the carrot. Catholicism turned the threat of everlasting torment into a masterful recruiting technique that used intimidation and redemption alternatively, forging the links in a chain to keep the faithful on a short leash. Public abhorrence at the ever-increasing corrupt trade in indulgences grew so intense that Martin Luther who published his "Ninety-five Theses" a year after Bosch's death, remarked: "If there is a hell, then Rome is built on it."

The most effective "Get out of Jail" card in Christendom's Monopoly (A Faustian Bargain, page 1).

Judaism, too, believed in hell on earth, and the Babylonian Talmud described hell as having three entrances: one in the desert, one in the sea and one in Jerusalem. The Jewish netherworld developed over the ages as it came into contact with other religions: from the Canaanite and Ugaritic mythologies, which were widespread around ancient Israel and Judah, to dualist theologies like Persian Zoroastrianism, which the Jews encountered during their Babylonian exile. In the beginning there was the Sheol, a place of neither punishment nor torture, just the abode of the dead. But this view evolved until, by the beginning of the third century AD, the angel on duty already had a choice of weapons – five types of flames – each with its own nutritional preferences. There was fire that neither eats nor drinks; fire that drinks but doesn't eat; fire that eats but doesn't drink; fire that both eats and drinks; and fire that eats fire.

A religion that found itself, along with many other philosophies and beliefs, at the centre of George Lucas' hyper-real faith (Force Majeure, page 135).

Jewish hell eventually expanded physically, too. Once Judaism received planning permission it was finally able to boast its very own seven highly specialized regions of hell, each with its own tortures and torments.

Bureaucracy, of course, was an infernal nuisance in its own right and had been ever since the ancient Egyptians. The entrance to the *duat*, their realm of the dead, was guarded by Ammit the devourer of souls, whose role was to consume those who failed to measure up to the feather of truth. It was not hard to find a way around this by timely acquisition of the *Book of Coming Forth by Day*, better known as the *Book of the Dead*. This included incantations and tips for the afterlife that could help the owner cheat his or her way into Aaru, the field of reeds, which the Greeks later picked up and turned into their Elysian fields.

It was the ancient Chinese who raised the bar, quantitatively speaking at least. Historically partial to bureaucracy, they created Diyu, a hell of almost infinite complexity consisting of a ramified subterranean maze with specific sub-specializations. Diyu has 18 levels of hell, each divided into different departments. For example, the Niu Keng hell is reserved for people who abuse animals – they are thrown into a pit where they will be trampled by the same animals they have been cruel to. All underworld sections are equipped with hot and cold running agonies.

As opposed to a labyrinth, which has a much simpler layout (A Rat in a Maze, page 147).

The Jewish hell Gehenna, with its modest seven sections, limited itself to heat only. Its name is derived from "the valley of the son of Hinnom", a site used for an Ammonite human sacrifice ritual, which King Josiah sought to eradicate, "That no man might make his son or his daughter to pass through the fire to Molech."[8] In time this accursed place became Jerusalem's main garbage dump and the memory of the burning altars, together with the heat from the compost causing occasional spontaneous combustions, turned hell into a place associated with eternal fire in the Eastern mind. Similarly, as befitted a religion that emerged from the desert, the Qur'an portrays Jahannam as blazing with fire in almost every verse where it is mentioned, describing it as 70 times hotter than the fires of earth.

She's not the only one (Force Majeure, page 135).

However, in the Western world the core of hell is frozen, an image some scholars attribute to a racial memory of the great Ice Age. Like Dante, who fitted out his inferno with lakes of fire and brimstone as well as the ice encasing Lucifer, Bosch managed to compose a song of ice and fire that does not lack any of them. While in the upper right part of his image of hell a city is in flames (perhaps a reference to his own city of 's-Hertogenbosch, which was nearly consumed by fire when he was 13 years old), this surrealistic work of art shows a fiendish-looking penguin skating down the middle of a frozen lake, skirting the unfortunates trapped in it.

The visions of Bosch's *Eden* and *Garden of Earthly Delights* are no less bewildering, whether it is the left panel depicting God scolding Adam and Eve or in the centre panel, where a host of naked men and women are cavorting in a variety of physical pleasures, from eating forbidden fruit to copulating in a dizzying array of positions, surrounded by fantastic structures and mythological creatures such as mermaids, griffons and unicorns.

With the serpent looped around a tree in the corner (Here Be Dragons, page 79).

Tempting men, as they customarily do (Heads or Tails, page 183).

But Bosch's representations of the Garden – like the rest of his works – are unusual in the figurative landscape of the Good Place, because although hell may be fiery or frozen, heaven is usually ... tepid.

Possibly running amok, considering the absence of virginity in the picture (The Lady and the Unicorn, page 179).

The ancient Egyptians who managed to get into Aaru found themselves on a chain of fertile islands, where those who passed the rigorous post-mortem obstacle course could lie back and relax while supernatural servants satisfied their every whim forever and ever. In the Greek Elysium the weather was always perfect, while in the apocryphal Happy Hunting Grounds imagined by the white man for the Native Americans, the bison were always plump and easy to catch. In the Norse Valhalla you could revel

Who admitted only the fiercest warriors (Wonder Women, page 37).

in bloodcurdling battles to the death over and over again. In Judaism, the Garden of Eden – where Adam and Eve were first brought and later expelled from – began as a physical place. Later theological conceptions, such as reincarnation and resurrection, have no explicit mentions in the Jewish Bible except for a few relatively vague references. The prevailing view was that "the dead know not anything, neither have they any more a reward; for the memory of them is forgotten. Also, their love, and their hatred, and their envy, is now perished."[9] Thus declares Ecclesiastes with the wisdom of Solomon and in his usual merry fashion.

Following Zoroastrian influences, Judaism also began to construct its own heavenly residence for the righteous where they receive their just rewards, which consisted mainly of gorging themselves on Behemoth meat while lounging under canopies made from the beautiful skin of the Leviathan by the Almighty.

When Christianity appeared, it inherited these readymade blueprints, but now they had a name. The word "paradise" rolled into English via a long and winding path from cuneiform in old Persian, where it was used to describe an enclosure and, specifically, a walled garden of the kind preferred by Assyrian emperors such as Ashurbanipal. From there it became the Hebrew *pardes*, meaning orchard or garden and now Christianity got to cultivate and expand it. According to Tertullian, the second-century-AD early Christian author, paradise is a vast gladiator arena where the wicked fight it out to the delight of the faithful spectators, who refrained from wasting their time and corrupting their souls on such worldly pursuits when they were alive.

However, during the Middle Ages the physical aspect of the Sweet Hereafter faded, while the hidden light of the spiritual paradise intensified, as Dante expressed in *Paradiso*. Beatrice, his unrequited love, leads him among the planets, where the souls of the redeemed reside. Their radiance is so great that it becomes indescribable, like the worst torment.

And as with *Inferno*, a picture is worth a thousand words. In the case of paradise, the same image has been replicated a thousand times, from fresco to TV, from canvas to cinema, from Raphael to Robin Williams in the 1998 film *What Dreams May Come*. It has pastel-colored feather clouds replete with chubby, winged cherubs and berobed, serene humans treading lightly amid lush tropical vegetation or gleaming marble pillars or both

While "hell" comes from the Old Norse *hel*, which means "dwelling place" and the name of the goddess of the netherworld in Norse mythology (Twilight of the Gods, page 65).

Most paradises are gated communities (Best of All Possible Worlds, page 247).

Among his glorious construction projects was also a huge library, an institution that at least one librarian believed to be heaven (Ex Libris, page 9).

– and for some reason – they are often playing a lyre; all in an aesthetic-theological fusion very far from the bloodthirsty glee of Tertullian's depictions.

With the passing of the centuries, the Reformation, Protestantism and the Enlightenment, the very physical, detailed, hierarchical structure of Christian heaven and hell underwent a radical revolution.

Milton's *Paradise Lost* served as a turning point. His work depicted the protagonists of the great primordial drama – God and Satan, Adam and Eve – as believable characters full of angst and desire: Byronic Satan, passionate Adam, narcissistic Eve.

> Satan, specifically, was human, all too human (Number of the Beast, page 79).

> He himself was considered to be diabolical (Blood Lust, page 93).

Like Dante, Milton sought to reconcile Christian and pagan traditions to some extent, and even took an example from the works of Homer, another blind poet. Unlike Dante, who created and inhabited hell by the power of his imagination, Milton relied heavily on scripture. Yet, his immense talent stages dramatic scenes that are almost secular in tone. His Satan, who declares that it is "Better to reign in Hell than to serve in Heaven,"[10] is not a horrific three-headed monster, but a prodigal son trapped in an Oedipal struggle with a holy father.

Heaven, hell and everything in between never looked the same again.

Hell stopped expanding and started deepening, changing address from the underworld below to the hearts of humankind above. Shakespeare was proven right when he prophesized in *The Tempest*: "Hell is empty and all the devils are here."[11]

However, becoming an abstract concept only boosted its appeal. Hell stars in comics like *Spoon*, *Constantine* and *The Sandman*; it appears in its traditional horrifying role in films like *Drag Me to Hell*; it's a fixed location in TV serials such as *Buffy the Vampire Slayer* and *Supernatural*. *Inferno* has become the title of a Dan Brown thriller, in which the author of *The Da Vinci Code* examines the Malthusian fear of population explosion, which we may consider the most radical form of Sartre's misunderstood dictum, "Hell is other people".[12] In Brown's book, Dante's work and other artistic milestones of former times become a mere mystery to be deciphered if we want to defeat the forces of evil, who are no longer angels or demons but flesh-and-blood humans.

> Which has its own take on the Holy Grail (King of Cups, page 153).

Does our hectic and secularized world still have room for hell? Underneath our overpopulated cities, is there enough space for

Dante's nine circles? Do we still need Bosch's grotesque penal mechanisms? No longer a final destination, an ever-burning fire, hell is now an image or metaphor: the underworld as entertainment, pain as pastime. Unlike Dante's and Milton's contemporaries, we are not really afraid of hell. Our hearts have hardened to its imaginary horrors and we have outdone them with the horrors we perpetrate in reality by our own hands.

There is a whole genre of options (Fear Itself, page 237).

But while hell changes beneath our feet, Eden suffers (or, being paradise, perhaps it enjoys) the defect of perfection that makes all utopias static and dull. While descriptions of the worst torments of the underworld seemed to bring out the best in human imagination, the everlasting bliss of paradise is portrayed as timeless boredom. The fear of hell and the desire to avoid it gave humanity divine inspiration saturated with libidinal power, while the desperate, obsessive longing to return to where we were created, begging to be accepted back, seems childish by comparison.

Ever since their very first depiction (Best of All Possible Worlds, page 247).

Perhaps the true paradise we long for is lost forever and is not the one we return to after death. We were expelled from this paradise as soon as our lives began, as soon as we were born. This is the paradise of fetuses, the cradle of the womb, the state of utter innocence, the time before time and all knowledge of good and evil.

10
NUMBER OF THE BEAST

Please allow me to introduce myself: I was the one who afflicted Job with boils; I was there at Jesus' moment of weakness and it was I who signed bargains with Faust and Robert Johnson at the crossroad. I have suckled from witches' lady parts. Believe me. I am the father of lies, prince of hell, ruler of the netherworld, fallen angel, lord of darkness, Lucifer Morningstar. My number is 666 (or 616 according to certain versions of John's Revelation). Pleased to meet you, hope you've guessed my name.

> A misunderstanding (Weird Sisterhood, page 25).

The speaker, here, started his career as a low-ranking adversarial angel, a mere speed bump in the Book of Numbers. But by Job's time, he had already been promoted significantly to inquisitor, charged with breaking the faith of a man whose only apparent sin was being too perfect and upright.

When trying to date the composition of the Book of Job, Bible scholars have seized on the presence and function of Satan in the text as proof that it was written in the era of the Second Temple after the Babylonian exile, which exposed Jewish thought to Zoroastrianism with its dualistic approach. Its sacred writings feature two opposing powers forever vying to gain the upper hand in the world: Ahura Mazda, the light of wisdom, the holy spirit, creator of all that is good, and Angra Mainyu, the evil spirit who dwells in the dark, also known as Ahriman, the source of evil. Traces of this notion of evil, alongside the afterworld and final judgment, trickled through to Judaism and from it onward to Christianity and Islam. The division between good and evil was such an elegant solution to the ancient moral conundrum of the "suffering of the righteous" that even monotheism took it on board, though not without caution. For example, Isaiah puts the following words in the mouth of God, "I form the light, and create darkness: I make peace, and create evil: I the LORD do all these things."[1] Christianity, too, initially adopted the notion of a Satan who does the Maker's dirty work, like confronting Jesus with three temptations.

> The light and the dark sides of the force (Force Majeure, page 135).

However, his position began to change under the influence of Gnostic theology, which rocked the fledgling religion's cradle.

Which brought the population of Europe to its knees, causing people to seek redemption from the Devil's horns in the unicorn (The Lady and the Unicorn, page 179).

It made its way into Christianity and to an extent filtered back into Judaism, the two intersecting at one point. It became further entrenched in the Middle Ages, especially after the plague and the eschatological sects that washed over a panicked Europe, a third of whose population was wiped out. The calamity stirred up an existential crisis, which left room for Gnosticism's Satan to creep in: the demiurge who was considered an autonomous, active force in the world with his own (though not equal) power – that our plane of existence is his turf and he created it. It was a belief that generated images of Satan as the king of this world, a hell on earth he ruled ruthlessly and an apocalyptic place of the kind prophesied in John's Book of Revelation.

Its plot suggests a war occurred in heaven between Archangel Michael and his forces and the Devil and his supporters, which ended with the Devil being cast out onto earth. If we go by the Christian reading of Isaiah's mysterious verse, "How art thou fallen from heaven, O Lucifer, son of the morning! How art thou cut down to the ground, which didst weaken the nations! For thou hast said in thine heart, I will ascend into heaven, I will exalt my throne above the stars of God."[2] This was not just any war, but a full-blown palace coup. In the Hebrew Bible, the name of this son of the morning is "hêylêl", which may be derived from the word "light". The Vulgate, the late-fourth-century Latin rendering of the Old Testament, introduced the name "Lucifer" into the realm of Christianity. Originating in Roman folklore, Lucifer (meaning "light-bringer" in Latin) was the son of the goddess Aurora – dawn personified – and the name of the planet Venus, the brightest star in the heavens. Only decades later was it discovered that Venus' orbit around the earth forms a pentagram, the geometric shape that would one day be associated with the Devil himself. Coincidence? We can neither confirm nor deny.

He wasn't the only pagan Dante put in his hell (Moving Heaven and Hell, page 71).

Who has read at least one book in which Satan appears in the lead role (The Body Electric, page 221).

However, Satan's appearance has been borrowed from other pagan sources. Dante possibly took his three-headed Satan in *Inferno* from Cerberus the Greek hell-hound and the guardian of Hades. The Devil's horns that began to adorn his head in Christian iconography may have been harvested from Cernunnos, the common epithet of the Celtic horned deity traditionally associated with wild animals, or from the head of Pan, the Greek god of panic, another god of the wild who also gave the Devil his goat's lower body. Thus, the Devil became a sort of Frankenstein's monster, cobbled together from the remains of vanquished deities. Since its emergence from Judaism's bosom, Christianity has advocated the commandment, "Thou shalt not waste, thou shalt not want." The ancient idols it encountered in its soul-redeeming quest were not obliterated, they were simply recycled.

Church fathers offered the pagans who adhered to the beliefs of their ancestors and worshipped trees, waterways, rocks and the forces of nature the perfect return. Instead of their crowded pantheons, filled with horned thunder gods and horny fertility goddesses, they received hundreds of alternate saints, whose remains would rest in churches to be built on ancient pagan altars. There is no need to relocate, as Pope Gregory I instructs in his sixth-century letter to Abbot Mellitus, "Tell Augustine that he should by no means destroy the temples of the gods but rather the idols within those temples. Let him, after he has purified them with holy water, place altars and relics of the saints in them. For, if those temples are well built, they should be converted from the worship of demons to the service of the true God. Thus, seeing that their places of worship are not destroyed, the people will banish error from their hearts and come to places familiar and dear to them in acknowledgement and worship of the true God. Further, since it has been their custom to slaughter oxen in sacrifice, they should receive some solemnity in exchange ... They will sacrifice and eat the animals not any more as an offering to the devil, but for the glory of God to whom, as the giver of all things, they will give thanks for having been satiated ... For surely it is impossible to efface all at once everything from their strong minds, just as, when one wishes to reach the top of a mountain, he must climb by stages and step by step, not by leaps and bounds."[3]

Thus, in an admirable combination of frugal practicality and deep insight into the psychology of the believer, Christianity captured the hearts of the pagans, while incorporating elements of pagan worship into its own mythology. Did you idolize Adonis, Dumuzid or Osiris, the dying-and-rising gods of the Greek, Mesopotamian and Egyptian pantheons respectively? You could replace them all with the resurrected Jesus. In your pagan hierarchy was there a chief god, a father of all, whether you called him Jupiter or Odin? Convert him, if you would, into the Creator, the only true God. Did you make sacrifices at the holy grove? Now you could worship a chip of different wood, a piece of the

Sometimes with monstrous threats (Here Be Dragons, page 79).

Who did not excel at turning the other cheek (Twilight of the Gods, page 65).

cross. And since demand always prevailed over supply, the bustling trade in relics meant that the fragments of this true cross, which appeared everywhere, were enough to form a ladder to heaven. Yet as long as it reached paradise, no one cared too much.

But what of the gods themselves? The more stubborn ones, who were not willing to change or who embodied traits that Christianity preferred to suppress, such as sexuality, female power or chaos, were relegated to demons and conscripted to the legions of hell.

The pagan holiday that Christianity annexed (as it did with Christmas) to celebrate the saints who did not get a special role or day on the calendar was the Celtic Samhain, whose name means "summer's end". This day, which fell on November 1, marked a time of important change in the ancient agricultural world – the beginning of deadly winter. This was the time of year when the screen between worlds grew thinner and various supernatural beings could cross over into our reality, perform antics, demand sacrifices, repay the worthy and punish sinners. Throughout the centuries, Samhain intersected with Parentalia, the Roman feast of the dead, which was celebrated in late October, thus offering Christianity a deal of two pagan festivals for the price of one and the perfect date for the Church to celebrate the memory of all its saints and the souls of the blessed. It started as All Hallows Eve and became Halloween. For the demons, the deposed gods, Halloween has become a holiday of necromancy, in which they are summoned from oblivion only to be exorcised again. Once a year they get to rise from the depths of the cultural liminal and show themselves in horror movies, costumes and terrifying carved pumpkins.

Unlike them, the Devil is here to stay. However, it took years for his now identifiable form to stabilize. In the *Codex Gigas*, also known as *Satan's Bible*, he is portrayed with vulture's talons, and facial features reminiscent of certain Hindu gods. Legend has it that this huge tome was written by a monk who broke his vows and was sentenced to be walled in and buried alive, as was the custom in the thirteenth century. The monk begged for mercy and promised that if absolved, he would produce a manuscript containing all human knowledge, in just one night, to praise God. Close to midnight, and probably not having reached beyond page three, the monk realized his chances were slim. He prayed, but rather than to God

From which Gutenberg longed to profit (A Faustian Bargain, page 1).

Although they had no problem undergoing metamorphosis (The Human Animal, page 189).

And even though he was probably not allowed to light a candle in the scriptorium (Ex Libris, page 9).

he directed himself to Satan. The latter appeared and helped him complete the volume, which weighs in at 75kg (165lbs), is 92cm (3ft) tall, and 50cm (nearly 20in) wide. Not exactly the kind of thing you'd want to land on your head – which is what happened years later to an innocent passerby, who had stopped to take a look at the great fire raging in the castle where the manuscript was kept. Just then, someone decided to save the precious book and threw it out the window. Though eight pages vanished and the manuscript's cover was damaged, the *Codex* survived the ordeal. We remain in the dark about the fate of the man who was hit and of the monk who was saved by Satan.

Pacts with the Devil traditionally culminate in a wholesale liquidation. While during the Inquisition, it was heretics like members of sects such as the Manicheans or the Cathars who bore the brunt of blame for such dealings, in the Renaissance culpability was shifted onto the witches and next came the intellectuals' turn. The sixth-century cleric Theophilus of Adana is the first to be named for having signed a pact with the Devil, selling his soul to land an ecclesiastic promotion. His story appeared in Germany in 1587, in a booklet called *Historia and Tale of Doctor Johannes Faustus: The sorcerer, wherein is described specifically and veraciously: His entire life and death, How he did oblige himself for a certain time unto the Devil, And what happened to him, And how he at last got his well-deserved reward.* It became the source of Christopher Marlowe's 1588 play *The Tragical History of Doctor Faustus* and Johann Wolfgang von Goethe's monumental *Faust*, whose first complete version was published in 1832 and became one the founding texts of Western culture. The story of the scholar who craves occult knowledge and sells his soul to Mephistopheles – "the spirit that negates"[4] – inspired many musical works for opera and the ballet by great composers such as Schumann, Wagner, Berlioz and Liszt. It was also the impetus for great literature: for example, Thomas Mann's *Doctor Faustus* and his son Klaus Mann's *Mephisto*. It also left its mark on Bulgakov's *The Master and Margarita*, in which Satan turns up in Moscow calling himself Woland, a nod to Goethe who introduced the name as one of the Devil's aliases in his *Faust*.

However, not all Satans are sleek salesmen. Throughout the centuries, the Devil has appeared in various guises that allow us to feel some sympathy for him or, at the very least, to recognize his human traits. Examples include his jealousy of the Son of God,

Did they make their way to the Ninth Gate? (Flame and Moth, page 17).

In at least one case, that of the possessions of Loudun, France in 1634, an entire convent packed with Ursuline nuns supposedly came under the Devil's thrall, after a priest named Urbain Grandier summoned him. Grandier was convicted of sorcery and burned at the stake (Weird Sisterhood, page 25). The 1952 title *The Devils of Loudun* by Aldous Huxley, author of *Brave New World* (Best of All Possible Worlds, page 247) and subsequently Ken Russell's 1971 movie *The Devils* explore this unusual story.

how he envied humankind for the preferential treatment they received from God, his arrogance in assuming himself superior to those of flesh and blood and declining to bow his head before Jesus. Islam ascribed similar sentiments to him. Iblis, whose name seems to derive from the Greek *diabolos*, which means "devil", also refused to bow and is full of contempt for humans created from "dried clay of black mud".[5]

In *Paradise Lost* John Milton, who was described by his admirer William Blake as "of the Devil's party without knowing it",[6] fashioned his Devil in the guise of a rebel willing to suffer the agonies of hell as long as he avoids the shame of surrender. His Devil speaks in the voice of Milton the republican, who distanced himself from the tyranny of Charles I and supported regicide. Deeply influenced by his encounter with Galileo in Italy and the great scholar's suffering, Milton allows his Devil to express his own aversion to Catholic dogma, his admiration for this visionary individual (who, like him, was going blind) and his passionate defence of the freedom of thought.

By contrast, the Catholic Church saw the Devil as battling against humans rather than God, as affirmed in 2018 by Pope Francis when he warned his followers that "we should not think of the Devil as a myth, a representation, a symbol, a figure of speech or an idea. This mistake would lead us to let down our guard, to grow careless and end up more vulnerable. The Devil does not need to possess us. He poisons us with the venom of hatred, desolation, envy and vice. When we let down our guard, he takes advantage of it to destroy our lives, our families and our communities."[7] The competition – the "Church of Satan", founded in San Francisco by Anton Szandor LaVey in 1966 – started an offensive. Even though they related to Satan as "a symbol of pride, liberty and individualism, and it serves as an external metaphorical projection of our highest personal potential,"[8] they did not turn a blind eye when members of "The Satanic Temple", whom they saw as "imposters" and "political activists", sullied their good name. To defend their bad reputation the satirical organization of the Temple sued Warner Bros and Netflix for 150 million dollars, claiming that their use of a sculpture of Baphomet, the satanic goat, in the TV series *The Chilling Adventures of Sabrina* breached their copyright. The most recent incarnation of the Sabrina character, which first

Who got in trouble with the Catholic Church after refusing to denounce heliocentric ideas and other newfangled notions like the fact that the moon was not as pristine as Aristotle preached and had a spotty face (Man in the Moon, page 115).

And it is not wise to violate the copyrights of those who cooperate with the Devil (Weird Sisterhood, page 25).

appeared in 1962, centres on a figure who is part-witch in an attempt to combine the cult of Satan and female empowerment, joining feminism and human sacrifice. The Satanic Temple claimed Sabrina encouraged a view that the series was all about a "patriarchal, cannibalistic cult",[9] whereas the Church of Satan did not seem to care that much: "These actions are not in any way representative of the apolitical, individualistic and atheistic religion of Satanism. Please do not attribute their actions to us."[10] The pope was right to warn his flock they should not assume the Devil was "a myth, a representation, a symbol, a figure of speech or an idea". Nowadays it would be difficult to find people who venerate Satan outright. Modern Satanism is a blend of Gothic aesthetics, free choice, nihilism and atheism, which in many ways takes Lucifer's name in vain. If he does exist, then surely the Devil dwells in our heart, our mind, which is "its own place", as Milton wrote, "and in itself can make a heaven of hell, a hell of heaven,"[11] because surely the greatest trick the Devil ever pulled was not to convince the world he didn't exist, but to make them think he was merely a metaphor.

HERE BE DRAGONS

It is a truth universally acknowledged that wherever medieval cartographers had to draw uncharted land that was still to be "discovered", they inscribed the Latin words *Hc Svnt Dracones* (Here Be Dragons) to warn seafarers. Unfortunately, like the dragons themselves, this is nothing but a myth.

And not the only myth that maps enshrined (The Territory and the Map, page 47).

In fact, there is not one ancient map that carries these words. They occur only twice in the entire history of cartography: on the Hunt-Lenox Globe, a sixteenth-century copper sphere the size of a grapefruit, which is one of the oldest extant globes, and on an engraved ostrich egg, its presumed prototype. The belief in the widespread existence of such maps is stubborn, like the grip of a dragon's talons dug into the human brain. This is also a particularly picturesque reminder that maps are fantastic objects, and the territory they sketch is the wild landscape of fiction.

In the course of their millennia-long hibernation in the caves of the imagination, dragons passed through an amazing physical and psychological evolution. They went from an archaic, Mediterranean monster to European devils; from moronic giant lizards to creatures with supreme intelligence; from using virgins as mere toothpicks, to sucking at their breasts. Borne aloft on huge bat wings they moved from the hidden recesses of J R R Tolkien's Lonely Mountain to G R R Martin's Gates of Westeros, from the mind's eye to screens, large and small. They were blessed with the capacity to spray acid, to spit fire, to emit shock waves, to bring luck and to levy blood tax. They were assembled from fossilized dinosaur bones, the horns of long-forgotten gods and the scales of ill-reputed snakes, all welded together into terrifying chimeras that showed off their amazing technicolour form and figure.

The dragon defeated by George of Lydda, better known as Saint George the dragon slayer, was small enough to be tied by its neck to a young lady's garter, and she proceeded to lead it along like a dog on a leash. Warriors returning home from the crusades relayed this story about the young Roman soldier and Christian convert, and it was widely and warmly embraced. George turned into the patron saint of countries like England, Montenegro, Catalonia, Ethiopia, Georgia and Lithuania. Directly borrowing from Ovid's story about Perseus, Andromeda and the sea monster, Christian mythology tells of a dragon that dwelled on the shores of a lake whose surroundings it had poisoned. In order to placate this dragon a whole succession of virgins were offered to it, until eventually the only young woman left was the king's daughter. As he was passing by, valiant George subdued the dragon and he and the princess tied it to her undergarment, as mentioned above. They walked the monster to the town where George proceeded to blackmail the residents to convert at dragon-point. Facing the complex choice between coping with a nervous monster wearing a woman's garter or putting their faith in the merciful Son of God, they all chose to be baptized. George then slayed the monster and gained eternal glory, and hundreds of stained-glass windows, paintings and sculptures, which all celebrate the moment he pierced the dragon with Ascalon, his sword or lance. The name derived from the Judean seaport of Ashkelon, established at a spot used in the distant past by people who belonged to the Mesopotamian civilization. It was a place that George, who was from the neighbouring town of Lydda, might well have known.

Which had its own scaly creatures – for example, a goddess with a fish-tail (Heads or Tails, page 183).

In the Canaanite creation myth, dragons were the servants of Yam, god of the oceans, lakes and rivers. Abrahamic monotheism declared war on these monsters and on the idolatry that spawned them. Canaanite El was vanquished by the Hebrew Elohim; Tiamat, the great goddess of primordial chaos, was called to order in Genesis, while Elohim, the god with the capital G, "with his sore and great and strong sword", comes down on "leviathan the piercing serpent, even leviathan that crooked serpent; and he shall slay the dragon that is in the sea,"[1] as Isaiah poetically puts it.

However, the dragon returned in John of Patmos' revelations, "Behold a great red dragon, having seven heads and ten horns, and seven crowns upon his heads."[2] It threatens the kingdom of God: "And there was war in heaven. Michael and his angels fought against the dragon; and the dragon fought [Michael] and his angels,"[3] until "the great dragon was cast out, that old serpent, called the Devil, and Satan, which deceiveth the whole world: he was cast out into the earth, and his angels were cast out with him."[4] These prophets use the Greek word *drakōn* to describe the scaled creature, a word that refers to a huge, fantastic serpent, such as the one that reveals himself to the Achaeans in Homer's *Iliad*: "Then appeared a great portent: a serpent, blood-red on the back, terrible, whom the Olympian himself had sent forth to the light."[5]

The Europeans who translated the Old Testament from the Greek simply transcribed the word as it was, and so the "dragon" joined the Christian bestiary.

The dragon turned into evil incarnate and St George's victory became a re-enactment of Archangel Michael's struggle against the Church's eternal foe. Hence the dragon's culinary preference for the flesh of flawless virgins: it is a corrupt creature that tries to gnaw at the very roots of innocence, like its progenitor the serpent, which seduces Eve to eat from the fruit of the Tree of Knowledge.

Furthermore, the dragon is associated with another of the seven cardinal sins – greed. It lounges on a bed of plundered gold as it guzzles the virgins.

The association between the serpent, the most phallic of all beasts, and the loss of virginity and innocence is not limited to the Judeo-Christian religions. In Ovid's *Metamorphoses* Medusa was a beautiful girl whom Neptune coveted and pursued, finally capturing her and forcing himself on her in the temple of Minerva. The goddess, jealous of Medusa's virginity and chiefly troubled by the girl losing her maidenhood on the floor of a temple, "Turn'd her eyes away, nor durst such bold impurity survey," and in a shocking demonstration of divine victim-blaming, she cursed the girl with an evil eye so that from then on she turned anyone who looked at her directly to stone, while also changing "her shining hair"[6] into hissing snakes.

According to the Talmud, the Jewish rabbinical text, it all started when someone did *not* turn his eyes away. The serpent saw Adam and Eve naked, unashamed and engaging in intercourse for all to see, and he lusted after Eve. But the serpent was also subtle. The Talmud describes how the serpent sought to kill Adam and marry Eve, seducing her into more than a bite of the forbidden fruit – an unholy act that produced Cain, the first murderer.

The biblical serpent is not the limbless creature we know today, but an entity with consciousness, intelligence, a voice and hands and feet, all of which got taken away from it in punishment. But it is the woman who paid and is still paying the heaviest price in cultures that draw on the myth of the fall from grace. In the eyes of Christianity, woman was the source of original sin and, in Judaism,

As they did when they translated the Greek *monokerōs* (The Lady and the Unicorn, page 179).

Which, in turn, passed on its name to Vlad Tepes' family, i.e. "Dracula" (Blood Lust, page 93).

Other mythologies found them useful. The *Nibelungenlied* hero Sigurd killed the dragon Fafnir, took the *Nibelungenschatz* – its treasure – and bathed in the dragon blood, thus making his skin impervious to harm (Twilight of the Gods, page 65).

Lucifer (Number of the Beast, page 79).

women must be hidden, they must not be touched or their voices heard. Woman is responsible for the expulsion from paradise, for carnal lust, for our race's mortality. All the hardships of femininity, from menstrual cramps through labour pains to the rule of men, came upon her because of her deadly curiosity and weakness of spirit and flesh.

As the author of *The Witches' Hammer* made abundantly clear (Weird Sisterhood, page 25).

But before we start pointing fingers at the snake, it turns out that we owe it some thanks as well. In her book *The Fruit, the Tree and the Serpent: Why We See So Well*, Lynne A Isbell, a professor of anthropology and animal behaviour, explores the theory of "snake identification" and argues that certain aspects of human evolution developed in response to a threat these reptiles presented to our ancestors. Without the serpent, she says, "we would not have had the foundation of excellent vision, a sense that enables us to develop written languages, draw up blueprints and build complex structures … recognize the difference between good and evil in another person's face, or detect a dangerous snake resting camouflaged in the grass."[7] In this, at least, it looks like the author of the book of Genesis has a point: the snake did bring us knowledge. Another point that Genesis seems to get right is God's promise to the serpent, "I will put enmity between thee and the woman, and between thy seed and her seed."[8] Masahiro Shibasaki and Nobuo Masataka discovered that a woman's ability to identify snakes is at its peak when she is in the luteal stage of her ovulation cycle – when her body prepares itself to conceive – and therefore needs to be especially careful of potential risks, such as a snake.

And if a woman is particularly bad, she herself can be turned into a snake by identifying the seduced with the seducer, the victim with the instigator. In *The Silver Chair*, the sixth book in C S Lewis's *The Chronicles of Narnia*, an evil witch morphs into a huge, venomous snake. In the Old English epic poem *Beowulf* the monsters Grendel and his mother are the descendants of Cain, son of the serpent, and after he subdues them Beowulf is forced to face a third enemy, the dragon. Robert Zemeckis' adaptation of this Anglo-Saxon legend has Grendel's mother, digitally modelled after the actress Angelina Jolie, looking serpent-like and hiding her naked curves under a scaly veil and a twisting tail. The movie portrays Beowulf being seduced by the saucy serpent, an experience that leaves him unmanned and alludes to the possibility that the dragon that eventually brings about his demise is their son.

One of the great scholars and authorities on this very poem also happened to be the man who was more responsible than anyone for the central role of dragons in modern popular culture – even though his particular dragon was the last scion of an extinct race. Smaug, J R R Tolkien's fiery worm in *The Hobbit*, is a character with his own voice and distinct personality: wily, arrogant, clever, surprisingly lonely but not especially wise, rather than a violent, mindless lizard. And even though his presence in the book is slight, he has cast his shadow over all subsequent fantasy writing.

The Western dragons from whom Smaug descended and whom he spawned, mated with the Asian variant, which was of a distinctly different disposition: unwinged, good-natured, justice-and-law abiding. A good example is Falkor, the lucky white dragon Atreyu and Bastian ride in Michael Ende's *Neverending Story*. Their union brought us the modern dragon, a far more complex being than the one envisioned in Revelation's apocalypse. Today, there are Dungeons that teem with Dragons as well as computer games such as *Dragon Age* and its ilk, which crawl with them. There's a dragon for every season, from the depths of a winter night to autumn's twilight, and countless serials unfold the complex taxonomy of these fire-breathing, bat-winged creatures.

And labyrinths (A Rat in a Maze, page 147).

Some dragons hark back to aliens – like the ones in Anne McCaffrey's science fantasy series *Dragonriders of Pern*, while others are the product of genetic engineering. There are sweet, colourful dragons such as those in Cressida Cowell's book series and animation films *How to Train Your Dragon*, which turn into the protagonist's best friends, and novels like *His Majesty's Dragon* by Naomi Novik, an alternative history in which dragons serve as an air force in the Napoleonic wars. In Ursula Le Guinn's *Earthsea* books they are independent creatures of pure magic and sublime beings who speak in the language of creation itself, while in the animated film *Flight of the Dragons*, much like humans, they are divided into good and evil dragons; and in Rob Bowman's film *Reign of Fire* they are an intelligent but cruel race, seeking the annihilation of humankind.

But not the kind that abduct people (We Come in Peace, page 123).

The more advanced we become at filling in the gaps in the maps of pluralism and liberalism, the more the evil dragons are dying out. Smaug in *The Hobbit* was truly the last of his kind. Nowadays racial discrimination is not welcome, even in the case of dragons. It is hard, if not impossible, to find modern dragons that are simply bad, evil by birth and by nature – the genuine heirs to the monstrous creature in John's visions. Today authors make very sure they balance out a nasty dragon with an enlightened, good-natured one. The nice dragons fight the not-so-nice ones to the bitter end and triumph as a matter of course. Alternatively, the author makes a sincere effort to help us get to the bottom of their badness so that we realize they have endured years of persecution, discrimination and prejudice against scales, or maybe they fell victim to bullying knights with an insatiable lust for strife and/or ladies' unmentionables.

No longer a dumb and destructive beast or an incendiary devil with unusual dietary preferences, the dragon has evolved into a layered entity all of its own. At times it might be faithful to the point of symbiotic, like a type of huge, winged, fire-breathing dog, and the best friend of the human who gains its loyalty. Archangel Michael and St George could hardly have dreamed of such a triumph over the great serpent.

12

BLOOD LUST

Late in 1922, Florence Balcombe received a letter franked by the Berlin post office. Inside was an invitation to a celebratory screening at the Marble Room in the famous Berlin Zoological Garden. Invitees were asked to wear fancy dress and to expect an evening of sublime horror, courtesy of Prana Film. The name Prana – or "life force" in Sanskrit – was chosen by Albin Grau, one of the studio's founders. A member of the respectable secret society "Fraternitas Saturni", his declared objective was the production of films about the supernatural. But none of the magical symbols and satanic rituals the fraternity adopted (one of their advisors was the infamous sorcerer Aleister Crowley) was to any avail. When Balcombe received an invitation to *Nosferatu*, which was directed by Friedrich Wilhelm Murnau and was the first and only film Prana Film ever produced, she saw it casually described as freely adapted from Bram Stoker's novel *Dracula* and immediately realized that someone was trying to exploit and live large on her dead husband's work.

Vlad III, Voivode of Wallachia, the man who inspired Stoker's vampire, was born around the middle of the fifteenth century. His father, known as Dracul because he belonged to the "Order of the Dragon," passed on the name to his son, who was known as Draculea, or "little dragon". But there was nothing small about Draculea's scale of operations. He was one of Christianity's most bloodthirsty warriors against the Islamic enemies of the faith. Bishop Nicholas of Modrus, who was stationed in Buda, informed Pope Pius II of the activities of this loyal defender of the Cross in 1464: "40,000 people of both sexes, and of various ages, who belonged to the enemy faction, had been killed a short while ago on [Vlad's] orders ... Some of them died [on being] crushed under the wheels of carts; others, naked, had their skin flayed off down to [their] entrails; others were placed on stakes, or roasted upon burning coals; others were impaled through the head, the breast, the navel; others through the bottom (which is shameful to relate) ... And, so that no form of cruelty be missing, he placed stakes in

When designing tarot packs allowed him spare time (King of Cups, page 153).

Considering the reputation of dragons, this epithet could otherwise be understood as "the Devil" (Here Be Dragons, page 79).

mothers' breasts and impaled their infants there."[1] A janissary, one of the Ottoman Sultan's elite infantry soldiers, wrote a letter home describing the forests of impaled victims Draculea left behind lining the roads near Targoviste – the casualties were thousands of his brothers in arms. This is what earned Vlad the epithet of *Tepes* – "the Impaler".

The Church turned a blind eye to Draculea's deadly deeds against its earthly enemies and focused its attention instead on Christendom's other-worldly adversaries. It called the vampire to order. From being just any old folkloric creature lurking in cemeteries, the Church gave it a respectable status all of its own – the vampire now occupied a place next to the witch and the werewolf in the evolving monotheistic pantheon of medieval Europe. In 1645, the Vatican's librarian and theologian Leo Allatios published *De Graecorum hodie quorundam opinationibus*, a work surveying the beliefs of his fellow Greeks. In this, rather than describing the vampire or *vrykolakas*, as the Greeks called it, as a remnant from pagan days, he calls it a satanic creature. "It is impossible that a dead man should become a *vrykolakas* unless it be by the power of the devil,"[2] he writes. The book became the standard handbook of vampire hunters, much like the *Malleus Maleficarum* (*The Hammer of Witches*) became the chosen guide for all who persecuted lonely old women.

For a religion that sought to preserve the soul's eternal life and had a complicated relationship with the body – whether tortured, broken, crucified, pierced, abstemious or ascetic – the vampire's quest for physical immortality was a total abomination, a perversion of human as well as heavenly nature. And so, under the rule of Mother Rome, everything to do with vampires became the antithesis of Christianity. On the one hand we have the Saviour, Son of God, redeemer of virgins, who rose from the grave and whose faithful flock drink His blood and eat His body (by transubstantiation) as part of the Eucharist. And on the other is the vampire, tempter of virgins, begotten by Satan, who also rises from the grave but prefers to drink the blood of others. This is why items such as holy water, crosses and stakes are extremely efficient against him, especially when the later is made from buckthorn – specifically *Ziziphus spina-christi*, the tree Christ's crown of thorns was made from.

Like everything related to the Devil, Christianity ascribes vampires a rampantly satisfying sex life (at least to them). If

Of the two, the Church only took a resolute approach toward the first (Weird Sisterhood, page 25). The second tended to be perceived more as a superstition (Lupus Est, page 93).

One of the few who were allowed a peek at forbidden books (Flame and Moth, page 17).

94

witches hang out in the company of Lucifer, then the vampire is a sharp-toothed sex-machine, at least in his literary manifestations. James Malcolm Rymer's mid-nineteenth-century Varney the Vampire enjoys an almost exclusively female diet. *Carmilla* (1871) by Joseph Sheridan Le Fanu centres on a female vampire who prefers her own gender, "She would press me more closely in her trembling embrace, and her lips in soft kisses gently glow upon my cheek. ... I experienced a strange tumultuous excitement that was pleasurable, ever and anon, mingled with a vague sense of fear and disgust. ... but I was conscious of a love growing into adoration, and also of abhorrence."[3]

In John Polidori's *The Vampyre*, the novella that inspired the modern literary version of the vampire, the protagonist of the title is a serial womanizer (and serial killer), and the conversion of love and admiration into loathing were also typical of its author's own relationship with the man who served as his inspiration. John William Polidori was the son of an English woman and a translator, author and ghost-writer of Italian origin. His Catholic father sent young Polidori to be educated at a convent, and he began his medical studies at Edinburgh University, Britain's leading scientific centre at the time, when he was only 15 years old. However, in the early nineteenth century the forefront of medicine "was largely based around the study of 'antiphlogistics' – learning how to master the various ways of ridding the body of noxious substances in the quickest way possible – and so John became skilled in blood-letting, vomiting, enemas, blistering, and plunge-baths,"[4] recounts Andrew McConnell Stott in *The Poet and the Vampyre: The Curse of Byron and the Birth of Literature's Greatest Monsters*. Hating his medical studies, Polidori concentrated on the field's more esoteric subjects – he graduated with a thesis dedicated to the phenomenon of sleepwalking and couldn't wait to leave university. He received his degree when he was just 20 years old. When he reached London, he was dismayed to discover that local regulations forbade him practising until he was 26. Unemployed, lost, ambitious, penniless and extremely handsome, Polidori decided to try his hand at poetry.

It was a business profile that perfectly suited George Gordon, Lord Byron, who happened to be looking for a personal physician-cum-secretary to accompany him on a grand tour of the continent. His messy divorce from Anne Isabella Milbanke had just come through, his short and tempestuous affair with Caroline Lamb was over and the dissolute Romantic poet needed a change of scenery. However, Polidori's relations with his employer clouded over very rapidly when he committed the worst faux pas a fledgling poet can make – asking Byron if he would read something Poldori had written. Caroline Lamb had already said it: he was mad, bad and dangerous to know. Byron publicly mocked his private physician's poetic attempts and Polidori was deeply offended. Putting a brave face on it, he wrote to his sister, "I am with him on the footing of an equal, everything alike."[5] But when the two men reached Villa Diodati on the shores of Lake Geneva, where Byron was to spend a long, rainy summer in the company of his friend Percy Bysshe Shelley, his wife Mary and her step-sister Claire Clairmont, the doctor found himself drifting away from the employer who continuously humiliated and provoked him. Instead, he spent most of his time with Mary. They had a lot in common: both were very young (Polidori was 21 and Mary 19), brilliant and had powerful fathers who were writers. He recorded in his diary that he read aloud to her in Italian on 31 May and on the following days he took her rowing on the lake. He also had her infant son inoculated with Edward Jenner's smallpox vaccine. They had long, existential conversations about madness, idealism and "whether man was to be thought merely an instrument".[6] It was a few days after this conversation that Byron came up with his famous idea of a writing competition, and on 18 June the good doctor noted down, "Began my ghost-story after tea. Twelve o'clock, really began to talk ghostly."[7] Could it have been during the very same night when Polidori created his vampire that Mary Shelley awoke from her dream about a doctor and the monster he made?

About whom she subsequently wrote her novel *Frankenstein* (The Body Electric, page 221).

While Mary's reading list consisted of scientific tomes, Polidori was reading Lady Caroline Lamb's sensational *Glenarvon*, a *roman-à-clef* whose protagonist, the dour and charismatic Lord Ruthven, is based on her treacherous lover, Byron. Lamb was by no means alone in falling for the poet's bewitching personality and, according to another one of his lovers, his voice was "such a voice as the devil tempted Eve with; you feared its fascination the moment you heard it".[8] Polidori, too, was vulnerable to Byron's charms but he felt equally put out and degraded, believing that Byron robbed him of any sense of self-worth. So Polidori named one of the characters in the novella he had written "Ruthven" – not the hero, but the villain and undead creature that married

And apparently other attributes (The Pleasure Principle, page 195).

the miserable narrator's sister, who ended up dead. And Lord Ruthven? He "had disappeared, and Aubrey's sister had glutted the thirst of a VAMPYRE!"[9]

Even though the mysterious nobleman and the narrator eventually reach Greece and hike there in the countryside – the same happens in Byron's abandoned effort at winning the writing competition, "Fragment of a Novel". Ruthven is the first modern vampire, smooth-talking and sleek-mannered, hunting for his prey among the *haut ton*. Here we have the urban undead enjoying the bright lights of the big city rather than skulking in the wilderness. This is entirely unlike the vampires of folklore, who were merely odious tomb dwellers, and is much closer to Christianity's seductive Lucifer, the most beautiful angel in heaven before the Fall. Polidori had no intention of publishing his story, but some years after the competition at the lake the manuscript fell into the hands of a journalist, who published it under the title *The Vampyre; A Tale by Lord Byron*. It was enthusiastically received, writes McConnell Stott, "Goethe proclaimed it Byron's greatest ever work and popular hardback editions went through numerous reprintings, leaving Polidori scrambling to assert his rights as its author in the face of accusations that he was either a plagiarist or misusing Byron's name to further his own reputation."[10]

> Exactly the kind of place that Gothic writers preferred (Fear Itself, page 237).

This erroneous attribution also made its way into other literary creations. In Alexandre Dumas père's *The Count of Monte Cristo*, a countess at the opera remarks that the elusive count, who is in fact Edmond Dantès, "is no other than Lord Ruthven himself in a living form". This allusion to Byron draws a smile from her companion, "Although he could but allow that if anything was likely to induce belief in the existence of vampires, it would be the presence of such a man as the mysterious personage before him."[11]

Desperate, scandalized, robbed of his achievement by having it attributed to the person he perceived as a dangerous, soul-sucking vampire, Polidori took his own life. At the age of 25 and just one year before he would have been allowed to practise as a physician, the doctor drank a vial of cyanide. "Poor Polidori," wrote Byron on hearing the news of his death, "it seems that disappointment was the cause of this rash act. He had entertained too sanguine hopes of literary fame."[12]

Unlike Polidori, Bram Stoker's widow Florence Balcombe was most definitely not going to give up. She sued Prana Film, bankrupting the company and making it shut down. She demanded – and got – compensation, and the court ruled that all copies of *Nosferatu* were to be collected and destroyed. But such was the life force of Prana's first and last film that a copy distributed before the ruling survived, was reproduced and has stayed alive until this very day, which goes to show that vampires really aren't so easy to get rid of.

One person who must have seen the film before it was removed from the screen by court order (and who clearly was struck by Max Schreck's terrifying appearance as the bald Count Orlok, with his sharp teeth, pointed ears and hooked nose) was Julius Streicher. He started his newspaper *Der Stürmer* (*The Stormer*) and became its editor-in-chief. The newspaper excelled in explicit, coarse and pornographic anti-Semitism, and made its name by printing caricatures of Jews appearing as leeches guilty of horrifying sexual crimes whose aim was to soil the pure Germanic race – in short: vampires. They were depicted as absolute Others, absolute anti-Germans, the ultimate polluters of Aryan blood and carriers of plagues. Adolf Hitler made the connection as early as 1925, "The black-haired Jewish youth lies in wait for hours on end, satanically glaring at and spying on the unsuspicious girl whom he plans to seduce, adulterating her blood and removing her from the bosom of her own people … But the final consequence is not merely that the people lose all their freedom under the domination of the Jews, but that in the end these parasites themselves disappear. The death of the victim is followed sooner or later by that of the vampire."[13]

The poster announcing Fritz Hippler's 1940 film *The Eternal Jew* shows hideous Jewish faces that are the splitting image of Count Orlok. In the same year, the director Veit Harlan, placed his *Jud Süss* (*Süss the Jew*) in a threatening and bloodthirsty position behind a blonde Aryan virgin, an exact reproduction of Bela Lugosi's stance when he approaches one of his unsuspecting female victims from behind in his role of Count Dracula (1931).

But the baneful link between Jews and blood predated Hitler and Streicher by centuries. It is a frequent motif in narratives that circulated in medieval Europe. Blood libels were accusations against Jews of ritual murder and using the blood of Christian children to bake their ceremonial bread at Passover, a holiday that coincides with Easter, when Jesus also fell victim to the Jews according to the Christian thinking of the time. The first such

Which many of its members believed originated in the most legendary of islands (No Man's Island, page 57).

documented libel was told in *The Life and Miracles of St William of Norwich* by Thomas of Monmouth, a Benedictine monk. According to his account, written some six years after the events of 1144, a young apprentice tanner named William was sacrificed by the Jews of the town, "having shaved his head, they stabbed it with countless thornpoints, and made the blood come horribly from the wounds they made ... some of those present adjudged him to be fixed to a cross in mockery of the Lord's Passion."[14] These accusations, as well as those raised against the Jews of Lincoln in 1255, caused a growing hostility toward them in England. This was reflected throughout the ages in works such as Geoffrey Chaucer's thirteenth-century book *The Canterbury Tales;* Christopher Marlowe's *The Jew of Malta* and Shakespeare's *The Merchant of Venice* from the sixteenth century; and Sir Walter Scott's nineteenth-century *Ivanhoe*, which is set in twelfth-century England. But this hostility ran deeper than mere artistic influence. In 1290, all Jews were expelled from England to Spain (only to be expelled in 1492 from there, too) and elsewhere. They were not allowed to return until Oliver Cromwell's reign.

In his article, "Marking the Social Other by Blood: The Vampire Genre", filmmaker, photographer and scholar Haim Bresheeth argues that the identification with vampires imposed on two of Europe's liminal communities that suffered under the Nazis' iron fist – the Jews and the Gypsies – can be traced back to Stoker's novel. In the book the Gypsies are Dracula's faithful servants and it is they who bring his coffin to London. The person who receives the coffin is Immanuel Hildesheim, "a Hebrew ... with a nose like a sheep, and a fez ... and with a little bargaining he told us what he knew,"[15] writes Stoker. "The two eternal minorities of Europe (and of England) are thus defined as agents of diabolic evil on earth,"[16] comments Bresheeth. The great late-nineteenth-century Jewish migration from eastern to western Europe was perceived as a threatening invasion of foreigners. Evidence of the widespread suspicion against Jews can be found in the accusations aimed at the Jewish community regarding the activities of Jack the Ripper, who was roaming the streets of London in search of victims just as *Dracula* was being written. One theory about the killer was that he was a Jewish butcher seeking to eradicate prostitution.

Corruption and prostitution go wherever the vampire treads. "Dracula is the lover no woman can resist," writes Bresheeth.

They were not merely expelled and this occurred not just in England. Throughout the Middle Ages and beyond, blood libel was responsible for the persecution, accusation, torture and execution of tens of thousands of Jews across Europe, a fate they shared with other minority groups (Weird Sisterhood, page 25; Lupus Est, page 93).

"Through his bite, his uninhibited eroticism passes on to the women, his victims."[17] And so, the vampire is the great peril always threatening not just religion, but also patriarchy and the institution of marriage. The novel's preoccupation with "strong young manhood",[18] "manly fervour",[19] "stalwart manhood"[20] and with masculinity in general, as opposed to generous mentions of "voluptuous wantonness"[21] linked to the vampire and the women who serve him, gives us a sense of how threatened Stoker and his fellow Victorian males must have felt by any transgression of the boundaries kept with morals and conventions, especially by women. For what woman could remain indifferent to those piercing eyes and that bewitching voice? The titillating tangle of sex and death, Eros and Thanatos? This identification of the vampire with the radical Other, the alien dripping with potency who is out to debase the sacrosanct virgin, makes him into someone who can only be subdued by the Cross.

> Which licensed the vampires to be cast in countless paranormal, erotic novels (The Pleasure Principle, page 195).

Vampires of Ruthven or Dracula's type lacked morality. They were impervious to regret or compassion and took pleasure in their victims' suffering no less than they enjoyed the red essence of life they yielded. They looked like humans but had no shred of humanity, no soul and no reflection.

But why do vampires have no reflection? Although the invention of this trope is usually attributed to Stoker, apparently the first to include it in a vampire story was Dumas in a little-known novella called *The Vampire of the Carpathian Mountains or The Pale Lady*, published in 1849, "He came into this room to ask if my women were sufficiently attentive. He was standing with his back to that mirror, and I could swear that his image was not reflected in it!"[22] This became one of the most recognizable characteristics of vampires.

Mirrors are weird things. Their ability to reflect our appearance while seemingly reversing it from left to right stimulated many superstitions. For example, some believe that breaking a mirror brings seven years' bad luck; Jews cover the mirrors in a house of mourning; and according to Greek folklore a mirror reflected a person's spirit, so it was a bad omen to unexpectedly catch a glimpse of your own reflection. Literature is littered with mirrors operating as portals to other realms or revealing the truth in this world: from Snow White's talking mirror to Alice's looking glass; from the mirror revealing your deepest heart's desire in the *Harry*

Potter series, to one reflecting things that are not, as in The Trap by H P Lovecraft. The word "reflection" comes from the late Latin *reflexio* – the act of bending backward – and denotes not only the image produced by a mirror but also the act of cogitation, hence its many representations in art where mirrors indicate self-examination and even the divine.

In Christianity the mirror is associated with the Virgin, who is often shown reflected in it. In *The Book of Wisdom*, she is compared to "a reflection of the eternal light, and a stainless mirror"[23] (*speculum sine macula* in Latin). In the Catholic Litany of the Blessed Virgin, Mary is named the Mirror of Justice.

If the Blessed Virgin is a mirror of God, then it follows that the vampire, as the embodiment of evil, will have no reflection. And if it is the soul that is mirrored, then he has none. But psychology may offer another reason.

Jacques Lacan, one of psychoanalysis' most original thinkers, theorized that from the age of about six months, infants begin to recognize themselves in the mirror. This enables the formation of the ego via the process of apperception (identification), in which the self becomes an object viewed from outside and reflected upon from inside. The ego is the result of identifying with our mirror image. But before Lacan there was Freud, and before the ego there was the id – libidinal, aggressive, impulsive – the pleasure principle writ large. The id desires immediate gratification and dwells in "the dark, inaccessible part of our personality" as Freud put it, for "what little we know of it we have learned from our study of the dream-work ... We approach the id with analogies: we call it a chaos, a cauldron full of seething excitations ... There is nothing in the id that corresponds to the idea of time."[24] The id "knows no judgements of value: no good and evil, no morality".[25]

Does that sound like someone we know? Vampires are pure id. They are stuck forever at an early developmental stage, in infinite infancy. Orally fixated on suckling – especially from women – the vampire is unable to delay gratification, knowing nothing but his impulses and the need to satisfy them, without any concept of morality or time. The creature has no reflection, and this is what allows him to live forever.

Enter Anne Rice, who raised a different species of vampire from the grave: the good vampire. Vexed by thoughts about crime and punishment, good vampires suffer ad nauseam from the pangs

In which a boy is sucked into a magic mirror, a fourth dimension where everything is reversed, including perspective, colour and even body parts, all created by a seventeenth-century glazier who sought forbidden knowledge – a common theme with Lovecraft (Fear Itself, page 237).

Like the one performed by the lady looking in the mirror in the tapestry known as "Sight" in *The Lady and the Unicorn* series (The Lady and the Unicorn, page 179).

of their conscience. If Dracula and his ilk were id then the new vampire is super-ego: super-human and all too human at the same time; forever young, accursed in perpetuity; beautiful and miserable till the end of time. It may not be entirely surprising that it was a woman who brought about this change. In addition to being the vampire's victims, women are liminal creatures in their own right, living on the margins of a world ruled by men and perceived as eternally sinful voluptuous wantons (ever since Eve). Who better than a woman understands that to stay attractive one needs to remain forever young? Who else will love someone who can't bear to look at his own reflection in the mirror?

The genre of the moody, forlorn vampire has its own heroes, such as Louis in Anne Rice's *Interview with the Vampire* and Angel in the TV series *Buffy the Vampire Slayer*, but nobody comes even close to the magnificent, Christ-like, demure, vegetarian Edward Cullan, fashioned by Stephenie Meyer in her *Twilight* saga. Fittingly for an author of Mormon persuasion – the one true Christianity in its own eyes – Meyer's Cullan clan are "holier than thou". Carlisle, the family patriarch and the son of a clergyman, is a physician who devotes himself to saving human lives, while Edward constantly rejects Bella's sexual advances. *Twilight* takes the equation sex = death, which runs through Christian puritanism, to its extreme and beyond. Edward is willing to turn his beloved Bella into a vampire – and thereby kill her – only after they are married (in a church, needless to say). Bella, on the other hand, having given up trying to seduce Edward, insists on consummating their marriage before she turns into a vampire (which is to say, before she dies), thereby transforming their intercourse into an act of inverse necrophilia. As a result, Bella finds herself miraculously pregnant. The amazing success of the *Twilight* books, especially among young women, must be credited not only to its slow-burning unfolding and its gothic-romantic ambience, but to the constantly rehearsed message about the value of delayed physical gratification, which resonates with deeply ingrained female indoctrination. Their success was also augmented by the books' constant nod to the sado-masochistic basis of the vampire mythology: the magical transformation of blood into life, of flesh to food and of pain to pleasure. This combination produced a flourishing branch of paranormal erotica, like the leather-bound *Anita Blake* series written by Laurell

At least the heroine of her *Sleeping Beauty* quartet got a happy ending after all her suffering (The Pleasure Principle, page 195).

Whose sin was greater than just biting into forbidden fruit, at least according to some (Here Be Dragons, page 79).

K. Hamilton, Charlaine Harris's *Southern Vampire* series, which oozes sensuality, and many more.

The fairy godmothers who gathered around the vampire's coffin were nothing if not generous with their gifts. The Christian "bear-hug" delivered him from the outposts of folklore where he had lurked, granting him diabolical powers that made him incalculably stronger; political theology cast him in key roles; and art gave him the title of Count and pictured him in over 300 films, scores of TV series and thousands of books, housing him in vibrant city centres, showering him with sex appeal. In our eagerness to create the perfect Other and our attempt to produce the physical embodiment of a Devil who can be killed (with the right implements), we have come up with a magnet that eternally attracts and repels, an object of both desire and disgust. We have turned the vampire from beast to beauty, from horror to hero, from the spirit of evil to the soul of virtue.

In this case, at least, there was no fear of anyone being abducted (Paper Fairies, page 161).

13

LUPUS EST

First, they put him on the wheel, limbs splayed, and tied him to the spokes. Then the executioner used tongs to strip off his skin. Next followed the procedure which lent its name to the Breaking Wheel. Using the blunt end of his axe, the executioner set about breaking his limbs in various places, and wove the broken bones between the wheel's spokes. Only then he turned his axe and severed the head. The body remained on the gallows and the Wheel was put on display, the head mounted upon it beneath a crudely carved image of a wolf.

It all began in 1582, when the good burghers of Badburg in Germany noticed that their cows, goats and sheep were being expertly dismembered by what they believed was a wolf. But then came the milkmaids. And the children. And the pregnant women whose bellies were slashed, and their fetuses removed and devoured. Panic broke out and the community embarked on a hunt that led them not to a wolf but to a man. He was a prosperous farmer by the name of Peter Stumpp. He confessed under torture to all the monstrous acts they accused him of. Worse, he claimed he had struck a pact with the Devil when he was 12 years old; he had given him his soul in return for neither wealth nor other earthly delights, but an enchanted belt made of wolf skin. Whenever he would strap it on, he explained, he transformed into "the likeness of a greedy devouring Woolf, strong and mighty, with eyes great and large, which in the night sparkled like brands of fire, a mouth great and wide, with most Sharpe and cruel teeth, A huge body, and mighty paws". For 25 years, he preyed upon anything that came his way, including children's hearts "hot and raw, which he accounted dainty morsels and best agreeing to his Appetite".[1] Among those children was his own son whose brain he consumed with pleasure. Stumpp was also accused of sexual crimes: raping and murdering women while in his wolf form, seducing his own daughter and committing adultery with a relative. The two family members were sentenced to death. They were flayed, with their bodies hoisted alongside his on to the pyre

The sign of St Catherine, who appeared to Joan of Arc and guided her (Wonder Women, page 37).

Perhaps if he had entered this diabolical covenant at a more mature age, he could have derived knowledge from it. Or at least a musical talent (Number of the Beast, page 79).

on 31 October 1589. The accounts report that at no point in this horrific trial did Stumpp ever express regret. On the contrary: he told his inquisitors how he had enjoyed strolling around town and greeting his victims' families, titillated by their ignorance.

The belt was never found.

In 1852, a man was admitted to the Asile d'Aliénés de Marévill asylum in Nancy. Even though the doctors didn't see anything unusual in his appearance, he insisted he was growing fangs, parting his lips to show what he considered to be overgrown canines, and convinced he had fur covering his body. He demanded raw meat to eat, but when it was offered to him he refused it because it wasn't rotten enough. In 2009, the Dutch psychiatrist Jan Dirk Bloem saw a young man who complained of "increased hair growth on the arms (as perceived by him, not by others), 'hardening' of his jaws and facial muscles and the growth of fangs that caused small wounds in the corners of his mouth"[2] – none of which Bloem could see. Though the patient's appearance did not seem to alter, he was convinced he was turning into a wolf.

No evidence that the moon influences human (or wolf) behaviour has been found (Man in the Moon, page 115).

What persuaded these men they were transforming into beasts of prey that howled at the moon? What caused Stumpp to commit murders, rapes and cannibalism for decades? Robert Eisler, the Jewish Austrian art critic, historian and philosopher of culture, religion, economics, mythology, science and more, believed the answer could be traced back to the mists of our prehistory. Eisler, who interacted with and influenced luminaries such as Carl Jung, Sigmund Freud, Karl Popper and Walter Benjamin, was arrested following the Anschluss in 1938 and sent to Dachau concentration camp as prisoner number 16547. Later that year he was transferred to Buchenwald, another camp, then released 15 months later. He subsequently made his way to England and in 1948 delivered a lecture to the Royal Society of Medicine, which also came out as a book, *Man into Wolf: An Anthropological Interpretation of Sadism, Masochism and Lycanthropy.* In it Eisler makes the controversial argument that up until the onset of the Ice Age, we hominins were peaceful, tree-hugging vegetarians. Driven by hunger, some of our ancient forefathers were forced to make the evolutionary step from herbivores to carnivores, and to achieve this they had to imitate predators. They had to start both hunting them and hunting like them, to learn how to be rapacious meat-eaters. In the wake of Jung, Eisler argued that this development left its paw prints on our archetypes, myths and folklore and became encoded in our ability to enjoy pain – both inflicting and enduring it. This leads to the "derivation of all crimes of violence, from the individual attack on life known as murder to the collective organized killing which we call war". Well versed in what he called the "fleeting dreams and lasting delusions of contemporary Humanity",[3] Eisler ends with a warning about the annihilation we will bring upon ourselves unless we learn to tame the wolves we have become. As one who was incarcerated in the *Konzentrationslagers* of Nazi Germany, he saw how humans turn against their fellow humans like wolves, and knew first-hand how likely we are – as a race – to prey upon our own flesh and blood.

This was the sin of the first werewolf. His name was Lycaeon, King of Arcadia, and he tried to deceive Zeus the Omniscient himself by feeding him the flesh of his own son. When Zeus discovers this, Lycaeon is punished:

> "Howling he fled, and fain he wou'd have spoke;
> But humane voice his brutal tongue forsook.
> About his lips the gather'd foam he churns,
> And, breathing slaughters, still with rage he burns,
> But on the bleating flock his fury turns.
> His mantle, now his hide, with rugged hairs
> Cleaves to his back; a famish'd face he bears;
> His arms descend, his shoulders sink away
> To multiply his legs for chase of prey.
> He grows a wolf, his hoariness remains,
> And the same rage in other members reigns.
> His eyes still sparkle in a narr'wer space:
> His jaws retain the grin, and violence of his face."[4]

This gruesome tale was passed on to us in the eighth century by Pūblius Ovidius Nāsō in his *Metamorphoses*. According to Ovid, Zeus changes the king's visage so his appearance reflects his internal nature. This is a metamorphosis into metaphor, with the image turning into reality.

Lycanthropy is the most popular version of therianthropy or the transformation of a human into an animal. However, according to the Diagnostic and Statistical Manual of Mental Disorders (DSM), the "bible" of psychiatry, in its clinical manifestation lycanthropy

It appears frequently in Ovid's classical works (The Human Animal, page 189).

is a condition in which patients believe they are turning into, or already are, an animal – any animal. In the Bible, Nebuchadnezzar, ruler of Babylon, may have suffered from this syndrome. The Book of Daniel states that: "He was driven from men, and did eat grass as oxen … till his hairs were grown like eagles' feathers, and his nails like birds' claws."[5] Many years before, the good people of Uruk, an ancient city of Sumer (and later of Babylonia), had had to deal with a man who exhibited similar symptoms, "He ate grasses with the gazelles, and jostled at the watering hole with the animals."[6] His name was Enkidu and he would become the companion of the first great hero, Gilgamesh.

Whose story was discovered in the excavations of the great library of Nineveh (Ex Libris, page 9).

Doctors Aldebaky Younis and Hamdy Fouad Moselhy published a study in 2009 entitled *Lycanthropy Alive in Babylon: The Existence of Archetype*, announcing that they had identified eight cases of lycanthropy in the past 20 years, an extremely dense rate of incidence for this rare psychiatric disorder and, by strange coincidence, all occurring in the vicinity of what had once been Babylon. In seven cases the patients had felt they were turning into dogs. The authors argued that clinical lycanthropy had been largely influenced by the patient's cultural environment and what species of animals represented evil in it.

In medieval Europe no animal caused more anxiety than the wolf. For thousands of years, it had been the most dangerous and common predator on the continent. Hunted aggressively, wolves were gradually eradicated, their habitat overrun by humans by the time of the Industrial Revolution. And the fewer wolves there were, the less likely people were to fear them. As Nadine Metzger observes in her article, "Battling Demons with Medical Authority: Werewolves, Physicians and Rationalization", by the end of the fifteenth century the wolf was extinct in England, where consequently fewer werewolf trials were held than in continental Europe.

In France alone, about 30,000 people were accused of being werewolves and hundreds of them were executed. Their persecution coincided with Europe's witch-hunts; where most accused of witchcraft were women, those charged with lycanthropy were far more likely to be men.

This time, at least, the Church was not to blame. Unlike the belief in witchcraft, which it upheld, Christianity had a problem with werewolves, because according to its doctrine they could not exist – even the Devil cannot turn a human into a beast. The Church therefore treated reports of animal transformation as illusory. The inquisitor Heinrich Kramer, author of the bestselling *Malleus Maleficarum* had an unequivocal answer to this conundrum, "It is to be said that this sometimes has a natural cause, but is sometimes due to a glamour, when it is effected by witches."[7] In territories where folklore was still battling ecclesiastical lore, the rural population was not interested in fur-splitting and had no compunction about crying wolf. Kings such as James I had the divine right to interpret such cases as involving the mind or psyche rather than some supernatural phenomenon. Even he, a fanatical witch-hunter, writes in his 1597 *Demonologie*: "If any such thing has been, I take it to have proceeded but of a natural superabundance of melancholy, which as we read, that it has made some think themselves … one kind of Beast or other."[8]

> Which Shakespeare used as one of his sources for *Macbeth* (Weird Sisterhood, page 25).

People's perspectives on werewolves differ in relation to how the wolf is perceived or represented in their culture. Roman mythology attributes many positive qualities to the wolf, after all legend has it that the city of Rome itself was founded by Romulus and Remus, two brothers who suckled from the breasts of Lupe, the she-wolf. Not all werewolves are described as evil incarnate. At times, the evil one in the story is the human. For example, Bisclavret confesses to his wife that he turns into a wolf for three nights every month and he can only become a man again when he puts on his human clothes. His treacherous wife duly sentences him to the life of a wild animal in the forests by hiding his clothes. When King Arthur happens to cross paths with him, he is impressed by the wolf's polite demeanor and brings him to his court. Bisclavret's wife then appears in the palace and when the mild-mannered wolf attacks her and rips off her nose, the king realizes there might be something behind this. He interrogates the woman and she admits her crime. Bisclavret receives his clothes back and is restored to his human shape.

> Whose origins lie in the Celtic and Welsh mythologies where therianthropy abounded (King of Cups, page 153).

We know very little about Marie de France who wrote this story (the name suggesting she wrote her stories in England) in the twelfth century; but it is one of the earliest versions of the werewolf legend in writing, with the author referring to wolf-men and the tales about them as common knowledge. "It hasn't happened lately, but then every once in a while some men were transformed into werewolves and went into the forests where they spent their lives doing mischief. They would eat anybody they happened to meet."[9]

The Enlightenment's powerful spotlight eventually cast belief in werewolves into the darkest margins of culture where it took refuge among folklore; there, within the confines of legend, it was allowed to roam only within the cage of the imagination.

In an early version of the tale that we recognize today as the story of Little Red Riding Hood, the wolf – probably a latter-day descendant of Lycaeon – persuades the heroine to eat her grandmother's flesh. The wolf claims that Grandmother's ear is a dumpling and her teeth are grains of rice, while her blood is nothing but wine. In addition to being a rather terrifying parody of the Catholic Eucharist, this version also carries sinister sexual overtones. The wolf asks the girl to perform a slow striptease: "Get undressed, my child and come to bed with me," he coaxes. "Where should I put my apron?" she asks. "Throw it into the fire. You won't need it anymore," the wolf replies. And she gets the same answer about her bodice, her dress, her petticoat, her shoes and stockings – "Throw them into the fire, my child. You won't need them anymore." Finally, she joins him in bed and exclaims, "Oh, Grandmother, how hairy you are!"[10] In Charles Perrault's *Tales of Mother Goose*, first published in 1697, the girl similarly takes off her clothes before getting into bed with the wolf. A moralizing writer, Perrault does not trust his readers to draw their own conclusions and spells out his point, "Children, especially attractive, well-bred young ladies, should never talk to strangers, for if they should do so, they may well provide dinner for a wolf. I say 'wolf,' but there are various kinds of wolves. There are also those who are charming, quiet, polite, unassuming, complacent, and sweet, who pursue young women at home and in the streets."[11] So, in contrast with Lycaeon, who turns inside out, here the wolf represents the human. In the Grimm brothers' 1812 version, there is a human inside the wolf, longing to come out. Or rather, two human beings – two women, Little Red Riding Hood and her grandmother – and they are finally set free by the hunter.

Those who fell prey to the "Beast of Gévaudan" were not so lucky. In 1765 the town witnessed scores of deaths (the number is estimated as being between 60 and 210) among residents whose throats were apparently ripped out by sharp, rapacious teeth. According to those who survived to tell the tale, the perpetrator

An accusation sometimes levelled at the Jewish people (Blood Lust, page 93).

was a huge wolf with supernatural strength, clever and wily like a human and capable of walking on his hind legs. Louis XV's two wolf hunters were sent out to take care of the problem after the local militia had failed to trap the animal, but they had no success either. Then the king's personal guard tried his hand. He actually caught a large wolf, which was stuffed and sent to Versailles as proof; the man received a generous reward, was knighted and showered with praise. However, the attacks continued. Eventually it was Jean Chastel, a local huntsman, who managed to shoot the monstrous wolf. According to the ever-growing legend, he covered his bullets in silver, a metal believed to have purifying powers that were especially effective at dispatching baneful creatures. A post-mortem came up with remains of neither grandmother nor granddaughter, but the wolf's stomach still contained parts of his most recent victim. In Christophe Gans' film *Brotherhood of the Wolf* (2001), which portrays a radically fanciful version of these events, the wolf is a metal-armour-wearing lion made to look like a wolf, and he is used by members of a secret society, who are seeking to dethrone the king, to strike fear in the hearts of the population. Claims about the wolf's political ambitions were already made by Robert Louis Stevenson in 1878, in his *Travels with a Donkey in the Cévennes*; he called the Beast Gévaudan "the Napoleon Bonaparte of wolves".[12]

Stevenson, too, released the beast inside the man, seven years later in his character Mr Hyde, who lurks inside Dr Jekyll. Jekyll and Hyde are both humans, the same man whose personality has split thanks to Jekyll's scientific experiments with a potion. His personality splits into good and evil, light and dark, one who saves lives and one who destroys them. The contrast also shows the divide between the cultured person, bound by social and religious conventions, and the wild creature, id unbound, whose sole aim is to satisfy his desires.

Definitely not the only monster that suffers (or enjoys) this condition (Blood Lust, page 93).

Gothic horror literature – a genre Stevenson joined late in the day – produced bands of werewolves. For example, Sutherland Menzies wrote *Hugues the Wer-Wolf* in 1838 and Catherine Crowe published *A Story of a Weir-Wolf* in 1846. Bram Stoker was responsible for forging the link between wolf-men and vampires in his iconic *Dracula* novel of 1897 and in the short story, "Dracula's Guest", when he presents the werewolf and wolves in general as collaborators with Dracula. According to Stoker, Dracula himself can turn into a wolf, as he does while ravishing Lucy Westenra in Francis Ford Coppola's 1992 film, *Dracula*.

While Stoker drew inspiration from the stories his Irish nanny told him, the Germans had their own antecedents. Adolf Hitler and his sect took their great passion for wolves from ancient Nordic sources like the Icelandic Völsunga saga, and they identified with the ancient Teutons, seeking to bring about Ragnarök, when the great wolf Penryr eventually swallows the sun. Wolfsschanze, the Wolf's Lair, was the name of the Führer's headquarters in East Prussia, while the Nazis called a guerrilla unit that tailed the Allied Forces on their way into Germany, Werwolf. The Nazis saw the wolf as pure, physical and directly connected to the earth and the natural order of the world. The wolf was a part of nature to the same extent that the vampire was perceived as outside it, just as they – the natural Aryans – were the antithesis of the decadently cerebral, feeble-bodied Semites. For them the vampire was a representation of the Jew, an abject, blood-sucking parasite, with the werewolf in the role of the Aryan warrior incarnate, as Robert Eisler and millions of his people discovered to their horror when the wolves led them like sheep to the slaughter.

This was not the only time that vampire and werewolf found themselves on opposing sides. Often, they are immortal enemies, such as in the film series *Underworld* where werewolves start as servants of the vampires but rise up against their oppressors; or in Stephenie Meyer's *Twilight* books in which the loyal wolf-men are the dogged guardians of humanity, protecting them against the vampires.

But from its earliest conception, this animosity had an erotic undertone. Meyer's books and the films they were turned into, *The Wolves of Mercy Falls* by Maggie Stiefvater and many others pick up on the werewolf's vehement virility. As with the accusations levelled at Peter Stumpp or tales that feature the motif of an animal bridegroom, the werewolf also stands for the wild, terrifying and tantalizing aspects of sexuality.

Of all the supernatural creatures that traverse human culture, perhaps the wolf-man dwells closest to the margins of our reality, sniffing about to find the entrance and sometimes leaving his scent trail on its threshold. His essence – his proximity to both the natural and the supernatural – and the fact that he can move among us without us noticing, both attracts and alarms us. We are

Established in 1918 and dedicated to the study of the Aryan race's origin, the Thule Society was named after the ancient Greeks "Ultima Thule", meaning "farthest north" or the proverbial "Ends of the Earth" (No Man's Island, page 57).

"*Götterdämmerung*", the last part of Wagner's cycle *Der Ring des Nibelungen* culminates with Brünnhilde singing for 20 minutes before she leaps into the fire and her death, and from there the opera proceeds directly to the flames consuming Valhalla. The image of the well-endowed Valkyrie sporting a breastplate and brandishing a spear gave rise to the colloquialism "It ain't over till the fat lady sings" (Twilight of the Gods, page 65).

quite familiar with the violence that always threatens to erupt from the beast. It is alive in us and we need no potion, magic belt or pact with the Devil to call it forth from the dungeon of domestication we have built for it. The whiff of bestiality, which is exploited and honed in innumerable paranormal novels, doesn't merely serve to spice things up. It is the thing itself: an invitation to touch, stroke and surrender to big, hairy, teeth-baring desire.

14

MAN IN THE MOON

King Frederick the Great made a pilgrimage to Swedish Pomerania on 15 July 1756. His purpose was to visit the modest hut of Aul Jürgens, a local farmer and folk healer renowned for his miracles. About a month and a half later Frederick's forces invaded Saxony and the Seven Years' War began. Legend has it that the king believed his military victories were due to the old man's blessings and so, in gratitude and as a token of his respect for loyal services, Frederick bestowed the moon on Jürgens and his family until the end of time. Imagine the surprise of Martin, a direct descendant of Jürgens, on discovering in 1996 that a keen American entrepreneur by the name of Denis Hope had officially registered the rights to the moon and was selling deeds at the rate of $40 (£25.50) apiece. Hope made good business from a 2,159-mile (3,447-kilometre) lacuna in the international Outer Space Treaty, which stipulates that no country can lay claim to ownership of the moon and other celestial bodies.

Hope said that because the treaty did not mention private ownership, he was entitled to sell to anyone who showed an interest, including three former US presidents: Jimmy Carter, Ronald Reagan and George Bush Jr. But Hope wasn't the only businessman mooning over Luna. Even more excessive was an eccentric millionaire with an outer-space obsession, who scouted investors with especially deep pockets, engaged in crowdfunding, sold his property, destroyed his marriage and made it known that he was willing to "cheat, lie, steal, beg, bribe"[1] to realize his objective. This man was not one of the three multi-billionaires who launched their egotistic–altruistic space ventures in 2021, but Delos D Harriman, the protagonist of *The Man Who Sold the Moon*, a novella by science fiction writer Robert A Heinlein.

Having grown up in the USA during the New Deal era (1933–39), Heinlein developed a deep mistrust of large government enterprises and a certain fondness for libertarianism. He created his hero in 1949 – 13 years before J F Kennedy stated in his historic speech at Rice University, "We choose to go to the Moon in this

Mars had one of those, too. Malachi Constant is the richest, most depraved man in the world and the protagonist of Kurt Vonnegut's *The Sirens of Titan*, a satirical space romp that includes a war with the Martians (We Come in Peace, page 123) among other things.

decade and do the other things, not because they are easy, but because they are hard."[2] And hard it was. The space race, which began on 4 October 1957 with the Soviet launch of Sputnik 1, fired up the Cold War, fuelled by ideological testosterone and an unquenchable competitive impulse. This was captured well by Kennedy's vice-president and successor, the rough-hewn Lyndon Johnson, when he said: "Control of space means control of the world."[3] In a memorandum sent to the president in April 1961, he also dwelled on the psychological aspect and the effect on morale of such an achievement: "If we do not make the strong effort now, the time will soon be reached when the margin of control over space and over men's minds through space accomplishments will have swung so far on the Russian side that we will not be able to catch up, let alone assume leadership."[4]

The National Aeronautics and Space Administration (NASA) was far from catching up. Established in 1958 with the aid of aerospace engineer Werner von Braun and other former Nazi scientists who had been smuggled into the US during Operation Paperclip at the end of World War II, NASA was caught with its pants down and the scramble to be first at the final frontier initially appeared rather like a potato sack race.

Some believed that in this type of competition women might have an edge. William Lovelace was an expert in aerospace medicine and in charge of testing the astronauts who participated in the Mercury programme. Lovelace wanted to find out how suitable women would be for space travel. He invited 19 highly trained and experienced female pilots to take his tests, including some who had served in transport and intelligence functions in the military during World War II. Thirteen passed. The documentary *Mercury 13* by David Sington and Heather Walsh unveils that they outdid their male counterparts on some of the tests, such as prolonged stay in a sensory deprivation tank. However, none of this seemed to the liking of the good old boys in NASA, who ordered Lovelace to stop the tests once they discovered that he had been conducting them, citing the authority of President Johnson.

And didn't have to hide their gender in order to be drafted (Wonder Women, page 37).

The Americans lost that race because the first woman in space was Russian. Like Lyndon Johnson, Nikolai Kamanin, the director of Soviet cosmonaut training, was obsessed with the idea of supremacy; and like Lovelace, he also believed that women might be more suited to the task. On reading that the Americans were considering sending women into space he said, "We cannot allow that the first woman in space will be American. This would be an insult to the patriotic feelings of Soviet women."[5] He put out the word and a special committee headed by Gagarin himself sorted through the applicants. The physical requirements were that the candidates had to: be less than 30 years old; be less than 5ft 7in (1.70m) tall (the Vostok spacecraft was tiny); and weigh less than 154lbs (70kg). Khrushchev also had political stipulations, which were that the candidates should be card-carrying party members from a working-class background, with no higher education. This would allow him to prove to the Americans that not only privileged university graduates could get to space. Among the 400 women who applied for the programme was a young textile-mill worker and enthusiastic parachutist (with 126 parachute jumps behind her) called Valentina Vladimirovna Tereshkova, who had the advantage of a history of party activism and a war hero for a father. And so, she became one of the five women selected for the training.

On the morning of 16 June 1963, Tereshkova was taken by bus to the launch pad. Following the tradition originally started by Gagarin, who had needed to relieve himself against the bus tyre after a long wait cooped up in his spacesuit, Tereshkova duly squatted down and followed the precedent like one of the boys. It was a good thing she did, too, because two more hours passed until the countdown was completed and Vostok 6 launched. Tereshkova had to contend with a dangerous error of calculation that pushed the craft further from the earth than planned, which was then kept secret for 44 years. But her voice remained steady when she radioed "It is I, Chaika! (Russian for 'Seagull' and Tereshkova's call sign.) Everything is fine. I see the horizon; it's a sky blue with a dark strip. How beautiful the Earth is ... everything is going well."[6] She became not only the first woman in space but also the youngest at 26 years of age. To this day she remains the only woman to fly to space solo, and she logged more flight time than the American astronauts who had flown before her, combined.

But eventually, she became a token: a tool in the hands of strong men engaged in a race for dominance with other strong men. It would be another 19 years before another woman − Svetlana Svitskaya − was allowed to fly into space.

If Tycho Brahe had relieved himself in time, the history of astronomy might have looked different (We Come in Peace, page 123).

117

On hearing about Tereshkova's exploits, the astronaut Gordon Cooper blithely commented, "Well, we could have used a woman on the second orbital Mercury Atlas that we had. We could have put a woman up, the same type of woman, and flown her instead of the chimpanzee."[7] John Glenn, the first American to orbit the earth, was a little less blunt in his reaction when he said that it simply "goes against our social order".[8] The social order Glenn meant was American capitalism's secret weapon against the Soviets' threatening, non-hierarchical egalitarianism, the same social order that Tom Hanks' mini-series *From the Earth to the Moon* clings to and embraces. It is precisely this order that on 20 July 1969 resulted in a small step for one man and a giant leap for "man-kind".

In contrast to the competitive relations with Russia, mighty China and its billions of communists wasn't on the Americans' radar in 1969, or at least not enough so as not to poke fun at its folklore. While the crew was preparing for the lunar landing on the fifth day of the Apollo 11 mission, NASA mission control in Houston asked them to "watch for a lovely girl with a big rabbit. An ancient legend says a beautiful Chinese girl called Chang-O has been living there for four thousand years. It seems she was banished to the Moon because she stole the pill of immortality from her husband. You might also look for her companion, a large Chinese rabbit, who is easy to spot since he is always standing on his hind feet in the shade of a cinnamon tree. The name of the rabbit is not reported." Astronaut Michael Collins replied, "Okay. We'll keep a close eye out for the bunny girl."[9] The unnamed rabbit was the mythical Jade Hare, Tu'er Ye, who was later commemorated by the Chinese themselves when they named their 2013 lunar rover after him.

From its infancy human culture has been torn by the question of the moon's gender. For the Greeks and Romans, the moon embodied feminine divinity, due to the perceived connection between its cycles and women's menstrual cycle, and the moon's light being borrowed from the sun, which is several times its size and often associated with masculinity. Lunar goddesses like the Greek Selene or the Roman Luna and other female deities such as Diana, Juno and Hecate, who were associated with the moon, came to represent its mystical aspect in Western culture. However, in Mesopotamia the moon god, Sin, was male; and in ancient Egypt the moon came under the rule of Thoth, god

And numerous circles of hell (Moving Heaven and Hell, page 71).

The triple-faced goddess of crossroads and witchcraft (Weird Sisterhood, page 25).

Author and occultist Aleister Crowley created "The Book of Thoth" Tarot deck after experiencing mystical revelations in Egypt (King of Cups, page 153).

of writing and magic, who manifested himself as a baboon. In Germanic mythology, which gave English the word "moon", he was Mani, whose great powers ruled the ebb and flow of the world. He was the man whose human-like shape can sometimes be observed during full moon, as a result of the contrast between the lunar surface and its seas. In other traditions the Man in the Moon was someone who committed a heinous crime and was banished, as with Cain, the wanderer and first murderer, who was doomed to circle the earth for all eternity according to Dante's *Inferno* and *Paradiso*.

And many days of the week (Twilight of the Gods, page 65).

Son of the serpent (Here Be Dragons, page 79).

The moon's effect on water led some to believe it also affected the fluids in the human body, especially in the brain; Aristotle and later the Roman historian Pliny the Elder argued that weak brains containing an excess of moisture became unsettled when there was a full moon, an insight immortalized in the word "lunacy". It was to the moonstruck, the tragic lovers, the wild women, the wolf-men, that the moon, that fickle and changeable ruler of the night kingdom, spoke.

The first is much more popular for obvious reasons (Moving Heaven and Hell, page 71).

Not everyone needs the moon to undergo change – for some a belt will do the job (Lupus Est, page 93).

Although this claim is contradicted by modern knowledge (for one, the moon's gravity remains constant whether it is full or waning), this belief became firmly entrenched in our cultural consciousness. It has survived the tides of time to the point where some police stations increase their personnel on full moon nights. A meta-analysis conducted in 1985 by psychologists James Rotton and Ivan W Kelly and astronomer Roger Culver found absolutely no connection between psychiatric outbreaks, suicide, crime, calls to help lines and more, and the phases of the moon.

But the paranoia that attacked Bill Kaysing in 1974 and gave rise to one of the most bizarre conspiracy theories ever, may nevertheless indicate a connection between Luna and lunacy. Kaysing claimed that Aldrin and Armstrong's moon landing, during which they left behind their footprints, bags full of bodily waste and the Star-Spangled Banner, had never happened. In his book *We Never Went to the Moon*, Kaysing argued that the American people had been misled and that the moon landing was nothing but a clever hoax for political gain. In 1980 the Flat Earth Society accused NASA of getting Stanley Kubrick to stage the landing using a script from the famous science fiction writer Arthur C Clarke and sound and visual effects courtesy of Disney studios. Believers in this conspiracy theory claimed that the moon landing

One of the most useful products on other planets, it turns out (We Come in Peace, page 123).

was useful ammunition in the propaganda war between the US and the USSR and also served to lift the low spirits of the US people, who were taking the brunt of the Vietnam war. All this could have been achieved, they said, in a well-equipped studio without people having to sit in the actual rocket, waiting until they fired tons of jet fuel under their seats.

The detailed conspiracy theories and the no-less-detailed counter-arguments that followed are closely connected to the importance Americans still attach to the erect national flag forever frozen on the lunar surface. And the possibility that the resulting patriotic orgasm was the result of someone faking it has shocked some and enraged others for decades. This image of the flag's pull is so powerful that Damian Chazelle, the director of the Neil Armstrong biopic *First Man*, was taken to task for not including the historic flag-planting scene in his film. Republican senator Marco Rubio wrote, "This is total lunacy. And a disservice at a time when our people need reminders of what we can achieve when we work together. The American people paid for that mission, on rockets built by Americans, with American technology & carrying American astronauts. It wasn't a UN mission."[10]

And these are times when space is returning to private hands, just as Heinlein foresaw. We have no way of knowing whether the grandiose plans of the current NASA director (appointed by Donald Trump) for a permanent station on the moon will ever materialize, but its future builders had better remember the penal colony and forced labour camps Heinlein wrote about in *The Moon Is a Harsh Mistress*.

Way before any human being who is not a white American man employed by the US government set foot on the moon, Luna was bought, sold, colonized, abandoned, bombed, its population enslaved and liberated under the tides of the imagination. Fascination with the moon has never stopped since 1609 when Johannes Kepler wrote one of the earliest works of science fiction, *Somnium,* in which the moon is populated by demons. The protagonist of *Cyrano de Bergerac* reached the moon on goose wings; Baron Munchausen met people who held their head under their arm on his visit there; Jules Verne's space explorers fired their cannon at it; and in one of the first moving pictures ever made, according to George Méliès the early explorers got stuck in the moon's round face. In Fritz Lang and Thea von Harbou's German

Who applied his unique perspective on earth – as seen from another planet (We Come in Peace, page 123).

That may have had something to do with his mother being accused of witchcraft (Weird Sisterhood, page 25).

Creatures that also appeared on ancient maps (The Territory and the Map, page 47).

Expressionist film from 1924, the "woman in the moon" makes an appearance, while in Arthur C Clarke's *Space Odyssey* there is a more masculine influence when scientists discover a monolith in the Tycho crater.

From male to female, maddening to magical, the moon accompanies us from its orbit, seemingly just out of reach. Only 12 men (and not one woman) have so far walked on its surface, leaving an imprint that will survive long after they themselves have turned to dust. Will these traces be erased in a building boom? Will the evidence of our earliest attempts be buried under the mines, resorts or prison facilities that will emerge on our most faithful satellite? In our attempt to keep the moon out of the struggle between nations bent on colonizing it, we have forfeited it to the rich entrepreneurs who want to use it as they see fit. From a common vision uniting an entire nation under its flag to proof of what enlightened capitalism can achieve for the benefit of all, will the moon turn into an exotic vacation destination for individualists with more money than countries, people who have sampled everything earth has to offer? If so, surely this will be lunacy.

15

WE COME IN PEACE

On a chilly autumn morning on 30 October 1938, a war of the worlds broke out: "Ladies and gentlemen, we interrupt our programme of dance music to bring you a special bulletin from the Intercontinental Radio News. At twenty minutes before eight, central time, Professor Farrell of the Mount Jennings Observatory, Chicago, Illinois, reports observing several explosions of incandescent gas, occurring at regular intervals on the planet Mars. The spectroscope indicates the gas to be hydrogen and moving towards the earth with enormous velocity."[1] The tune of "Star Dust", which was broadcast following the announcement, kept being interrupted by reports of landings, aliens and poisonous gas. The actor Orson Welles had begun the broadcast by announcing this was a version of H G Wells' 1898 book *The War of the Worlds*, but not everyone had tuned in at the beginning of the programme and the *New York Times* reported that tens of thousands of people had run into the streets holding wet towels or handkerchiefs to their faces.

The month following this sensational radio event saw no fewer than 12,500 articles about it, and the then German Chancellor, Adolf Hitler, was cited as saying that the phenomenon was "a testament to the decadence and corrupt condition of democracy".[2] Less than a year later it turned out that the world's citizens had good reason to be fearful. On 1 September 1939 the Nazis invaded Poland and World War II began.

On the morning of 7 December 1941, when war was raging in Europe, a pensioner in his late sixties woke up in his home in Hawaii to the sound of explosions that seemed to be coming from the harbour. Rather than Martians in silver cylinders, these turned out to be Japanese in silver fighter planes, which did not make them appear any less alien to Americans. In spite of his advanced age, the man asked to be employed as a military correspondent and got his wish. After all, he was the author of more than 70 books and the creator of one of the most popular icons of all time: Tarzan of the Apes. His name was Edgar Rice Burroughs and he

The venomous propaganda directed against the Japanese during World War II, including the incarceration of more than 100,000 Americans of Japanese descent in concentration camps, was expressed in posters that emphasized, exaggerated and ridiculed their Asian facial features, and also in maps depicting them as rats or as monsters with blood on their hands, preparing to destroy the land of the free (The Territory and the Map, page 47).

wrote a thing or two about Mars as well. In his *A Princess of Mars*, published in 1912, an officer from Virginia in the Confederate Army, named Captain John Carter, reaches the planet that local inhabitants call "Barsoom". Together with a four-handed alien warrior and a gorgeous princess, he gets involved in some hair-raising adventures.

From the moment Mars was first spotted by humankind, its red hue caused by the high amount of iron oxide on its surface has given the planet an aura of bloodstained danger. For the Babylonians it was known as Nergal, the god of destruction and fire, while the Chinese saw it as a bad omen. The Greeks named it after their god of war, Ares, and the Romans, who changed the god's name but not his essence, called it Mars. The planet's own irregularly shaped moons were discovered by astronomer Asaph Hall in 1877 and named Phobos and Deimos – meaning fear and terror – after the sons of Ares.

Misinterpreting an anagram Galileo used to hide the fact that he had discovered two protrusions on either side of Saturn (which were, in fact, its rings), Johannes Kepler believed that he was referring to the moons of Mars and deciphered the message as saying: "Hello, furious twins, sons of Mars". They were both right. Mars was a source of fascination for generations of astronomers, from the ancient Egyptians to the medieval Europeans. But Kepler was the first man to declare war on it. He believed with almost religious fervour in a solar system of celestial harmony that could be represented by geometric bodies neatly nestling within each other, encompassed by a sphere. He believed the aesthetics of the idea were so appealing that in February 1596 he offered to make a model for his patron Duke Frederick of Würtemberg, which would essentially be a vending machine dispensing alcoholic beverages, to celebrate the harmony and symmetry of the heavens. The planets would be made of precious gems: Jupiter was to be fashioned from sapphires, Saturn from diamonds and the moon, naturally, would be studded with pearls. The drinks in each planetary sphere – vermouth for Mars, mead for Venus, brandy for Mercury, and so on – would come out of seven taps around the rim of the contraption, fed by invisible pipes.

Fearing that someone would steal his model, Kepler scattered the orders for the pipes for the beta version among several different goldsmiths, but when they arrived and he tried to assemble them,

Ares/Mars' daughters received less kudos (Wonder Women, page 37).

All three, in fact, were right. The first literary representation of these two celestial bodies appears in *Gulliver's Travels* by Jonathan Swift, who knew that to make his most outlandish inventions appear credible he must give them a semblance of scientific veracity and therefore included the measurements and orbits of those moons, ostensibly taken by the astronomers of Laputa, his flying island. Surprisingly, his data is so close to the truth that the Soviet spacecraft designer V G Perminov believed that Swift had managed to find and decipher records that Martians had left on earth (The Territory and the Map, page 47).

Although there were those who had reservations about his piety (Weird Sisterhood, page 25).

his design failed. There was a problem with his calculations, but it would take time for him to realize that Mars was the one that was causing him trouble.

A year after the failure of his machine, Kepler accepted an invitation from Tycho Brahe, the bad boy of astronomy, to be his assistant at his new observatory.

It is hard to imagine two more different men – the thin, ascetic German and the flamboyant Danish bon vivant who owned his own island inhabited by beautiful women, a fortune-telling midget and a pet moose that Brahe killed accidentally by giving it beer. At one time, the funding granted to Brahe by Frederick II, the King of Denmark, reached 1 per cent of the kingdom's budget. But by the time Kepler met him in Prague, Brahe was no longer the same playboy who had boasted an impressive collection of prosthetic noses – one of them of pure gold – after losing his own in a passionate duel over mathematics. The king died and Christian IV, his son and heir, disliked Brahe and his ostentatious lifestyle. After ceremonial humiliations and a funding drought, Brahe decided to accept the invitation of Czech Emperor Rudolf II and move to Prague.

But if Kepler had hoped for a fruitful scientific relationship with the great astronomer he was soon proved wrong. Brahe guarded his observation tables like a mother hen and was unwilling to let Kepler peek at his golden eggs. Perhaps to distract his frustrated and overly enthusiastic assistant, Brahe posed a challenge to Kepler: to predict the orbit of Mars. No problem, Kepler told him – in Latin, presumably – and promised to return with an answer within a week. It took him six years. This he called his "war with Mars".

But then, on 13 October 1601, Kepler's stars changed. Brahe went out to attend a great feast in the presence of the Czech emperor. Eleven days later he died in agony. According to the official version, Brahe was reluctant to offend the emperor by excusing himself and visiting the lavatory. After he had drunk a lot and refrained from relieving himself, his bladder simply exploded. The events surrounding that night were immortalized in prose by author Max Brod in his 1936 book *Tycho Brahe's Path to God* and the Czech writer Milan Kundera in the novel *Immortality*.

Who refused to comply with the last request of his friend, Franz Kafka, to destroy his writings after his death (Flame and Moth, page 17).

Kepler now had unfettered access to Brahe's tables. Perhaps this is why, over the years, theories arose that Kepler had poisoned

Brahe. But there were other suspects, such as Christian IV, who was outraged by rumours that the astronomer was sleeping with the queen, his mother. There are also those who claim that the murder plot inspired Shakespeare's *Hamlet*, which is set in the contemporary Danish royal court. The question whether or not there was anything suspicious about Brahe's death intrigued historians for 300 years, and in 1901 his body was exhumed and examined, to reveal abnormal amounts of mercury. This finding suggested he had been poisoned or had been taking medication for his kidney problem.

With Brahe's observation tables on Mars at his disposal, Kepler could finally make good on his brash promise to the now dead man. He made 2,007 complicated calculations to discover not only the unexpectedly elliptical orbit of the red planet, but the fact that what keeps the planets in their orbits is the power of the sun. To do that, Kepler used Mars in his words, as "a watchtower". His biographer Max Casper writes "Now here again Kepler's inventive genius was active and suggested an ingenious trick," continuing, "he, so to speak, transposed his eyes to a particular position of Mars' orbit and from there found out directly the relative values of the distances from sun to earth."[3] After delays arising from disagreements over rights to the deceased Brahe's calculations, he published his *Astronomia Nova* in 1609.

On 5 September 1887, the Italian astronomer Giovanni Schiaparelli got closer than anyone before him to fulfilling Kepler's vision of standing on Mars. With the help of his powerful telescope, he noticed something he called *canali* crisscrossing the surface of the planet. These lines appeared to be tracks or conduits of water. Due to an error in translation, the original Italian was rendered as "canals" rather than as "channels". While channels tend to refer to natural waterways, canals are by definition unnatural and they don't evolve by themselves. Canals require brains to plan them and limbs to dig them – in this case an astronomical feat of engineering. That was what Percival Lowell, a nineteenth-century American orientalist, mathematician and astronomer, thought. He was so intrigued by Schiaparelli's network of canals that he published three books: *Mars* (1895), *Mars and Its Canals* (1906) and *Mars as the Abode of Life* (1908), insisting that Mars was home to an ancient, languishing civilization, which had dug canals to transport water from its poles to its dry zones.

Lowell's theory sparked the public imagination. Subsequent observations that revealed peculiar and picturesque formations such as "the face" and "the pyramids" further boosted belief in the existence of a Martian culture. Martian fever spread. Literary works, scholarly articles, music albums and a slew of B-movies (for example, the 1964 *Santa Clause Conquers the Martians*, considered the worst film ever made) were dedicated to life on Mars. Socialist artists were apparently drawn to its reddish tint, as in Alexander Bogdanov's book *The Red Star* (1908), in which a visitor from earth discovers a workers' utopia on Mars. In Alexei Tolstoi's *Aelita* published in 1923 and adapted for the silent screen as one of the first Soviet sci-fi movies in 1924, Mars is the site of a communist revolution.

There's close competition between it and Ed Wood's zombie movie *Plan 9 from Outer Space* (Head Hunters, page 231).

A modern incarnation of Thomas More's remote island (Best of All Possible Worlds, page 247).

The masters of the genre all popped over for a visit, leaving their footprint in the planet's ruddy dust: from Ray Bradbury with his *Martian Chronicles* to Philip K Dick's psychedelic *Martian Time-Slip*. But over and beyond imagining Mars' subsiding civilization, these books yielded an impression of earth's ebullient culture. One of the most influential was Robert A Heinlein's book *Stranger in a Strange Land*, whose hero, Valentine Michael Smith, is a human raised by Martians who comes to earth and redeems it. The novel became a cult phenomenon for the hippie generation and was a favourite of the scientologist mass murderer, Charles Manson. It also inspired another monumental creation that brandished Mars in its motto: "The Rise and Fall of Ziggy Stardust and the Spiders from Mars", David Bowie's 1972 revolutionary concept album. Six years later, Jeff Wayne recorded the electronic music version of Wells' *War of the Worlds*, sending hits like "Forever Autumn" to the top of the charts.

The 1960s were good years for extraterrestrials. They were also fertile ground for conspiracy theories, which were spreading like wildfire. If you believed that your country could stage the murder of its own elected president or fabricate a landing on the moon (supposedly filmed at a secret military base called Area 51), it wasn't so hard to accept that thousands of Americans were kidnapped annually and probed anally by aliens. And that furthermore, national authorities were fully aware of these goings-on but were keeping mum because in exchange they received advanced technology from another world (which was being researched at the same Area 51 facility).

With the kind help of science fiction writers' generous imagination (Man in the Moon, page 115).

Barney and Betty Hill were an unusual couple for the early 1960s. Betty was a social worker and Barney a postman, but they spent their free time on one the greatest national struggles of their era – alongside the protests against the US war in Vietnam – the fight for advancing the rights of "American people of color". It was, for them, a personal issue because Betty was white and Barney African American. In 1961 Betty and Barney claimed they were pursued by an unidentified flying object, only to wake up hours later 37 miles (60 kilometres) from where they had last been; they also claimed that the extraterrestrials used hypnosis to drag them on board their spacecraft and subject them to bizarre experiments.

Americans wanted to believe. Though it was not the first story of its kind, Barney and Betty's account came along at the right moment – at the height of the Cold War and the space race. They received a lot of public attention, reports of similar abductions rose significantly, and their descriptions of aliens became paradigmatic: small, grey beings with large pear-shaped heads and almond-shaped, slanted eyes – just like the thousands of aliens depicted in popular culture ever since. Their experience, too, became standardized. Many abductees reported that they had been forced to undergo strange experiments with the use of mysterious anal probes. It was generally assumed that what the extraterrestrials had in mind was to eventually create a hybrid creature, an alien–human cross, but their specifically anal interest in us humans is harder to explain.

According to one of the period's bestsellers, *Chariots of the Gods?*, aliens have been visiting us for thousands of years. Erich von Däniken, a Swiss hotelier, was convinced there are references in sacred texts and the beliefs of ancient civilizations such as the Maya, the ancient Egyptians and the people of Easter Island, to "gods" who were in fact extraterrestrials who had made early contact with the earth's ancient cultures. The scientific community rejected his findings as fraudulent and him as a charlatan. His next book, *Gods from Outer Space*, he wrote from jail where he was serving a sentence for tax evasion – and fraud. Von Däniken unsurprisingly argued that he had fallen victim to a conspiracy aimed to silence him and hide evidence about the presence of aliens on earth. Still, many people enthusiastically embraced his ideas, which were in tune with newly emerging New Age thought and spirituality. This created a lively, evolving subculture that offered support groups

Since the dawn of time, it seems, the human race had been fascinated and threatened by the idea of hybrid creatures (The Human Animal, page 189).

He also found confirmation of this, he claimed, in Norse mythology (Twilight of the Gods, page 65), the epic of Gilgamesh and the ruins of Tiwanaku (No Man's Island, page 57), and believed that the need to hide this forbidden knowledge was behind the burning of ancient libraries (Flame and Moth, page 17).

A place that has historically proven itself inspirational (The Pleasure Principle, page 195; King of Cups, page 153).

for people taken by aliens, as well as insurance in the case of abduction, though the burden of proof – obviously – was on the claimant. So far, such a policy has been taken out by about 20,000 people, offering cover for alien pregnancy, experiments carried out by extraterrestrials and death by aliens. To date the insurance company has agreed to pay out in only two cases (whose details are classified).

The voluminous mythology (believers will say: accurate descriptions) concerning abductions and government-led efforts to cover them up coalesced in the 1970s. The crash of a US military test balloon in 1947 near New Mexico – which at the time had been investigated because of suspicions of alien involvement – returned to the headlines. The name of the US Air Force base where the remnants of the crashed balloon had been taken – Roswell – entered the conversation about UFOs. Conspiracy theory adherents argued that what the Air Force had found, rather than a test balloon, was an alien spaceship. The military had removed small grey bodies from the wreckage and subjected them to a thorough post-mortem. The argument was that the incident had marked the start of contacts between the US government and aliens.

Phil Schneider, a government geological engineer turned ufologist, argued a contract was signed between the US government and the "greys", as part of a deal in which they received technology that enabled them to develop stealth aircraft. Schneider was found dead in his home, a catheter tube wrapped around his neck. Many other investigators of aliens were similarly unlucky, dying in a variety of bizarre circumstances: an LSD overdose, a sudden stroke, unexplained suicides and accidental shootings by the police, which – their followers claimed – were delivered by the hands of those loyal conspirators, the Men in Black. With their expressionless faces, timeless black suits and black shades, the MIB were the government's go-to tool for cleaning up, cross-examination and intimidation. Lowell Cunningham's comics bearing their name present them as devoted to gaining control of the ignorant masses and keep the American people in the dark about the truth. But as Chris Carter, the creator of the conspiracy-laden TV series *The X-Files*, knew, the truth is always out there.

Unfortunately, the truth, at least as far as Mars is concerned, was disappointing. The Mariner space probes launched in the late 1960s, forever disproved Lowell's "canals". There were wonders on Mars, such as Valles Marineris, the largest canyon in the solar system, or Olympus Mons, the highest mountain (three times as high as Mount Everest). But no crumbling ancient alien civilization or, indeed, any signs of life have been found. Yet.

It took literature, film and science some time, but they got over the worst of their disappointment and rekindled their interest in Mars. *The Martian* by Andy Weir, which was turned into a motion picture of the same name, is the story of an astronaut who is left for dead by his friends who return to earth. He is forced to use his colleagues' dried faeces as manure to grow potatoes to survive. In the film *Total Recall* based on the short story "We Can Remember It for You Wholesale" by Philip K Dick, the TV series *Babylon 5* and *The Expanse* by the writers Daniel Abraham and Ty Franck (aka James S A Corey), the humans living on Mars rebel against the rulers of the earth and demand autonomy. And Robert Zubrin, an American author and space engineer, established the Mars Society in 1988, whose objective it is to send a manned mission to the red planet. Elon Musk with his SpaceX enterprise has detailed colonization plans. Humankind will set out for Mars, colonize it and establish the advanced civilization of its dreams. We constantly re-invent and imagine life on Mars, but now the life we picture there is our own.

One of the first to think about turning another arid planet – not only into a dwelling place for the human race, with bubble cities or underground burrows – but into a place similar to earth itself, with its atmosphere, flora and fauna, was British philosopher and author Olaf Stapledon. He was one of the most original and daring thinkers about the future. The scope of his vision not only impressed science fiction writers but equally scientists such as the evolutionary biologist John Maynard Smith, and the mathematician and physicist, Freeman Dyson. Even a politician, who tried his hand at writing between the two world wars, found solace in Stapledon's capacious imagination. His name was Winston Churchill. In his first book, *Last and First Men*, published in 1930, Stapledon tells the story of human history from his own times to its absolute end, covering two billion years. Applying jaw-dropping feats of Hegelian dialectic, he sketches the rise and fall of no less than 18 human species, each of which evolves (or is created and engineered by their predecessors) and subsides to clear the stage for the next. Some of them resemble us, others are feline and

It is a pity that it was not possible to invite him to join the "Human Interference Task Force" of 1981 (Remember to Forget, page 139).

there are those whose bodies have evolved to support their huge brains. In the course of these millions of years, humans set out for the stars and, after destroying the local inhabitants, populate them. On these planets they conduct a titanic feat, which Stapledon conceived but was named by another science fiction writer, Jack Williamson, in a story published in 1942: "terraformation". This process requires aggressive geological intervention, extreme atmospheric adjustments, changes to the temperature with the aim to either heat or cool the planetary surface and ecological cultivation to enable plants to grow, animals to flourish, and so on. In 1961 the astronomer Carl Sagan proposed sowing seaweed in the dense atmosphere of Venus to absorb carbon dioxide and reduce the greenhouse effect on our lustrous neighbour, thus making it possible to develop a life-supporting biosphere. In 1973 he also made suggestions concerning the terraforming of our archaic object of fascination and terror: Mars.

During the US–Soviet space race, Soviet scientists managed to generate artificial biospheres for training their cosmonauts. They spent months in them, breathing oxygen harvested from seaweed and munching hydroponic food.

The US answer to these Soviet efforts was a project that began operating in Arizona in 1991. Typical of any American enterprise, it was bigger, more capitalist and a lot wilder. It had three acres of geodesic domes and pyramids containing a variety of ecological environments, from a rainforest to a desert; about 4,000 species of plants; pollinating insects like bees; primates of the Galagidae family, which are small and nocturnal; and some much bigger primates – seven humans who volunteered to be locked in and try to live in a closed ecological system as long as they were able to by growing their own food and recycling their waste via the soil. Biosphere 2 was the product of a generation that saw itself as humanity's last great hope to correct its mistakes. "Western culture is not just dying," said John Allen, one of the founders. "We are digging around in the rubble to take everything useful so we can build the new culture that will replace it."[4] The launch of the experiment was celebrated in the proper spirit, with a huge psychedelic party attended by celebrities of the movement like the prophet-junkie Timothy Leary. And tourists were invited to purchase admission tickets, wander around and peep in through the hothouse walls to catch a glimpse of the experiment's participants.

Three years later, on 4 April 1994, two of them broke their way out of the hermetically sealed complex fearing for their own and their cohabitators' lives, after the plants and animals began to die, food was running out and oxygen levels dropped.

More than 20 years have passed since the Biosphere project was abandoned and its findings disappeared, never to be seen again. NASA's statement on 27 September 2012, about evidence of liquid water on the red planet brought the discussion about the economic, operational and political–ethical issues of terraformation back to the forefront. A relatively nearby planet that has precious water on its surface? Keen entrepreneurs are already rubbing their hands in anticipation, architects are drawing up plans for affordable housing, nimble opportunists stake out plots with a view on Vallis Marineris. Then there are the starry-eyed scientists and engineers who are all excited about Herculean projects such as: a chain of giant mirrors interlinking across the planet and helping to reflect the sun's radiation; the distribution of millions of nano-robots, which will be engaged in planetary engineering or drilling into the planet's frozen heart; and controlled nuclear explosions to jump-start geological processes. All these enthusiasts are faced with the pragmatic sceptics mumbling their memento mori: we don't have enough money; we don't have the technology; nor do we have sufficient time to get all these ventures rolling. These projects make the word "grandiose" look small and are only the beginning of a process at the end of which another planet will be created in our image and likeness. Full terraformation, assuming it is technologically feasible, is bound to be economically exorbitant and will carry on for centuries.

There are other ways to enable long-term extraterrestrial colonization – rather than adjust the planet, change the colonists – whether by genetic engineering, cloning or mechanically, as in Frederik Pohl's *Man Plus* and *Mars Plus* novels whose protagonist has been adjusted to survive in a toxic atmosphere by undergoing a procedure that turns him into a cyborg. Still, in Larry Niven's *Footfall*, it is humans who fall victim to terraforming, when aliens drop a huge asteroid into the ocean as a prelude to an invasion. The writer who did the most in-depth research about long-term terraforming is Kim Stanley Robinson in his *Mars* trilogy, in which he observes the moral and political aspects of the conquest of Mars, over decades.

Having already sold all of those on the moon (Man in the Moon, page 115).

Tiny versions of our ancient mechanized slaves (Ex Machina, page 213).

These aspects are now coming up for discussion due to the probability of finding the unicellular life that might be joyfully swimming in Mars' saline water and the concern about their fate once earth's water engineers set up their first desalination plant there. The question of what would befall the native populations on planets slated for terraforming already troubled Stapledon's contemporary, C S Lewis, the creator of the *Narnia* novels. He admired Stapledon's work, but as an observant Christian couldn't accept his pragmatic attitude to the effect that such a population would inevitably go the dodos' way and become extinct in a planetary genocide.

Do unicellular aliens have rights? Who owns a planet: the micro-organisms that inhabit it, or the brave astronauts who make their way to it and plant their flag? And which flag should that be? Will China or the US announce their respective imperialist projects to settle other worlds in the solar system? Or will we have to face corporate colonialism? Richard Taylor, the British mathematician, has coined the phrase "Make way, microbes", while Greenpeace activists urgently argue that life that hasn't developed on earth, no matter how small, has rights. And there are those who wonder what is the point of tying humankind's fate to the gravity of some huge rock? We should be content with space stations and leave other planets alone, spare them our bothersome presence – especially given our rather sad record in the field of environmental conservation. Opponents of terraforming think of it as a dangerous (even if still largely hypothetical) form of terrestrial ethnocentrism and planetary chauvinism.

Whether we choose to build our home on a nearby planet or move beyond the boundaries of the solar system; whether the aliens come to us or we come to them, we must remember that we are the stuff of stars and each of our atoms began somewhere in the great vacuum of space. If indeed the stars are our destination, we must come in peace.

16

FORCE MAJEURE

A long, long time ago, in a galaxy far, far away (more precisely, it happened in 2009, in the small Welsh town of Bangor), shoppers at the local Tesco were surprised to see a robed and hooded Jedi knight in full regalia, strutting into the supermarket. It wasn't petrol for his spaceship he was looking for or a battery for his lightsaber – just a sandwich for lunch.

He was a 24-year-old whose name was Daniel Jones and he had established the Church of Jediism a year earlier. Very ungallantly, staff drew his attention to the fact that patrons were requested to remove hoods on entering the premises, as they offer ample cover from the prying eyes of security cameras to those who wish to illegally remove objects from the shop. The knight refused to yield, arguing that not wearing the hood was against his religion. His catechism (which he himself had formulated) stipulated that knights must cover their head in public. Jones went on to accuse the supermarket chain of religious intolerance and announced that he was considering taking legal action.

The retail empire, not to be outdone, struck back: "Obi-Wan Kenobi, Yoda and Luke Skywalker all appeared hoodless without ever going over to the Dark Side and we are only aware of the Emperor as [some]one who never removed his hood," a Tesco spokesperson explained. "Jedis are very welcome to shop in our stores although we would ask them to remove their hoods … If Jedi walk around our stores with their hoods on, they'll miss lots of special offers."[1]

Jones was inspired to found his church when he discovered that in the 2001 census 390,000 British citizens stated they adhered to Jediism, the fictitious religion George Lucas created for his *Star Wars* saga. For the first time in the national census's history, the option to identify as a Jedi had been made possible with the inclusion of a voluntary, open question about religious beliefs. Being a Jedi ranked fifth on the list of most popular religious affiliations, behind only Christian, None (having no religion), Muslim and Hindu. The source of this phenomenon, it seems, was an internet campaign that (wrongly) claimed Jediism would receive official recognition as a religion if enough people put it down on their census forms.

In Australia 75,000 people registered as Jedi knights and the number of followers of "the Force" in Canada rose to 21,000. The phenomenon kept growing. In 2006, two knights of the honourable order of the Jedi in the UK demanded that "International Day of Tolerance" should henceforth be "Interstellar Day of Tolerance". In April 2015, thousands of Turkish students in Izmir called for the establishment of a Jedi temple with the aim: "To recruit new Jedi and to bring balance to the Force". In a provocative press release the students explained that "uneducated Padawans are moving to the dark side ... To find the balance in the Force, we want a Jedi temple."[2] This was a protest against the construction of hundreds of mosques on university campuses throughout Turkey and the ever-increasing Islamization of the government led by Recep Tayyip Erdogan, who increasingly acts like an absolute ruler.

The intriguing relations between Lucas' epic space opera and the infamous Middle Eastern dictator who ruled over Turkey's neighbour, Iraq, were explored by the Iraqi-American artist Michael Rakowitz. In his amusing and thought-provoking exhibition, *The worst condition is to pass under a sword which is not one's own*, he traces "links between Western science fiction and military–industrial activities in Iraq during Saddam Hussein's regime".[3] Using elements such as the similarity between megalomaniac urban sculpture in Baghdad and the iconic Star Wars poster, Rakowitz forges an alternative interpretation of the force that fuelled the deposed dictator's ambition. He points out that the design of Hussein's elite units' helmets emulate those of the film's stormtroopers. And the special screening of the film for a select audience of senior party members, along with Saddam and his then 15-year-old son Uday, which took place only six months before he declared war on his neighbours, all give credence to Rakowitz's reading.

It was Saddam's great rival, Iran, that supplied one of the key elements in Lucas' fictional mythology: Zoroastrianism, the religion of the country's ancient inhabitants, the Persians. For thus spoke Zarathustra: our world is ruled by two opposing powers – good and evil, light and darkness – and they are locked in eternal struggle. Lucas was very happy to adopt this dichotomy as the division at the heart of his narrative, while he took the need to balance the two tendencies against each other from Taoism, together with the elusive mystical nature of the Force.

Also, into the shopping trolley of Lucas' theological supermarket went Carlos Castaneda, Zen Buddhism, the medieval European code of chivalry, dualist gnostics and reactionary technophobia. And all of this is suffused by the spirit of the comparative mythologist, Joseph Campbell and his *The Hero with a Thousand Faces*. Lucas confessed that Campbell's notion concerning the "monomyth", a pattern that weaves right through the heroic narratives of all mythologies, is what got him out of a writer's block when he was writing the screenplay.

The "hero's journey" that Campbell describes helped Lucas create his reluctant messiah, Luke Skywalker, a boy who finds he doesn't know his origins – as could only be expected from the spiritual offspring of Moses, Jesus and King Arthur – and the milestones he must pass on his journey toward personal and galactic redemption. Luke's ancestor, it turns out, was not only Anakin/Vader but also someone at the centre of another modern mythology: Paul Muad'Dib Atreidis. He is the protagonist of Frank Herbert's science fiction epic *Dune*, adapted into a mini-series directed by John Harrison in 2000, and into two feature films, the first in 1984 directed by David Lynch, and the second directed by Denis Villeneuve and released in 2021. Lucas acknowledged the enormous impact Herbert's novel had on his thinking, which Herbert resented. It is apparent on every level, from the barren landscape of Tatooine, the Skywalker family's home planet and its resemblance to the dunes of Arakis, to the villains of these pieces, who are both patriarchal figures – Paul's grandfather and Luca's dark father.

But the similarities aren't exhausted by aesthetic details or plot. They are also reflected in the works' ambitious scope, in their dizzying blend of religion and science, theology and technology. Spaceships, laser weapons, aliens and robots exist side by side with knights and concubines. The organic powers of the good and enlightened Force, whose knights wear white linen robes as if they were performing *Lawrence of Arabia* in outer space, struggles against the evil ghost in the machine, whose soldiers are locked into rigid plastic suits with articulated limbs, like gas-mask-wearing Nazi insects. This is the war between the sons of light and the sons of darkness in its most simplified version.

Which took shape primarily in romances about courtly love and the exploits of King Arthur (King of Cups, page 153).

"The suspicion of technology is a manifestation of larger fears about the erosion of traditional individualism,"[a] writes Cyrus Patell. This is expressed in the representation of the Empire as a hyper-technological dictatorship and of its faceless stormtroopers imposing the rigid order that every dictatorship must uphold (Best of All Possible Worlds, page 247).

A work that also greatly influenced many of the comic book writers of the 1940s (No Man's Island, page 57).

In 1125, William of Malmesbury wrote that like Moses' grave, Arthur's burial site was unknown, but "whence antiquity of fables still claims that he will return"[b] (King of Cups, page 153).

Where Herbert experimented with imagined religions (Remember to Forget, page 139).

It is not by coincidence that our first encounter with the Jedi religion occurs in a sand-swept land, for many a religion emerged from the desert: it is a blistering crucible in which humanity has undergone some of its formative spiritual experiences.

Lucas certainly did not intend to establish a religion, but he did seek to create a world. And while Jediism might be an invented religion – aren't all religions, in the end, and indeed, right from the start? – *Invented Religions: Imagination, Fiction and Faith*, by the historian Carole M Cusack, discusses Jediism as a hyper-real faith. She follows Jean Baudrillard, who observed that entertainment, information and communication technologies provide experiences more intense and involving than the scenes of banal everyday life. The realm of the hyper-real is more real than real. Even though Jediism doesn't consider Lucas' works to be holy writ or see Master Yoda as its prophet, it carries a spiritual truth for its followers that is no less true for them because it was created artificially – on the contrary. The dividing line between fan and devotee has never been thinner.

The word "fan", most likely short for fanatic, derives from the Latin *fanaticus* meaning mad, enthusiastic, inspired by a god. The god in question was the great god Pan, protector of wild nature. But the fanatic also originally pertains to a temple, from the Latin *fanum* meaning shrine or consecrated place.

Shopping centres are our modern shrines and consumerism is consecrated. The *Star Wars* saga, with its sacred merchandise, novelization, comics, prequels and sequels, computer games, endless parodies and diverse cultural products – is a palimpsest, a new myth from a long time ago, scribbled on the pages of earlier religions it erases. From being a monomyth, Lucas' mythical collage has evolved into a neomyth, which renews and resets everything and can move back and forth in time to images of the future cast as the remote past.

Its combination of a rigid adherence to the rules of universal myth and the series' eclectic, intergalactic flexibility is what makes Jediism a subversive alternative and not merely a humoristic homage. It offers itself as an icon for all who wish to defy the authorities' interference in how they choose to define themselves, in what they believe, or just simply in their freedom to wear a hood – self-proclaimed rebels against the empire.

May the Force be with them.

As opposed to others who did mean to (Remember to Forget, page 139).

Who expands on the concept of hyper-realism in his influential book *Simulacra and Simulation* (1981), and the relationship between the real and the symbolic as expressed, for example, in Jorge Luis Borges's "On Exactitude in Science" (The Territory and the Map, page 47).

Perhaps that's the reason why fans are often considered childish (Paradise Lost, page 171).

Modern-day pilgrims' mirrors (A Faustian Bargain, page 1).

17

REMEMBER TO FORGET

Under the hooves of the reindeer covered in their ragged winter furs, their breathing leaving white puffs of cloud in the frozen air; under the clean white shroud of snow; under the black soil; under the roots of the naked trees; under the cold rivers flowing into the dark; under the rocks a secret is buried. A secret we must remember to forget. Forever.

The burial chambers of this secret are in the depths of a huge granite cathedral, reached through a winding tunnel 520 metres (569 yards) deep, in a region that has been geologically stable for the past two million years. This is crucial, because the secret buried here must stay untouched through 100,000 more years. Once the gates close, the tunnels are blocked and the entrance is sealed, the soil will cover the opening once more, trees will again grow their roots around it, snow will blanket it and the reindeer will stamp the ground, unaware of the eternal fire underneath them. It is a fire that we lit with our own hands and that we must now smother.

In physics, the halving time of military-use plutonium is 24,110 years, and during this time the material continues to discharge its lethal radiation. But radioactive waste is not only produced by military industries: medical and other industries make their contributions, too. They are life threatening and likely to poison the environment for long periods of time. And so, the prosaic question, "Who is taking out the trash?" turns into a matter of life and death. Over and beyond being a technically challenging matter of removal and burial, this is an abstract issue of signposting, with possibly fateful consequences. Because if the time it takes certain types of radioactive waste to decay can be tens or even hundreds of thousands of years, then we must find a way of marking our radioactive material to make sure the labels will remain meaningful throughout a span of 30 generations of human development. How are we to make a message that will still be understood – assuming there will still be someone who *can* understand – in scores of thousands of years? How do we convince them to believe us? How are we to speak to the future?

It is said that in 1872, when self-taught Assyriologist George Smith managed to decipher the Mesopotamian flood story on a clay tablet from excavations at the library of Nineveh, he was so elated that he started taking off his clothes and running around the reading room (Ex Libris, page 9).

Who slays a monster that was a descendant of Cain, the first murderer (Here Be Dragons, page 79).

The most ancient continuous human culture, China, has endured for about 5,000 years. Sumerian cuneiform, the earliest system of writing we have so far found, dates back to 3500 BC, but not all languages have had their own Rosetta Stone and a persistent Champollion intent on decoding them. Some of them, like the undeciphered symbolic language of the Indus Valley culture, the mysterious "Linear A" of Crete and the only half-understood glyphs used by the Maya seem to have lost their meaning forever. Currently used languages, inevitably including English, the contemporary lingua franca, have all undergone dramatic change during their existence. No modern English speaker can read the greatest Old English epic, *Beowulf,* without special training – a poem only written at the end of the tenth century. And they will not find it much easier with Chaucer's *Canterbury Tales,* composed in Middle English. Even early Modern English is not always easy to read: for example, William Shakespeare's sixteenth-century writings. All this covers a span of no more than 1,500 years. What will the English language look like in another 10,000 years (assuming it survives)? How will it be written? How will it sound? How will it be read?

Or should we set our sights on signs instead, hoping that in addition to being worth a thousand words, one picture can also last for thousands of years – and thereby let signs speak for us? The white hand against a red background, currently the common sign for "Stop!" has only fulfilled that function since 1915. The trefoil warning symbol for radioactivity was created by the members of the radiation laboratory at Berkeley University in California in 1946. Marie Curie wouldn't have been able to make sense of it and it is too risky to assume that those who inherit the earth will either. Pictographs are inherently artificial and culture-dependent constructs.

And even if we manage to find the language or the specific objects able to withstand the gnawing teeth of time, how can we be sure that our warnings will be heeded? Museums worldwide are bursting with objects carrying ancient warnings telling people "Don't touch!", "No entry" or "Caution! Danger!" – such as the ancient Egyptian inscription in the National Museum in Scotland, dating from between 1295–1069 BC that cautions "beware of forcefully removing this stone from its place. As for he who covers it in its place, great lords of the west will reproach him very very very very very very very very much."[1] Contemporaries knew to take such warnings extremely seriously – the same words that the Egyptologists of the nineteenth century ignored with such enlightened arrogance. Who says that the archeologists of the future will not shrug off the superstitions of the savages of the past with their preposterous warnings against some invisible, lethal radiation?

Aren't we savages of the present familiar with tales of illusive will-o'-the-wisps luring us away from the straight and narrow down into perdition? In Finland's epic poem, *Kalevala*, they are called *Aarnivalkea* and they burn with an eternal flame to mark the place where treasure is buried. Maybe this is what the Finns were thinking of when they came up with a solution for nuclear waste that will endure for millennia, even until the stars in the night sky will have changed position. A model of their massive nuclear storage facility, made in collaboration with ArkDes, Sweden's national centre for architecture and design, was displayed in an exhibition at London's Victoria and Albert Museum, entitled *The Future Starts Here*. And it illustrates the movements of astronomical bodies and constellations relative to the earth over the course of time that the storage facility is expected to exist. Onkalo, meaning "little cave", seems a monstrously ironic name as we see Michael Madsen, the director of the documentary *Into Eternity*, wandering through its vast interiors. The facility will eventually contain about 250,000 tons of the radioactive material Finland will have produced up to that point, and the plan is to fill and seal the place by 2100. From the moment its gates close, Onkalo's role will be passive. It will require neither maintenance nor monitoring. Finland's abundant nature will be allowed to grow wild and cover the location and the potential horrors that are buried there. No mythic flame will mark this unknown burial place. Those who conceived of this huge engineering enterprise, its planners and builders, intend their creation to be wholly erased from memory. As one of the scientists says to Madsen in the film, human curiosity knows no bounds. Even the tiniest trace of something having been hidden here will make someone want to dig it up and expose it. The best approach therefore is for nobody ever to suspect its existence. And what if someone manages to make their way in? asks the director. The scientist shifts uneasily, expressing his hope that any culture sophisticated enough to unearth this underground hiding place is

In the library where the clay tablet deciphered by Smith was unearthed there were no less terrifying curses (Ex Libris, page 9).

A work that – alongside Norse mythology – greatly influenced J R R Tolkien's Middle Earth (King of Cups, page 153).

likely to have some insight into what might be buried in there. "Onkalo must last 100,000 years. Nothing built by man has ever lasted even a tenth of that time span, but we consider ourselves a very potent civilization. If we succeed, Onkalo will most likely be the longest lasting remains of our civilization."[2]

Others believe that fear will overcome curiosity. That is the conclusion of the American government, who in 1991 employed 13 linguists, archeologists, psychologists and historians to come up with creative solutions to the quandary of how we warn future inhabitants. Two years later they published a report splendidly named: "Expert Judgment on Markers To Deter Inadvertent Human Intrusion Into the Waste Isolation Pilot Plant", which proposes a system of many warnings and defences in the shape of a labyrinth. The landscape where the labyrinth starts is dominated by enormous concrete thorns positioned in all directions, behind which 8-metre-high (26ft) walls rise up, engraved with images of human faces distorted in pain and terror (here the authors of the report mention they were inspired by the Edvard Munch painting *The Scream*) as well as arresting inscriptions in languages including English, Arabic and Navajo, which offer comprehensive information about the contents of the site. The wording of the proposed message fluctuates between hints of Percy Bysshe Shelley's "Ozymandias", mourning the splendours of a lost world and dire warnings reminiscent of the Biblical prohibition against eating from the Tree of Knowledge: "This place is a message ... We considered ourselves to be a powerful culture. This place is not a place of honor ... no highly esteemed deed is commemorated here ... nothing valued is here. What is here is dangerous and repulsive to us. This message is a warning about danger. The danger is in a particular location ... it increases toward a centre ... The danger is still present, in your time, as it was in ours. The danger is to the body and it can kill. The form of the danger is an emanation of energy ... . This place is best shunned and left uninhabited."[3]

With all due respect to the doubtful poetry, painful crown of thorns and work of Norwegian painters from the nineteenth century, the really interesting approaches to the problem were made in the 1980s. In 1982, the German Institute of Language and Communication presented the issue to the wider public, and this prompted a response by the Polish science fiction writer Stanisław Lem. He proposed creating genetically engineered "atomic flowers"

Already at the centre of the classical labyrinth lay a danger created by the actions of human beings (A Rat in a Maze, page 147).

Whicht, like his wife Mary's great work, deals with hubris and our human attempt to overcome nature (The Body Electric, page 221).

That since eating from it we have not ceased to miss our mythical lost childhood (Moving Heaven and Hell, page 71).

that would be sown in the vicinity of nuclear waste sites where they would naturally multiply. The DNA of these flowers would be designed to encode a message about the dangers of the place they were blooming in. Philipp Sonntag of the Berlin Centre for Science was concerned that a catastrophe might destroy the message, so he designed a foolproof message bearer. He came up with the idea of launching an artificial satellite carrying a warning on its surface into space. From its orbit the satellite would be eternally visible to earth's inhabitants. In a different approach, Vilmos Voigt from Lórand Eötvös University in Budapest thought of constructing a cross between the Tower of Babel and the Rosetta Stone. He proposed building concentric circles that could be engraved with the required information in all the main languages. At fixed intervals in time, the warning information would be refreshed by engraving the next circle using contemporary language. This would not only document linguistic changes across the generations, but also link the warning into a chain of evolving and accumulating meaning. French writer François Bastide and Italian semiotician Paolo Fabris, on the other hand, suggested harnessing the services of two of humanity's oldest companions: cats and folklore. They would breed genetically mutated cats. Exposure to radioactive material would make these cats change colour spectacularly – say, into purple. The supreme traits of these guardian cat would at the same time be celebrated in poetry and music, so that millennia into the future, grandmothers would still be telling their grandchildren the tale of the cats that changed colour and to get well out of the way when they go purple. This idea became known as "The Ray Cat Solution" and briefly went viral, eliciting a short documentary in 2016, which investigated its popularity in certain corners of the internet generally devoted to all things feline.

But the most dramatic solution was presented by linguist and semiotician Thomas Sebeok. He was a member of the "Human Interference Task Force", established in 1981 by the giant construction corporation Bechtel, contracted by the US government for the country's planned, deep geological, nuclear repository project. A motley crew of behavioural scientists, artists, engineers, nuclear physicists and anthropologists looked into the use of long-time warning messages to prevent future access to the site or, in the report's own words: "To design a reasonably fail-safe means of communicating information about the repository and its content, such that the system's effectiveness would be maintained for up to 10,000 years (about 300 generations)."[4]

Perhaps inspired by one of the fathers of nuclear energy, physicist Alvin Weinberg, who viewed nuclear power as a "Faustian bargain", Sebeok's idea was astonishingly simple. Establish a religion. Only the fire of faith would match the flames of radioactivity. An artificial religion, with its own theology and mythology, could define the disposal sites as taboo, anathema, and portray the atomic energy they held as divine power. Ritual and ceremonies would be the responsibility of an "atomic priesthood", a term first coined by Weinberg himself. They would be a secret dynasty of guardians of the forbidden chambers who would pass the occult knowledge of their true purpose down the generations. This radical idea was not included in the final report. "It is easy to see why," writes Sebastian Musch in his article "The Atomic Priesthood and Nuclear Waste Management: Religion, Sci-Fi Literature and the End of Our Civilization". "Besides the deeply antidemocratic nature of the endeavor to create a religious caste that deceives the public into believing in the supernatural power of nuclear energy", it isn't clear how feasible the programme is, or to put it bluntly, how dangerous, for "Every religion has its potential heretics and schisms."[5] As Musch mentions, many religions went to war; many religions didn't survive those wars, their temples were destroyed, their priesthood was wiped out and their untouchable holy implements were plundered and desecrated. From here the road to Raiders of the Plutonium Ark is not so long.

Thoughts about an atomic priesthood or religious engineering had been around well before Sebeok, but they had been expounded in a much safer medium – literature. Isaac Asimov, who along with Robert A Heinlein and Arthur C Clarke, is considered one of the "Big Three" of science fiction, prepared the ground in the short stories he published between 1942 and 1950, which became the immensely influential *Foundation* series. Inspired by Edward Gibbon's *History of the Decline and Fall of the Roman Empire*, Asimov wove a story featuring a mathematician struggling to save the Galactic Empire from a new dark age lasting 30,000 years, by establishing the "Encyclopedia Galactica", a repository of all human knowledge. With its original purpose forgotten by the people, science becomes a religion whose priests are the only ones who know its true meaning. Walter M Miller Jr explored

It's never a good idea to sign a deal with the Devil (A Faustian Bargain, page 1).

Or appropriated by other religions (Number of the Beast, page 79).

the worst-case scenario in his 1959 magnum opus, *A Canticle for Leibowitz*, in which the writings of a technician named Leibowitz are glorified in a religion formed in the ruins of a post-apocalyptic society. Basing itself on these texts, the new religion eventually leads back to nuclear annihilation many centuries later. Science fiction writer Arsen Darnay's 1978 novel *Karma* and his novellas such as the 1976 *Aspic's Mystery* all take place in a future history and seek to tell stories of redemption, reincarnation and rebirth, the corrosion of time and atomic priesthood. Frank Herbert, who put a lot of thought into the explosive potential of engineered religions and the evolutionary changes they might undergo, conducted his thought experiments in *Dune* (1965), in which the Missionaria Protectiva is responsible for planting a manipulative mythology aimed at supporting the order of Bene Gesserit with its selective breeding enterprise. In Roger Zelazny's *Lord of Light*, colonists from a destroyed earth use technology to transform themselves into seemingly immortal gods based on the Hindu pantheon, using their technological advantages to control populations and the process of reincarnation. Sam or Mahasamatman, the protagonist, is the Buddha who rebels against the gods. His original fellow crewmates are Brahma, the Creator, who was originally a woman named Madeleine; Kali, Goddess of Destruction and formerly Sam's lover; and Krishna who gets drunk in brothels.

This is neither the Krishna of the Bhagavad Gita, whose "majesty and radiance" are like a "sunburst of a thousand suns",[6] nor the Krishna whom the man in charge of the Manhattan Project had read about in the original Sanskrit. Though he worked with the leading US physicists of his time and the brilliance of his mind was beyond dispute, he wasn't the most obvious choice for the job. He was diagnosed with schizophrenia and suffered from depression and spells of violence, one of which led him to put a poisoned apple on his teacher's desk, and another to nearly choke a friend to death. He was a chain smoker who forgot to eat for days on end, immersed himself in Hindu theology, and supported radical politics, confessing in his security briefing that he "probably belonged to every Communist-front organization on the West Coast".[7] His name was Julius Robert Oppenheimer, the same Oppenheimer who observed the Trinity experiment from a safe distance, hypnotized by the enormous fireball going up into the sky that shone with the light of a thousand suns. "We knew

Following his experience during World War II Miller struggled for years with depression and PTSD. On the morning of 9 January 1996, the reclusive author placed a 911 call and told the police that there was a dead body on his lawn. When they arrived three minutes later, they found it. It was his. Only 72 years old, Walter M Miller shot himself in the head, leaving behind an unfinished sequel to *A Canticle for Leibowitz* named *Saint Leibowitz and the Wild Horse Woman*, which was published posthumously at his request in 1997 (Ex Libris, page 9).

Which had a significant impact on one of the most successful artificial religions in the world (Force Majeure, page 135).

the world would not be the same," he said years later in a TV interview in 1965, "A few people laughed; a few people cried. Most people were silent."[8] Oppenheimer himself was reminded of Krishna's words to Prince Arjuna, when he appeared before him as the incarnation of the eternal Vishnu, "Now I am become Death, the destroyer of worlds."[9] A few weeks later, the worlds of the people of Hiroshima and Nagasaki were destroyed.

However, Oppenheimer was wrong. A more accurate translation of Krishna/Vishnu's words is "Time," rather than "Death". Time is the destroyer, our eternal enemy; and deep time, which flows out into the unknown, is a future beyond our imagination. It is time to learn to control if we want to save our distant offspring and warn them of the hazards we have buried deep underground – our terrible heritage. It is our karma to ask forgiveness for the poisoned waste we have crowned with thorns.

Will you hear us? Have you heard us? Are you still there?

18

A RAT IN A MAZE

When he was 12, James Dallas Egbert III was asked to repair US Air Force computers; when he was 15, he enrolled in Michigan University and began his studies in computer science. About a year later, on 15 August 1979, he disappeared from his room in the dorms, leaving behind a suicide note and a cork board on which he had stuck 38 pins in a complex pattern. The family hired a private investigator who discovered that Egbert had been an enthusiastic participant in the popular role-playing game "Dungeons and Dragons" or "D&D". The investigator believed that a pattern formed by the pins was a map that would reveal the mystery of Egbert's whereabouts. The young man had used the pins to represent an underground labyrinth, a network of steam tunnels under the university buildings crisscrossing the campus in which he had been playing a "live" version of his favourite game with other students, which seemed eventually to have swallowed him whole.

They don't usually live in dungeons. They like caves, preferably under a lone mountain (Here Be Dragons, page 79).

With some maps you could just as easily get lost as find your way (The Territory and the Map, page 47).

The private investigator was right, but only in part. Egbert was a genius, but he was profoundly miserable. Hounded by his parents' impossible expectations, the high demands of academia and his confused sexuality, he began using his knowledge of chemistry to produce drugs that turned out to exacerbate his depression. He descended into the tunnels and hid, with a supply of milk, cheese, crackers, pot and sleeping pills. He took the pills. When his suicide attempt failed, he called the private investigator and turned himself in. It was a lot less sexy than "Youth Vanishes in Labyrinth Because of a Role-Playing Game."

The seeds of "Dungeons and Dragons" were sown during a fateful meeting at a conference at Lake Geneva, Wisconsin in 1972 between Dave Arenson, a writer and game developer, and Gary Gygax, an insurance agent who loved war games. It is difficult to overstate the impact of "D&D" on both the fantasy genre and the gaming industry. There had been role-playing games before, of course, but this game's structure offered unparalleled immersive possibilities. Immensely popular, it taught generations

The other Lake Geneva, in Switzerland, was also the location of a very dramatic meeting (Blood Lust, page 93; The Body Electric, page 221).

of gamers how to spin a plot and tell a story. It gave amateurs new liberties within their preferred genres, as well as the power to take active part in their favourite stories and join a world of imagination. Role-playing games formed the basis of the largest and most lucrative entertainment industry today – video, console and computer games.

Rising from 500,000 sales in 1977 when it was launched to 2,300,000 the year Egbert vanished, the sales of D&D reached 22,000,000 by 1982.

Egbert's disappearance may not have been a game-changer but it definitely had an effect.

One especially efficient writer took two weeks to produce a novel loosely based on his story, entitled *Mazes and Monsters*, which was turned into a TV movie starring Tom Hanks in his first role. An urban legend was born, mass hysteria was unleashed.

"Dungeons and Dragons" was the enemy. A Texan mother whose son shot himself, argued that a curse the dungeon master had put on him in the game was real, and sued TSR Inc., the publishers of D&D. She said the game "uses demonology, witchcraft, Vodou, murder, rape, blasphemy, suicide, assassination, insanity, sex perversion, homosexuality, prostitution, satanic rituals, gambling, barbarism, cannibalism, sadism, desecration, demon summoning, necromancy, divination and other teachings".[1] Small wonder young people got addicted. Fans were frenzied and parents were freaked out. Flocks of psychologists descended on the morning shows, explaining the game was interfering with young people's sense of reality, and religious preachers rushed to their pulpit to blast against this evil. William Schnoebelen, a Christian author and former Satanic priest, warned that "the materials themselves, in many cases, contain authentic magical rituals. I can tell you this from my own experience ... We studied and practiced and trained more than 175 people in the Craft. Our 'covendom' was in Milwaukee, Wisconsin; just a short drive away from the world headquarters of TSR, the company which makes Dungeons and Dragons .... In the late 1970s, a couple of the game writers actually came to my wife and I as prominent 'sorcerers' in the community. They wanted to make certain the rituals were authentic. For the most part, they are."[2]

It remains to be seen whether Schnoebelen's statements about the veracity of these rites have any merit, but at least one frequent

Unsurprisingly it's mentioned in the same sentence as sex perversion and satanic rituals (Weird Sisterhood, page 25).

Unsurprisingly it's mentioned in the same sentence as cannibalism (Head Hunters, page 231).

It is unclear if Schnoebelen belonged to the Satanic Temple or the Church of Satan (Number of the Beast, page 79).

It is possible Shakespeare himself used a similar tactic (Weird Sisterhood, page 25).

element of the game – the use of confusing, branching structures with secret passages – has a long history, dating to way before Egbert used pins to sketch it on the cork board in his room.

Labyrinths can be found painted on walls, erected from stones or carved in the rocks in Southern Europe, Native American cultural areas, northern India and on the shores of the White Sea. The labyrinth symbol first appeared around 4,000 years ago and more than 300 prehistoric labyrinths have been found around the globe.

In the West's formative myth of the labyrinth, the role of the subterranean complex is to capture a monster: the Minotaur, which literally means "the bull of Minos", the king of Crete who transgressed against the god Poseidon. As a punishment Poseidon made the king's wife Pasiphaë fall in love with a white bull that emerged from the sea. Head over heels in lust, the queen persuaded the legendary inventor Daedalus to construct a sex-doll version of the Trojan Horse – a wooden cow that she then entered, aiming to seduce the divine bull. Like Daedalus' other inventions, this one succeeded beyond expectation and its consequences were terrible. The queen became pregnant and gave birth to an abomination: half human, half bull. Sometimes he is portrayed with the hindquarters and legs of a beast like the satyrs and centaurs, and other times he has the body of a man and a bull's head. The Minotaur prowled around at the centre of the labyrinth that King Minos ordered Daedalus to build. And the citizens of Athens were forced to contribute human sacrifices to him, "Every nine years, nine men come into the house so that I can free them from all evil,"[3] recounts Asterion the minotaur in the story by Jorge Luis Borges, who more than any other writer was fascinated by the philosophical and artistic possibilities of the labyrinth.

Mazes and labyrinths are not the same thing: the passages of mazes fork and deceive by design and they are meant to make it difficult to get out; labyrinths consist of a series of connected concentric paths and aims to lead the visitor to their centre. This last feature attracted the Christians, who turned it into a two-dimensional rosary, embedded in cathedral floors. The labyrinth in Chartres invites pilgrims who cannot afford to make the journey to Jerusalem to pray as they proceed on their knees along the winding path to the heart of the labyrinth, which represents the heavenly city. And so, Christianity baptized this symbolic icon and exorcized

Many folktales with the animal bridegroom motif carry a whiff of bestiality (The Human Animal, page 189).

This became much easier to do after the invention of latex (Valley of the Dolls, page 205).

the pagan ghosts of the Minotaur along with Theseus, the hero who annihilated him. Their battle was an echo of a more ancient religious conflict between the Hellenes and those who worshipped the horned god, to whom they married their queen in a ceremony that promised the death of winter and the rebirth of spring and may have included human sacrifice.

According to Robert Graves, representing, the white goddess (Weird Sisterhood, page 25).

The word "labyrinth" might derive from *labrys*, a Lydian word meaning "double-bladed axe", a symbol associated with Artemis, goddess of the hunt. This interpretation and the link with the feminine may be expressed in its architectural shape – a form that is penetrated and exited at the same point and has a womb-like cavity at its centre. For Christians this shape came to represent the house of a patriarchal and monotheistic god as seen in the many allegorical works using the labyrinth as a symbol for the pilgrim's progress.

While the maze was compared, at least in one very naughty work, to the female genitalia (The Pleasure Principle, page 195).

This kind of transformation from feminine to masculine is ubiquitous (Man in the Moon, page 115).

Labyrinths and mazes were not only used by the princes of the Church. The aristocracy cultivated beautiful ones made from plants and hedges in the grounds of their palaces as the perfect place for secular pleasure and inspiration. One of the oldest surviving mazes can be found at Hampton Court. Jerome K Jerome described it as "a very fine maze", in his *Three Men in a Boat*, "They picked up various other people who wanted to get it over, as they went along, until they had absorbed all the persons in the maze. People who had given up all hopes of ever getting either in or out, or of ever seeing their home and friends again, plucked up courage at the sight of Harris and his party, and joined the procession, blessing him ... They all got crazy at last, and sang out for the keeper."[4]

Psychologists noticed this effect of mazes on human conduct. In past decades they have been examining the learning patterns of white mice, which, according to Douglas Adams in *The Hitchhiker's Guide to the Galaxy*, took the opportunity to improve their understanding of what drives the human mind. The protagonist of the heart-rending science fiction story *Flowers for Algernon* by Daniel Keyes empathizes with the mouse when the two of them are forced to solve the same mazes to determine the extent to which their intelligence has been enhanced following an innovative experiment. In his *Amber* series, Roger Zelazny uses the maze to allow his characters to travel between worlds and realities. Jim Henson's 1986 film *Labyrinth* and – in a very different way –

While they use tarot cards in order to communicate (King of Cups, page 153).

Guillermo del Toro's *Pan's Labyrinth* from 2006, both draw from its mythological roots, populating it with monsters and mysteries that the young heroines must face and charting the topography of coming-of-age and the struggle for self-definition.

It is no coincidence that the maze has become a frequent part of works aimed at young adults, who are scampering mice-like through the complex and confusing mazes of the life their parents have passed on to them, just as Minos bestowed the labyrinth on his monstrous, rejected son. Harry Potter copes with total terror in the shape of Lord Voldemort who is awaiting him at the end of the magical maze in *Harry Potter and the Goblet of Fire*, while in Suzanne Collins' dystopian *Hunger Games*, young "tributes" are chosen, like the Minotaur's victims, through an annual lottery and forced to participate in a cruel game invented by adults who constantly observe them; the heroine of the video game *Portal* navigates a deadly maze managed by an evil artificial intelligence pretending to be using her in a scientific experiment; in Wes Ball's post-apocalyptic film *Maze Runner*, based on James Dashner's books, young people are thrown into a huge maze full of terrifying creatures, only to find out that they, too, are part of an experiment.

A sentiment also expressed in many dystopias aimed at young adults (Best of All Possible Worlds, page 247).

The real-life contemporary versions of these mazes are escape rooms, in which participants must solve a succession of riddles and clues if they want to find their way out. These don't merely point at the wish to escape, but also remind us of our desire to get lost and surrender to bewilderment and confusion. James Dallas Egbert surrendered. He attempted, once again, to kill himself, purchasing the ingredients needed to make cyanide. He mixed it with root beer and drank it. It didn't work. But he did not give up. One year after the "Dungeons and Dragons" incident he finally managed to escape his inner labyrinth. On the 11 August 1980, James Dallas Egbert III shot himself in the head. He died in hospital three days later, a year and a day after his disappearance.

19

KING OF CUPS

Jayne Braiden told the man who entered the office in Brighton where she offered mystical consultations to try and focus on an important question while he was shuffling the deck of tarot cards she handed him. After Star Randel-Hanson laid the ten cards face down on the velvet-covered table, Braiden heard him murmur, "It is terrible, it is terrible." She asked him to choose a card, any card. He turned over the first one. The image on the card was The Tower: a spire hit by lightning, a collapsing roof, a fire breaking out from the ruins and two figures falling from the windows. Braiden explained to Randel-Hanson that the card symbolized "lots of arguments, lots of bad feelings". The next card he flipped was "The Emperor": an old, bearded man holding a staff, seated on an ornate throne and wearing an appropriately severe mien signifying the "dominant male", she said. He turned over the third card. A skeleton, a scythe in his hand. "Death."

Her suspicions were aroused by the explosive combination of tarot cards and her client's vague words. Braiden stopped and said she could see that "something really bad has happened and that we need to discuss this further". Randel-Hanson answered: "It's terrible, I killed him." Braiden kept calm and carried on, asking her client's permission to phone the police. She told the woman at the other end of the line, "I have a man in my shop and I know it is hard to believe but I have just seen that he has murdered someone."[1] The woman at the desk who took her call – in equal good form – replied that if it wasn't an emergency, the officers would be there within the hour. Braiden tried to get across that the dead body seemed still to be at the site of the murder, but the policewoman asked her to try to relax and keep the murderer busy. So, taking a deep breath, and possibly making a nice cup of tea for herself and her client, Braiden returned to the room. The two engaged in polite banter for 55 minutes until the officers of the law arrived and escorted Randel-Hanson respectfully to his home, where they found the body of Derick Marney – a psychic – stewing in his own blood.

The two of them had met some years earlier at the Spiritualist Church. As confirmed during the court case, Marney had invited Randel-Hanson to come and live with him and keep him company. The two had shared a bed, but when Randel-Hanson had refused to share his body, Marney had sexually assaulted him.

The murder had happened ten days before Randel-Hanson turned up in Braiden's office, in April, the month T S Eliot called "the cruelest month, breeding/Lilacs out of the dead land, mixing/Memory and desire".[2] Randel-Hanson may not have been familiar with these opening lines of Eliot's dense and enigmatic masterpiece *The Waste Land* – but he and the poet did share an interest in tarot cards.

Tarot's first known mention is on the hilarious list of games that Gargantua, Rabelais' giant, amuses himself with, but legend points to ancient roots in Egypt and its god of wisdom and sorcery, Thoth. The mythology surrounding tarot's origin has it that the gypsies (also erroneously believed to have originated in Egypt due to their skin colour) were responsible for dispersing the cards around the world during their travels. In fact, it seems that the first decks arrived in Europe from the Muslim Mamluke region, appearing in Italy during the second half of the fifteenth century where they were used in proper card games throughout the Renaissance.

These ancient decks, such as the Visconti-Sforza deck, were commissioned by the nobility to celebrate military triumphs. They consisted of 40 cards with numerical values, as well as 16 court cards (King, Queen, Knight and Page) organized in four suits (batons, coins, swords and cups). In addition, there are 22 cards that carry an eclectic array of images (The Tower, The Chariot); elements (The Sun, The Star); functionaries (The Emperor, The Hermit); tropes (The Devil, The Lovers); attributes (Power, Justice); and so on.

The 22 cards are called the Major Arcana (meaning "greater secrets"), while the remaining 56 cards in the suits make up the Minor Arcana ("lesser secrets"). The cards acquired their names in the eighteenth century when occultists like Antoine Court de Gébelin and fortune tellers like Marie-Anne Adelaide Lenormand – whose clientele included murderers such as Jean-Paul Marais, Maximilien Robespierre and other instigators of the Reign of Terror – began to claim they had magical powers. Mystics such as Eliphas Levi – the pseudonym of Alphonse Louis Constant

The moon also fell under its auspices (Man in the Moon, page 115).

And perhaps in Atlantis (No Man's Island, page 57).

The Devil represents being seduced by the material and physical pleasures. Peter Stumpp was more interested in the latter when he signed a deal with him (Lupus Est, page 93).

– suggested that the 22 cards of the Major Arcana, the Hebrew alphabet and the Kabbalah's *sephiroth* were all tied together.

Eliphas Levi made his mark on the other side of the Channel in England. His doctrine and methods found their way into the magical-philosophical teachings of the "Hermetic Order of the Golden Dawn," a secret society that dealt with Kabbalah, astrology, ancient Egyptian ritual, alchemy and parapsychology, riding the crest of the Victorian taste for spiritualism. It was established by three renegade Freemasons, and among its members were highly acclaimed authors such as Bram Stoker, William Butler Yeats, Edith Nesbit and Arthur Conan Doyle, as well as more infamous characters, like the man known to his own mother as "the Beast". He experimented with every available drug, caught syphilis, believed himself to be a messenger of the Egyptian god Horus and was crowned "The Wickedest Man in the World". His name was Aleister Crowley. He was a sorcerer, a poet, a mountaineer and possibly a spy. Once, he supposedly made all the books at Watkins, London's oldest esoteric bookshop, disappear – and then reappear. In a libel suit, which he lost befittingly on Friday the 13th against a woman who claimed his occult practices were black magic, Justice Swift said, "I have been over forty years engaged in the administration of the law in one capacity or another. I thought that I knew of every conceivable form of wickedness. I thought that everything which was vicious and bad had been produced at one time or another before me. I have learnt in this case that we can always learn something more if we live long enough. I have never heard such dreadful, horrible, blasphemous and abominable stuff as that which has been produced by the man who describes himself to you as the greatest living poet."[3]

The deeds that so shocked the honest judge are too numerous to mention, but Crowley found the time to create his own tarot deck, named "The Book of Thoth" and painted by Lady Frieda Harris according to his instructions.

With Crowley, and later without him, the Golden Dawn became very well-known (for a secret society). With its own tarot deck (which didn't survive intact), the order saw The Fool card as a manifestation of Perceval, a figure who features in the quest for the Holy Grail. The Fool's journey among the cards of the Major Arcana runs parallel with Percival's search for the spiritual enlightenment embodied in the Grail.

In recent decades, literary scholars have reviewed his work in the light of his friendship with Oscar Wilde, his marriage to the woman Wilde courted and the homoerotic themes in *Dracula*, concluding it was an expression of his repressed sexual orientation at a time when homosexuals were the Other, threatening the social order (Blood Lust, page 93).

Who used her son's name, Fabian, as a pseudonym in some of the novels she wrote with her husband for adults – until the boy's death (Paradise Lost, page 171).

Even his friendship with American illusionist Harry Houdini did not cure Doyle of his belief in magic and supernatural powers (Paper Fairies, page 161).

Crowley worked as a British intelligence asset and agent provocateur during World War I. Douglas Rushkoff, media theorist and author of the graphic novel *Aleister & Adolf* (illustrated by Michael Avon Oeming) believes that Crowley resumed his post during World War II, using the fact that many of Hitler's henchmen were occultists (for example, his second-in-command Rudolf Hess) to influence the outcome of the war (No Man's Island, page 57).

The Grail made its debut sometime between 1180 and 1191, in the romance of *Perceval, ou le Conte du Graal*, by French poet and troubadour Chrétien de Troyes. At this point in its evolution, the Grail was just one of the mysterious artifacts (alongside a blood-dripping Lance, for example) that the Fisher King's pages carry before Percival's astonished eyes during a feast hosted at the court of the crippled king. The knight, who is afraid to speak much, fails to ask the king to explain the wondrous procession, thus missing the opportunity to bring him – and the waste land he rules – solace and renewal.

But the connection between the king and the land, and between the physical condition of one and the other, is much older. Its roots reach back to pagan rites when the king was ceremonially married to the land. From these traditions, through the Welsh *Mabinogion* and Celtic mythology, came the story of Brân the Blessed and his quest for a magical life-giving cauldron. Robert de Boron followed similar footsteps in his *Joseph d'Arimathie*, composed between 1191 and 1202, in which Jesus's undertaker took the chalice the Son of God drank from during the Last Supper, used it to collect the blood of Christ after he was pierced on the cross by the Lance of Longinus, and from there, carried it to England. This story was enlarged and embellished by authors such as Wolfram von Eschenbach, who associated the Grail with the Philosopher's Stone; the authors of the *Vulgate Cycle*, who introduced the character of Sir Galahad the Chaste into the mix; and by the man most responsible for shaping King Arthur's canonical character, Sir Thomas Malory, author of *Le Morte d'Arthur*. Morally far removed from the illustrious knights and the righteous deeds he wrote about, Malory had been imprisoned as a thief, bandit and rapist, and for the attempted assassination of the Duke of Buckingham. While incarcerated, Malory managed to distill history (at least what Geoffrey of Monmouth had reported as history), romance, myth and folklore into a cohesive narrative. His work tells the life story of Arthur, son of Uther Pendragon, from birth to death, featuring guest appearances by: the wizard Merlin; Morgana Le Fey, Arthur's half-sister; Queen Guinevere; Lancelot du Lac, the greatest knight in the world; Tristan and Iseult, the tragic lovers; and many more. *Le Morte d'Arthur* was published posthumously in 1485, becoming an instant bestseller to the great financial gain of its publisher, William Caxton.

There are more than a few claimants to being the real Lance, which was kept in different reliquaries (A Faustian Bargain, page 1).

An epithet literally meaning "Head-Dragon" in Welsh but in a figurative sense, as fitting for the nation that chose the red dragon as its symbol, it refers to "head of the army". (Here Be Dragons, page 79).

One of the most powerful legendary witches (Weird Sisterhood, page 25).

The widespread acceptance of the tales of Arthur and his knights had a political angle. The Wars of the Roses, in which Malory had participated, ended with the victory of Henry Tudor of the House of Lancaster, who took power in the same year that *Le Morte d'Arthur* came out. Like the kings of the Plantagenet dynasty who had come before him, Henry Tudor drew inspiration and absolute authority from the image of Arthur and his perceived connection to the fabled king. His son, Henry VIII, even displayed the (apparently fake) remains of the original round table at Winchester Castle. But Henry VIII's absolute authority, especially in matters of the heart, plunged England into religious conflict and among his many victims was King Arthur himself. *Le Morte d'Arthur* and the romances glorifying the quest for the Holy Grail were seen as Catholic propaganda, and from the middle of the seventeenth century Malory's book went out of print and stayed there for about 200 years. No one picked up the ancient king's gauntlet. It took the Romantics of the eighteenth and nineteenth centuries and their longing for the olden days to bring Arthur "*rex quondam, rexque futurus*" – "the once and future king" – back to life, and Malory's work back into print.

The greatest standard bearer of this Arthurian revival was Alfred, Lord Tennyson, who laboured for 30 years on *The Idylls of the King*. A quintessential Victorian, for him the focus of the work was the ideal king and his would-be gentlemen in suits of armour. The Holy Grail is a mere herald of the end of the glorious court of Camelot and the demise of its model monarch.

T S Eliot, on the other hand, was far more interested in the spiritual quest for the Holy Grail than in Arthur himself. The king who really fascinated him was the Fisher King. In Eliot's poem the Fisher King is represented by a card showing a man hanging upside down by one ankle while his other leg is folded, almost resting on his crotch – the location of the king's wound and the cause of the impotence that turned the whole realm into a barren waste land. The card is in the "wicked pack" which Madame Sosostris, a "famous clairvoyante,"[4] reads from in the first part of the poem. Some of the cards the poet mentions are real tarot cards, such as "The Hanged Man", as described above. Others he invented, because "I am not familiar with the exact constitution of the Tarot pack of cards, from which I have obviously departed to suit my own convenience."[5]

In his work, Eliot sought to engage with the deepest layers of the myth – the unconscious stratum of the legend – and he used the cards to penetrate their mysteries. "The hanged man, the tower, the sun … are sort of archetypal ideas, of a differentiated nature," explained Carl Gustav Jung to the participants in a seminar held in 1933, "… an intuitive method that has the purpose of understanding the flow of life, possibly even predicting future events."[6] Jung's many contemporary followers still use tarot cards, but mainly as an instrument for reflection rather than to foretell future events.

Many artists used the archetypal symbolism and the huge cultural resonance tarot cards acquired over the centuries. Some were attracted by the "wicked" associations they came to hold, like the Finnish metal group "Tarot"; others by the drama of the cards' spread unfolding or by the narrative they seem to tell.

One of these artists was American poet and writer Roger Zelazny. Like T S Eliot, he was greatly influenced by Jessie Weston's 1920 book, *From Ritual to Romance*, a largely unsubstantiated yet hugely tantalizing examination of the connections between the Arthurian myth – especially the parts about the Holy Grail – and pagan influences. In his portal fantasy, *The Chronicles of Amber*, Zelazny serves up a dazzling dish consisting of familial rivalry, magic and intrigue, Shakespearean quotes, Arthurian references and the obligatory tarot cards, which his warring princes use to communicate and teleport from one reality to the next.

And magical beasts like the unicorn (The Lady and the Unicorn, page 179).

Just in case there is no labyrinth available (A Rat in a Maze, page 147).

Arthurian mythology had an interesting history among Zelazny's countrymen in the former British colony. Jackie Kennedy compared her husband John F Kennedy and his White House to Arthur and Camelot, helping to canonize Kennedy by alluding to an Arthur-like messianic return. For authors who were the epitome of Americana, Arthur was a literary inspiration. John Steinbeck wrote how he encountered Malory's book for the first time as a child, "I started at the black print with hatred and then gradually the pages opened and let me in. The magic happened. The Bible and Shakespeare and Pilgrim's Progress belonged to everyone. But this was mine – secretly mine … Perhaps a passionate love for the English language opened to me from this one book."[7] Steinbeck attempted to rewrite Malory's work into *The Acts of King Arthur and His Noble Knights* but never completed it. It was published after his death in 1976.

Following his reading of Malory, Mark Twain wrote in his diary, "Dream of being a knight in armor in the Middle Ages. Have the notions & habits of thought of the present day mixed with the necessities of that. No pockets in the armor. No way to manage certain requirements of nature. Can't scratch ... Make disagreeable clatter when I enter church. Can't dress or undress myself. Always getting struck by lightning. Fall down, can't get up. See *Morte D'Arthur*."[8] From this nightmare came the time travel escapades of *A Connecticut Yankee in King Arthur's Court*.

The author and literary critic Samuel R Delaney, in his monumental *Nova*, sketched a futuristic and sensational version of the quest for the Holy Grail when one of its protagonists, a gypsy boy, steals a tarot card in an attempt to change the shape of things to come. Author Tim Powers in his *Last Call*, creates a secret history of the mythical struggle for the fate of the modern waste land, mixing memory and desire, poker games and gangsters, Arthurian legends and tarot, all surrounding the shining city of Las Vegas.

A modern fairyland in which time stands still (Paper Fairies, page 161).

These powerfully expressive cards pop up time and again, serving as narrative and thematic tools in hundreds of literary works, films and TV, in computer games and comics, where they are convenient shorthand for macabre hints of things to come or for a piquant mysterious mood. Still, in spite, or maybe because, of their frequent and extravagant cultural use, tarot cards offer a glimpse into the murky depth of our collective subconscious, showing us the ancient archetypes swimming freestyle.

Nowhere in our culture are those ancient ones more at large than in the modern genre of fantasy, where Arthur left an indelible mark.

The wise old wizard, the beautiful witch, the pure knight, the perilous quest – all these tropes and many more constitute the very essence of the genre as we know it today, headed by *Lord of the Rings*, with Gandalf as Merlin's incarnation and the Fellowship of the Ring as a version of the Knights of the Round Table. Tolkien himself shunned the Arthurian myth, after having researched it thoroughly. He translated the fourteenth-century Middle English *Sir Gawain and the Green Knight* and even embarked on writing a long alternative poem in the tradition of *Beowulf* about the fall of Arthur, but he never completed it. Nevertheless, he felt that the Arthurian work was not ostensibly English (though possibly located in England) and therefore was not befitting the Matter of Britain.

For him, fairies were much more natural than humans (Paper Fairies, page 161).

He also felt "its 'faerie' is too lavish, and fantastical, incoherent and repetitive. For another and more important thing: it is involved in, and explicitly contains the Christian religion. For reasons which I will not elaborate, that seems to me fatal."[9] However, he did not shy away from appropriating some of its more prominent motifs.

Not everyone agreed with him. Numerous writers were influenced by Arthur, from T H White, who dived into the legendary king's adolescence and inspired J K Rowling's Harry Potter, through Marion Zimmer Bradley, who contributed subversive feminist commentary, to Guy Gavriel Kay, who combined the Tolkien fantasy with the Arthurian saga after assisting Christopher Tolkien in editing his father's then unpublished work, *The Silmarillion*. The Monty Python gang preferred to follow Mark Twain's example and turn the quest for the Holy Grail into a wild farce, which resulted in the successful musical *Spamelot*. And the list of derivative works of literature, cinema and TV goes on and on.

The longing for Arthur and his knights is a longing for order in the midst of chaos, for a glorious spectacle of a noble brotherhood, for a leader who truly stands for honour and justice and knows how to swing a sword when necessary. An exalted king of the people, Arthur is human, sinful and betrayed – a dreamer and a warrior who promises that when the time comes, when the land needs him, he will come again.

20

PAPER FAIRIES

Elsie Wright's mother had had enough. Day after day that summer, when Frances Griffiths, Elsie's younger cousin was staying with them, the girls would go out to play by the stream at the bottom of the garden and return all wet and muddy. When Elsie's parents asked what they were up to and why they came home so filthy, Elsie and Frances answered that they were playing with the fairies. "Playing with the fairies," Elsie's parents assumed, was a euphemism for "Getting dirty near the stream", but the girls insisted. Since Elsie's father happened to be an enthusiastic amateur photographer with his own dark room, he lent them his box camera and the two girls set out to prove their case. It took them half an hour to return triumphant and Elsie's father removed the plates and started to develop the photographs. But as the chemicals began to slowly reveal the images, it was not only Frances' face, crowned by a wreath of flowers, that was revealed, but also four tiny but fantastically detailed figures, who were dancing and floating around her head. One of them was playing the cymbals, another a flute, they were all in classically styled dresses with their hair cut in the most recent Parisian fashion and had butterfly wings on their backs. Some months passed and then the girls borrowed the camera again, bringing back new photos, including one of Elsie stretching out her hand to a gnome. Frances included one of the photographs in a letter to a friend back home in Capetown, and on the back she inscribed: "It is funny I never used to see them in Africa. It must be too hot for them there."[1] Convinced that the photographs were forged, Elsie's father went as far as searching their room for evidence, but he found nothing. However, Elsie's mother was a believer. In 1919, two years after the photos were taken, she participated in a meeting dedicated to "fairy life" organized by Madame Blavatsky's Theosophists, a secret esoteric society. Once she showed the photographs in the meeting, the rumour about the two girls' encounter with the fairy folk took wing.

> She believed she had received arcane information about the legendary island of Atlantis (No Man's Island, page 57).

In "The Adventure of the Sussex Vampire" Sherlock Holmes remarks to the good doctor that "we seem to have been switched on to a Grimms' fairy tale … Rubbish, Watson, rubbish! What have we to do with walking corpses who can only be held in their grave by stakes driven through their hearts? It's pure lunacy."[a] (Blood Lust, page 93).

One of those wholly convinced that the pictures were genuine was the inventor of the most rational literary character at the turn of the century, Sir Arthur Conan Doyle, who created (and destroyed) Sherlock Holmes. Sir Arthur's beloved Uncle Dick was one of the great fairy illustrators of the early nineteenth century, and he had published a particularly famous series of drawings for the tales of the Brothers Grimm in which butterflies pull along a leaf the Fairy Queen is sitting on, dwarfs nap under a mushroom, and so on. Arthur's own father had been a gifted illustrator, too. His notebooks were full of imaginary creatures, many of which he sketched during his stay in the mental hospital where he also ended his life. From an early age, Arthur Conan Doyle felt an attraction to the world beyond; he spent years on a spiritual quest, and more intensely so when his son Kingsley died in 1918 after contracting pneumonia. It seems he believed in everything: communication with the dead, astral projection, telekinesis and yes, fairies, too. Conan Doyle advocated Elsie and Frances' photographs in an article he published in the *Strand* magazine, where he also published his Holmes stories – an article he concluded with these naïve words, "The experiences of children will be taken more seriously. Cameras will be forthcoming. Other well-authenticated cases will come along. These little folks who appear to be our neighbours, with only some small difference of vibration to separate us, will become familiar. The thought of them, even when unseen, will add a charm to every brook and valley and give romantic interest to every country walk. The recognition of their existence will jolt the material twentieth-century mind out of its heavy ruts in the mud, and will make it admit that there is a glamour and a mystery to life. Having discovered this, the world will not find it so difficult to accept that spiritual message supported by physical facts which has already been so convincingly put before it."[2] The article was received with embarrassment, which only the respect that many felt for its author prevented from turning into contempt. To find the true explanation for the fairies' presence in the pictures, an editorial in the *Truth* periodical declared on 5 January 1921, "what is wanted is not a knowledge of occult phenomena but a knowledge of children."[3] Conan Doyle died many years before it was discovered that he was familiar with the person who, unknowingly, had contributed to the great fairy fabrication. In 1898 Claude Shepperson made the illustrations for "The Story of the Sealed Room", a short horror story by Conan Doyle, and in 1914 he was commissioned to make drawings for *Princess Mary's Gift Book*, featuring dancing girls in flowing dresses on one of its pages. Elsie and Frances cut them out of their copy of the book, attached butterfly wings they drew themselves and used pins to get the cut-outs to stand up in the grass. In an interview recorded by a Yorkshire radio station in 1985, they admitted the hoax for the first time and marvelled at the way it had spun out of control, "Two village kids and a brilliant man like Conan Doyle – well, we could only keep quiet," said Elsie; and Frances commented, "I can't understand to this day why they were taken in – they wanted to be taken in."[4]

What made it easier for everyone to believe the story was not just that the two girls had so persistently confirmed it even well into their old age, but the novel way they had captured the fairies. These were exciting days for the fledgling technology of photography, which had only just made its first artistic steps some 50 years prior. Although there were works like "I Wait", Julia Margaret Cameron's composition of 1872 in which in a solemn-looking girl displays a pair of angels' wings apparently sprouting from her back, there were also other images that blurred the boundaries of reality and truth at that time: the trend for posthumous photographs prevalent in Victorian England, in which the recently deceased were dressed, coiffed and made to pose with the surviving family members. But still, the photographic image was perceived as the unassailable, authentic truth. As with fossils, another great passion of the Victorian era, they were seen as freezing time itself, as preserving the outline of a past reality. The photographic image was believed to document and literally re-present things as they were. Susan Sontag, in her essay "On Photography", tried to sketch the early relations between images and the things imaged and wrote, "photographs give people an imaginary possession of a past that is unreal."[5]

All fairy tales ever written yearn for this unreal past. Already in their earliest literary appearance in the West, in Chaucer's *Canterbury Tales*, we can hear the lament about the vanished rapture of the fairies who have withdrawn to their enchanted domain and barred its gates to anyone who does not believe in them. This elegy resonates directly or indirectly in many of the works dedicated to these creatures populating the realm between heaven and earth,

Many nineteenth-century authors including Charles Dickens and Alexandre Dumas among others, tried their hands at horror fiction (Fear Itself, page 237).

People always wanted to believe the truth is out there, as *The X-Files* creator Chris Carter knew well (We Come in Peace, page 123).

Much like maps are always perceived (The Territory and the Map, page 47).

Which gave rise to the belief in actual dragons (Here Be Dragons, page 87).

between men and gods, as in Alfred, Lord Tennyson's poem "The Splendour Falls on Castle Walls":

"O, hark, O, hear! how thin and clear,
And thinner, clearer, farther going!
O, sweet and far from cliff and scar
The horns of Elfland faintly blowing!
Blow, let us hear the purple glens replying,
Blow, bugles; answer, echoes, dying, dying, dying."[6]

These are the fair voices of the Elven folk who, at the end of the campaign for Middle Earth in J R R Tolkien's *Lord of the Rings*, "diminish and go into the West";[7] the voices, too, of the Sons of Don who leave Prydain and whose veins run with immortal blood in the five-volume cycle by Lloyd Alexander; and of many others in many other works. In all of these, the fairy race leaves us with a world bereft of miracles and wonders, and rich in nostalgia for an ancient, ahistorical time when "the world was young, the mountains green, no stain yet on the moon was seen,"[8] as Tolkien puts it. A world yearning for times when the children of man danced to the pipes of Pan in blessed Arcadia, alongside the wild, capricious and impenetrable nature embodied in the fairies. Tolkien believed that humankind "is, in contrast to fairies, supernatural; whereas they are natural, far more natural than [them]",[9] and their nature is neither bad nor evil. They exist in their own right, emerging and withdrawing through the gates between their lands and our plane of existence.

The reason for their visits is human children. Even though most fairies are blessed with unparalleled radiance and beauty, they covet certain things we create, such as fire in the hearth and other domestic comforts, and also what we cling to – our offspring. Folklore associates fairies with eternity: there they dwell frozen, like the image affixed to the photographic paper. They never age and cannot procreate. This is what makes them steal newborns and replace them with fairies pretending to be human. The fate of these stolen children – or changelings – is briefly described in Richard Allingham's poem "The Fairies":

"They stole little Bridget
For seven years long;

When she came down again
Her friends were all gone.
They took her lightly back,
Between the night and morrow,
They thought that she was fast asleep,
But she was dead with sorrow."[10]

One characteristic of fairyland often evident both in folklore and fantasy is that time acts differently there. Once you've made the mistake of falling in love with a fairy or joining in with one of their celebrations or eaten or drunk anything they've offered you – even a mere morsel – there's no going back. They might finally let you go after what appears like nothing more than a few days, but you'll find that decades if not centuries have passed in the world you left behind. Juliette Wood, a folklore scholar, has suggested many of these narratives may have been created to explain human actions and misfortunes, from infanticide to abandonment. Who would not prefer to believe that the toddler who was bumbling about on its chubby little legs while you nodded off was abducted by fairies rather than a wolf? Who would not choose to explain having abandoned his family for seven years by claiming, if they could, that it was the elves who took him? The association between childhood and the fairies was preserved in the image of the tooth fairy, who originates in Norse mythology and comes for the child but settles for its teeth; or in the figure of the fairy godmother who either puts a spell on the newborn or removes a spell from the child, which is widespread in European folklore.

Or a wolf-man (Lupus Est, page 93).

The Vikings were in the habit of paying their children for their milk teeth, which they would then put on a string and wear around their neck for good luck in battle (Twilight of the Gods, page 65).

It may be due to the practical use fairies had that they managed to survive the Christian onslaught reasonably well. As opposed to the gods and goddesses of the polytheist pantheons who were made to join the forces of darkness, fairies stayed relatively free. Their religious neutrality turned their realms into the Switzerland of the supernatural, a haven for all manner of mythological refugees, like the Greek dryads, the naiads and nymphs or the Celtic *tuatha de danann* who gave birth to the lords and ladies of the Aos Si, the fairies. One of them, Niamh of the golden hair, chooses Oisin, the son of the Irish hero Fionn MacCumhail to be her husband in a story documenting the transition from polytheism to monotheism. The couple leave for Tir Na Nog on an enchanted white steed and Oisin spends 300 years with her in this land of eternal youth, until

And are let loose only once a year (Number of the Beast, page 79).

an accident causes him to break his oath never to set foot on Irish soil. As he narrates to St Patrick, the new patron of his Emerald Isle, "Instantly a woeful change came over me, the sight of my eyes began to fade, the ruddy beauty of my face fled, I lost all my strength, and I fell to the earth, a poor withered old man, blind and wrinkled and feeble."[11]

Christendom butted heads with Fairyland not far from there, in Scotland, when on 8 November 1576 Bessie Dunlop was accused of witchcraft and claimed that the powers she wielded were not bestowed by Satan's gnarled hand but by the fairy queen's gentle one. The attempt misfired and she went up in flames. And she was not the only one. In the same century in Sicily 65 people stood trial for associating with fairies; and in Joan of Arc's trial, too, she was accused of possibly having consorted with them. Hadn't there been rumours that her godmother received knowledge from the fairies? And didn't she say she had a revelation beside a fairy tree? Also originating in Scotland was the division of the fairy realm between the glorious Seelie court and its accursed counterpart the Unseelie Court. And the strife among the fairies themselves between creatures of light and darkness, locked in ongoing internecine hostilities. Such struggles are sometimes fought out on our own, earthly plane – like in Emma Bull's pathbreaking urban fantasy, *War for the Oaks*.

Once the fairies became a source of inspiration to the mortals who forged them, these courts turned into the mirror images of the human courts of kings and queens. Now the fairies adopted aristocratic manners, leaving behind the wild for the urbane, and the figure of the fairy queen became a fixed cultural icon. In the seventeenth century she was Queen Mab for Michael Drayton and Ben Jonson; in Edmund Spenser's work she appears as Gloriana, while Shakespeare called her Titania. They all paid homage to her but not without some thinly veiled criticism, which comes as no surprise as their earthly ruler was Elizabeth I.

Though it might have been a blink of an eye in fairy time, it took more than a century for images of fairies to take shape. When in the late eighteenth century the first illustrated editions of Shakespeare's plays came out, among the most popular were Henry Fuseli's drawings for *A Midsummer Night's Dream*, especially those entitled "Titania and Bottom" and "Titania Awakening". From then on, as Elsie and Frances' photographs show, fairies were

A common spectacle in Scotland in those times (Weird Sisterhood, page 25).

But in her case, it was her clothes that decided her fate (Wonder Women, page 37).

Shakespeare outdid them all in this respect, by giving Titania an idiotic lover with a donkey's head (The Human Animal, page 189).

tiny, feminine and, as befitted an era obsessed with entomology, equipped with insect-wings, usually of butterflies or dragonflies. Countless artists in the eighteenth and nineteenth centuries were inspired by these fairies. Many stories like the ballad of Tam Lin, who wants to free himself from the fairy queen's rule, went through various versions; and artists such as the poet Cicely Mary Barker and illustrator Arthur Rackham, made their own depictions of those little people.

One of the strangest and most bewildering of these depictions was created by the man who, on a clear day in late August pulled a knife and slit his father's throat while walking in the green meadows of Cobham, Kent. His name was Richard Dadd and in 1842, a year earlier, he had been one of the most promising Victorian painters. He accompanied a wealthy adventurer, Sir Thomas Phillips, to the exotic provinces of Italy, Greece and the Holy Land, and his job was to make sketches and watercolours for the use of his patron. At one point, on the boat that took them up the Nile, Dadd began to hallucinate. His travel companions believed he was suffering from sunstroke, but the symptoms worsened, and by the time he returned to England it was clear that something deeper was tormenting the young man, who was then 26 years old. After murdering his father Dadd fled to Dover, where he boarded a ship to France. In Paris he attacked another man and wounded him severely before being taken into custody. Dadd believed that his father was the Devil, that he himself was the son of the Egyptian god Osiris, and that it was incumbent upon him as the messenger of the god to destroy people possessed by a demon. Dadd was returned to his homeland and confined first in Bedlam and later in Broadmoor, where he died in 1886, more than 20 years later.

The source of the Nile was only to be identified as Lake Victoria in 1858 by British explorer John Hanning Speke, as his fellow traveller Richard Francis Burton was recovering from an illness on the shores of Lake Tanganyika (The Territory and the Map, page 47).

Dadd's works from both before the murder and his hospitalization and during his many years in the institution, possess a bewitching quality. The light is almost blinding, the shadows sharp as if the scene is revealed in a flash. But of all his paintings, perhaps the most fascinating is the one he named "The Fairy Feller's Master-Stroke". Dadd worked on it for over nine years during his stay in Broadmoor and never completed it. The work is mesmerizing in its strangeness. It depicts a woodland gathering of the fairy court, rife with strange and mysterious creatures of greatly differing proportions, who almost blend in with the autumnal foliage. The painting's focus is unclear, as the figure in the title is almost invisible to the eye, somewhere in the lower half of the piece. And the angle the scene is presented from seems to suggest the artist was peeking through the tangle in the foreground.

Dadd wrote an equally enigmatic poem seeking to clarify his painting. This was not the only poetic expression of the artwork. It inspired the band Queen to write a song whose title is the same as painting, expanding on the characters depicted in it and in Dadd's poem. Terry Pratchett, who recreated the painting in scenes of his book, *The Wee Free Men*, and his friend and colleague the author Neil Gaiman believed that Dadd simply drew what he saw. They surmised that one day he stumbled into a clearing where the fairies were performing one of their wonders, and part of him, perhaps the part responsible for his sanity, remained there, amid the bizarre shadows, the strange light and the magical creatures – forever.

"Faërie cannot be caught in a net of words; for it is one of its qualities to be indescribable, though not imperceptible,"[12] Tolkien explained. And indeed, not all fairylands whose geographies have been charted over the centuries looked like slightly altered versions of our known world. Some had their own set of rigid rules, like the one in *The King of Elfland's Daughter* by Edward John Moreton Drax Plunkett, Lord Dunsany; and others had no laws at all, like Neverland, where Peter Pan and Tinker Bell, the fairy who loves him, reside. J M Barrie's book resurrected the components of the ancient fairy story with the lost children who fell out of their negligent nannies' prams, when they were taken out for a walk in Kensington Gardens. These are the changelings, which was just what Barrie himself had been, having to play the role of the poor substitute (in his mother's eyes) of his beloved and dead elder brother, Arthur, the eternal child who would never grow up. *Peter Pan* is the culmination of a trend started by the tales of the Brothers Grimm, which banished the inhabitants of fairyland to the relative safety of the nursery. Andrew Lang, who wrote the most popular books of fairies of the nineteenth century, stated that "he who would enter into the kingdom of Faerie should have the heart of a little child,"[13] and, according to Barrie, the fairies themselves were created because "every time a child says, 'I don't believe in fairies', there is a fairy somewhere that falls down dead."[14] And when his envious, unfaithful and much-loved Tinker Bell is dying, Peter turns to his readers (or his audience, in the original theatre play) breaking the fourth wall and the boundaries between reality

Joining a long tradition of representations of sites that never existed (The Territory and the Map, page 47).

Like other children who got stuck in fairyland (Paradise Lost, page 171).

And other magical creatures like mermaids (Heads or Tails, page 183).

and make-believe and asks them for Tink's sake to believe in fairies, and to clap their hands to prove that the heart of a young child was still beating in their chest.

These children did grow up, though, and like Wendy, their encounter with the fairies changed them. Gradually, in the twentieth century, the fairies began to return to the adult sphere: from Lord Dunsany, whose book, published in 1924, greatly influenced Tolkien; Hope Mirlees and her enigmatic *Lud-in-the-Mist* in 1926; and Tolkien himself; and through John Crowley's *Little, Big*; and Neil Gaiman's *Dream Country*, which reveals the truth behind the writing of *A Midsummer Night's Dream* and how it relates to the death of Hamnet, William Shakespeare's young son. Then there is Poul Anderson's *The Queen of Air and Darkness* in which a private detective by the name of Eric Sherrinford – the name which Sir Arthur Conan Doyle, the fairy godfather and progenitor of Holmes, originally intended to give his detective – discovers aliens in a strange new world, using telepathy to pose as fairies and to steal the planetary settlers' children.

They may not have had much choice. The human race seems bent on conquering other planets (We Come in Peace, page 123).

No holds have been barred in recent years, and the influx of fairies is only growing more powerful as ever more of them are finding their way into stories.

For the fairies are our only way out, the only creatures whose world is adjacent to ours. If we could only find the right mound, the right crack or crevice, we could reach it. We are eager to leave our own lands behind and travel abroad to that glorious court – as young Elsie and Frances knew only too well, we want to believe. But more than anything, what we want is to be taken back into that other place, that pure, crystalline time, in which childhood never ends.

21

PARADISE LOST

Some books have a heart that's alive and beating. An ardent, sweet, innocent heart that touches the hearts of its readers and pounds along with theirs. Yet this heart may have been torn out of the chest of an actual child, preserved for all time in pastoral formaldehyde, leaving the original owner hollow, void of substance or shadow.

To find this heart, we must descend: go downstream, down the rabbit hole, take the second star to the right and straight on till morning. There, amid the willows and well past the Hundred Acre Wood, innumerable miracles and wonders await. A wall encircles this arcadia and not everyone may enter. Only children can pass through its gates. This is the paradise from which we were expelled when we reached sexual maturity, like Susan Pevensie, one of the four children who discovered C S Lewis's Narnia and was "interested in nothing nowadays except nylons and lipstick and invitations. She always was a jolly sight too keen on being grown-up."[1] J M Barrie puts an end to our hopes forever when he writes, "we can still hear the sound of the surf, though we shall land no more."[2]

A very dangerous stage, especially for young women, as many sensual *Bildungsromans* featuring damsels in distress can testify (The Pleasure Principle, page 195).

The mythological Arcadia was the dwelling place of the Greek god Pan, whom Barrie's protagonist is named after. It is the home of the god of the woods and nature, where "The wolf also shall dwell with the lamb, and the leopard shall lie down with the kid; … and a little child shall lead them,"[3] as Isaiah prophesied. However, this same Pan was also a sexual god, vengeful and dark, a god of fear as suggested by the word he lent his name to – "panic". Dangers, too, lurk in literature's arcadia, and those who venture there find themselves in an infantile ghetto, facing the terror on their own with the grown-ups patrolling the boundaries, keeping them safely locked up.

One of the contributors to the Devil's iconography (Number of the Beast, page 79).

It was in the mid-nineteenth century that the foundations of our modern wonderland were laid. As Humphrey Carpenter describes in his *Secret Gardens: A Study of the Golden Age of Children's Literature*, its building blocks variously consisted of the fire-and-brimstone, Christian-pedagogical literature of the previous century on the one hand, and the fairy tales and fables made popular by the Grimm brothers, Charles Perrault and Hans Christian Andersen on the other. It was the Romantic movement, with its loathing of the *Sturm und Drang* of polluted, poverty- and corruption-ridden industrial cities, and its great yearning for everything natural, clean, pure and innocent, that cemented them together. Following Rousseau, Wordsworth and others, Romantic passion homed in on a single, idyllic figure: the child, who came to occupy the centre of a huge spiritual–social–economic revival. Reformers did their utmost to set children free from exploitation; preachers urged them towards the kingdom of heaven and educators made it their goal to cherish their free and untamed spirit. While traders attempted to sell parents the relevant merchandise, and painters and photographers tried to capture its image, writers followed the spirit of childhood to the haunts only they knew intimately how to reach: the secret gardens of the imagination.

The golden age of children's literature started in earnest with the publication of Charles Kingsley's *The Water-Babies* in 1863: Kingsley was Darwin's friend and served as Queen Victoria's chaplain. However, the water that Kingsley's followers dived so enthusiastically into was home to monsters, too. A murky undercurrent bubbled below the surface of Victorian and Edwardian children's literature and, among other things, it saturated the roots of the forest A A Milne invented, inspired by his young son's toy animals. Christopher Robin Milne's explanation of his father's success was simple, and its presence is felt throughout the three volumes of his autobiography: "my father had got to where he was by climbing upon my infant shoulders, … he had filched from me my good name and had left me with nothing but the empty fame of being his son,"[4] he wrote. Alan Milne, he argued, neither loved nor understood children. "Some people are good with children. Others are not," Christopher Milne wrote. "It is a gift. You either have it or you don't. My father didn't."[5] The marriage of Alan and Dorothy Milne was an unhappy one, riddled with mutual infidelities. Having hoped for a daughter, Dorothy insisted on dressing Christopher like a girl in the gingham smocks Ernest Shepard immortalized in his illustrations. And Christopher received most of Pooh's friends as part of a rather cold calculation. They were "presents from my parents, carefully chosen, not just for the delight they might give to their new owner, but also for their

With their heady mixture of sexual undertones and gratuitous violence (The Human Animal, page 189).

Who liked to emphasize the moral of his stories (Lupus Est, page 93).

Who baptized the mermaid (Heads or Tails, page 183).

literary possibilities,"[6] he observed with bitterness. The couple had little patience with their child and his beloved nanny was the one entrusted with his education and well-being. Eventually separated from her, he was sent to public school where his fellow school mates bullied him. He was not in Hundred Acre Wood anymore. Christopher Milne never forgave his father for having turned the bedtime stories he told him into public property, sacrificing the meagre parental intimacy he managed to scrape together for the sake of success. Despite these unhappy family ties, which included the total disruption of his relationship with his mother in the last 15 years of her life, Christopher Milne managed a happy adult life. He married, had a daughter and lived comfortably near the small bookshop he ran with his wife, in which one very small shelf was set aside for his father's books.

Alastair Grahame was less fortunate. The stories that made up *The Wind in the Willows* also began as the bedtime stories his father told his only child, a little boy nicknamed "Mouse". Kenneth Grahame was a 38-year-old virgin when he married, after having conducted a lengthy correspondence with his future wife, all done in baby-talk. The marriage was a failure. Elspeth, who suffered from hypochondria and was given to fits of hysteria, spent most of her time in bed, while Grahame, who had libidinal issues, tried to keep safely out of her way. Alastair was a sickly baby who, in addition to a congenital eye problem, also suffered from developmental delay. The couple adored their son and convinced themselves that all this only pointed to the child's genius; they indulged him endlessly and could not bring themselves to impose discipline. Alastair, who grew up without any boundaries, liked to lie down on the road and pretend he was dead. His time in boarding school was intolerable too, especially when it turned out that the "genius" had learning disabilities. He was moved from one educational institution to another until, just a few days before his twentieth birthday, he went back to playing his favourite childhood game, but this time on a railway line. He was found on the tracks the next morning, his head severed and everything indicating that the act was intended.

Peter Pan also decided to end his life on the train tracks. Peter Llewellyn Davies was the third of five children with whom the writer and playwright J M Barrie developed an unusually close bond, having adopted them all when their parents died. Like Grahame, Barrie had a hard time forging intimate relations with women and, although he was married for 15 years to the actress Mary Ansell, there is evidence that they barely had sex. Nicholas, or Nico, the youngest of the Llewellyn Davies children acknowledged that, "I don't believe that Uncle Jim ever experienced what one might call a stirring in the undergrowth for anyone," clarifying that he, "never heard one word or saw one glimmer of anything approaching homosexuality or paedophliacy [sic]... Of all the men I have ever known, Barrie was the wittiest, and the best company. He was also the least interested in sex. He was an innocent."[7]

But the age of innocence came to an end when George, the eldest of the children and the one who inspired the boy who never grew up, did indeed remain forever young. He died in service during World War I. Seven years later, Michael, the fourth child, drowned together with a fellow student in Oxford, a death accompanied by rumours of a suicide pact and the love that dare not speak its name. Many years later, the demons of this death revisited his brother, Peter, when he set about putting the family documents in order. These resurfacing memories, together with having recently learned that his wife and his three sons inherited the fatal Huntington's disease, brought on a deep depression which he ended under the wheels of a train at London's Sloane Square underground station.

The three children in Edith Nesbit's *The Railway Children* did not end their lives on the tracks. For them, by contrast, life near the railway station was a source of strength and pleasure. Despite their harsh living conditions, they found value and beauty in their sudden poverty and destitution. Nesbit, who cleverly inserted bits of her own childhood into the narrative, had three children but, like Barrie, she raised five – the number of protagonists in her *Five Children and It* and its sequels. This confusing detail reflects the fact that two of the children she raised were not her birth children. They were the outcome of a longstanding affair between her husband and her best friend, Alice Hoatson. Alice moved in to live with the couple and worked as their housekeeper, continuing her sexual relationship with Hubert Bland for decades. And Alice was not the only one Bland conducted extramarital relations with. He was a serial adulterer who had no compunctions about the friends of his adolescent daughter Rosemund, who many years later, poignantly commented: "He endowed every affair with the romance of his own imagination."[8] Inspired, perhaps, by her parents' secret lives in their chaotic country household, Rosemund tried to take refuge in a fantasy of her own, together with her parents' friend, the author H G Wells. He was married and she was but a young girl, which drove her father to an attack of inordinate hypocrisy. He chased the couple all the way to the train station where he "did what any gentleman would have done and thumped him [Wells], there being no horse whips to hand".[9] Then he proceeded to drag a weeping Rosemund back to the house that was buzzing with both her parents' secret love lives. Many of these lovers were associated with the Fabian Society, a group of socialist utopians, which in time evolved into the British Labour Party. The couple's home served as the Fabians' unofficial headquarters. As Alice looked after her own children – who weren't aware she was their mother – as well as those of her lover's wife, Edith Nesbit let her be the "Angel in the House"; this gave her time to conduct affairs with the likes of G B Shaw and provide for the whole tribe. This bohemian lifestyle took a severe toll in the form of neglect. In 1900, Edith's 15-year-old son Fabian – named for the society she held so dearly – had to have his tonsils removed, a procedure carried out in the patient's home in those days. Having forgotten about the entire matter, no one in the family thought to make sure the boy observed a fast before being anaesthetized. Some hours after the successful procedure, his father found the boy dead in his bed, having suffocated on his own vomit.

> Sexuality is a complex matter in utopia as well as in its mirror image (Best of All Possible Worlds, page 247).

If only a nanny had been around, you might say, thinking that everything could have taken a different turn. But that's not necessarily the case. Thirteen-year-old Helen Goff invented Mary Poppins one night when her mother was out of her mind with grief at the death of her husband and left their house in Australia to drown herself in a nearby stream. Helen stayed behind in charge of her two little sisters. Though her mother returned, Helen never forgot the dread of this terrible night. The death of her beloved father, an alcoholic bank clerk of Irish origin, caused the family to descend into poverty and all this left its scars on Helen's psyche. Changing her name into Pamela Lyndon Travers did not erase these scars of the past. Throughout her life, as an author of erotic literature for Australian magazines, a mediocre Shakespearean actress in London, where she moved aged 25, and finally, as the celebrated and much-loved author P L Travers,

> A genre previously reserved for men (The Pleasure Principle, page 195).

she found herself chronically attracted to older men. She had relationships with unattainable father figures, who carried a tragic aura and were shrouded in mystery, from the drunk and unfaithful Irish poet Francis McNamara to the Greek-Armenian mystic George Ivanovich Gurdjieff, who had seven children with seven different women. When she wasn't immersed in hopeless love affairs, there was her longstanding, tempestuous relationship with her flat mate Madge Burnand, daughter of a well-known playwright. Burnand is the one who took a picture of the author bare breasted on a beach during an Italian holiday.

When she turned 40 Travers decided that the one thing lacking in her life was a child. Like her capricious heroine, she appeared unexpectedly at the door of the Hone family – friends of her publisher – in Ireland. They had recently taken in the seven abandoned children of their alcoholic son and Travers wished to adopt one of them. Like a fairy-tale witch, she was after one single and singular child – in this case, a boy born into a literary dynasty (the child's grandfather was Yeats' biographer), with Irish blood (a gesture to her own father's Irish descent and her love of Celtic mysticism), and one singled out by the tarot cards of her faithful astrologer. The one complication was that this baby boy, Camillus, had a twin brother named Anthony. "Take two", begged their grandfather in despair, "they're small". But Travers refused and took only seven-month-old Camillus, introducing him to a life of material and cultural abundance but poor in kindness and structure.

Travers never told Camillus that he was adopted and had a twin brother, pretending she was his biological mother and he her only child. This façade was shattered when 17-year-old Anthony appeared one evening at Travers' door, dead drunk and demanding to see his brother. He had had no part in the fairy tale, the expensive education, the glittery bohemian social scene and exotic travel. Dysfunctional parents and abysmal poverty had been his lot. When Travers threw him out of the house, Camillus never forgave her and their already strained relationship was ruined. And as in a fairy tale, her punishment was to see her son – the ready-made baby she had brought home – spiral into the very illness that had brought down both his father and hers: alcoholism.

Alice Liddell, too, could be added to this list of unfortunate children. The nature of the interest Charles Dodgson, who is

Fairies themselves had their own reasons for taking human children (Paper Fairies, page 161).

More useful in unravelling crimes (King of Cups, page 153).

better known as Lewis Carroll, took in her was troubling and unclear, and their relationship has spawned reams of speculation and research. Or Mary St Leger Kingsley, who lived with a young cousin who also served as her female companion, lover and substitute daughter, and in her books investigated questions of gender identity and sadism – a very long way away from her father's sanctimonious sermons.

We might shrug off these biographical anecdotes as nothing but a bunch of all-too-human misfortunes or, at the most, as the kind of issues celebrities' children have to cope with. But they seem to be tied together by a darker thread. A S Byatt tried to unravel this tangled material in her extensive and disturbing work, *The Children's Book*. She models her novel's protagonist, a children's fantasy author, and the company surrounding her consisting of suffragettes, anarchists, zealots and more, on Edith Nesbit and members of her radical circle – for example, the renowned sculptor Eric Gill, associated with the Arts and Crafts movement, whose reliefs decorate London's Westminster Cathedral. Gill kept a record in his diary of the sexual "experiments" he conducted with his sisters, his daughters and – at least on the one occasion he documented it – with his dog, "Continued experiment with dog after and discovered that a dog will join with a man."[10] Byatt believed that the family ambience and the sexual and political mores, which many of the geniuses of this golden age were creating their works within, transformed the castles of wonderlands into pavilions of perversions.

Later, artists like Allan Moore in *Lost Girls*, the explicit comics he created with Melinda Gebbie, were fascinated by the sexual (or asexual) aspect in the lives of the child heroines who find themselves in these wonderlands, and literary scholars as well as biographers addressed the role of libido in those who created them. Meanwhile, the lost boys and girls were left to their own devices, babes forever wandering in the ancient fairy-tale wood, the magic potion-poison seeping into their veins and wreaking its damage. They were canaries in the mines of their parents' imagination, mirroring ponds to their narcissistic illusions and fantastic fixations. They robbed them of the names they were given, passing them on along with their toys, memories and bedtime stories to the preferred children of their fancy with whom they often spent more time than with their actual offspring: immortal children, forever young, forever charming. In their attempt to rewrite their own childhood, which was often damaged, harsh and isolated – especially in the cases of Kenneth Grahame, Edith Nesbit and Pamela Lyndon Travers – these authors constructed splendid kingdoms in which time stands still, doubles back on itself, regresses, freezes. In these shrines of fantasy millions of reading children could feel themselves welcome guests – make a quick visit and return unscathed – while the authors' children were forgotten, prisoners in a never-Never-Never land.

22

THE LADY AND THE UNICORN

In the 1486 *Peregrinatio in Terram Sanctam*, the first illustrated travel book, Bernhard von Breydenbach reports on his journey to the Holy Land and describes sighting a unicorn standing on a hill near Mount Sinai. His readers didn't bat an eyelid because any civilized person knew about the creature with one single horn, which had already been mentioned by the ancients. Ctesias, a Greek physician at the court of King Artaxerxes II of Persia, mentions that the unicorn originates in India. He describes it as about the size of a donkey, with a horn on its head that is white at the bottom, red at the top and black in the middle; and it also has miraculous qualities. Even though later historians such as Plutarch saw Ctesias as someone who "introduced in his works an immense collection of incredible and extravagant stories",[1] when it came to the exotic unicorn, his tales were accepted without further ado. Aristotle mentions the strange creature when he discusses why some animals grow horns; Pliny the Elder mentions him in his *Historia Naturalis* as "a very fierce animal", and depicts it as follows: "[it] has the head of the stag, the feet of the elephant, and the tail of the boar … [it] has a single black horn, which projects from the middle of its forehead … This animal, it is said, cannot be taken alive."[2] The animal these thinkers referred to might have been what we now know as a rhinoceros. On the other hand, it may have been a kind of oryx with long, straight parallel horns, which seen at an angle might just have appeared to be one single horn. This horn tickled the imagination of the 70 wise men who were ordered by Ptolemy II to render the Hebrew Old Testament into the Greek Septuagint, each of them in their separate cubicles. They translated the Hebrew word *re'em* into the Greek *monokerōs*, a word comprised of *monos*, meaning "single" and *keras* meaning "horn".

Early Christianity's tendency to look at nature as one great mirror of the divine order and search it for meanings is reflected in the second-century *Physiologus*, whose anonymous writer lists

Which appeared, along with other sites – both terrestrial and celestial – on the maps of the period (The Territory and the Map, page 47).

It was one of the initiatives to make the culture of the Great Library of Alexandria more accessible (Ex Libris, page 9).

As they did when they translated the Greek *drakōn* (Here Be Dragons, page 79).

animals and their specific moral virtues (or absence of them) as well as their symbolic features. Here we have the first written source advising how to go about catching the unicorn: "A virgin is placed before it and it springs into the virgin's lap and she warms it with love,"[3] as Jorge Luis Borges quotes in his *Book of Imaginary Beings*. Isidorus of Seville, a seventh-century scholar, further explains the technique: "If a virgin girl is placed in front of a unicorn and she bares her breast to it, all of its fierceness will cease and it will lay its head on her bosom."[4] These same sources reveal that the unicorn's horn can purify poisoned water sources and heal snake bites. But what really hypnotized scholars and lovers in the Middle Ages, the period during which the rare animal's worship reached its zenith, was the nature of its relations with virgins. With the force of a battering ram the unicorn made its way into the period's romance, later filtering down into popular culture too, as a symbol of the unimaginable – for example, when Sebastian witnesses the wonders of Prospero's island in *The Tempest* and exclaims, "Now I will believe that there are unicorns!"[5] The unicorn was everywhere: in medical treatises and in the bestiaries, in sculpture and in heraldry, embroidered onto dresses and woven into tapestries, like the famous series "The Hunt of the Unicorn". Probably made for a wedding, these tapestries consist of seven hangings crammed with action, presenting a metaphor for the way marriage "tames" the rampant male by "trapping" him in the protective but binding enclosure also known as a woman.

The jewels in the crown of medieval weavings are perhaps the six tapestries that make up the "The Lady and the Unicorn" series and form the subject of Tracy Chevalier's bestseller of the same name, and these also underline the link between the beast and the bestial, between the unicorn and sensual experience. In "Sight", the best known of the series, the lady holds up a mirror, which the unicorn gazes into. Her hairdo, in the shape of a braid sticking out and away from her head, is reminiscent of the unicorn's horn. This phallic motif – which arose as soon as a wild creature with a long, hard horn leapt into a virgin's soft lap – evolved into *amor*, the emblem of worldly love, But the unicorn came to represent another aspect of love: *caritas*, pure divine love. In the tapestries of "The Hunt of the Unicorn" he is killed and then resurrected; and in "The Lady and the Unicorn" series, some interpreters claim, the unicorn witnesses how the lady gives up the pleasures of the senses for the sake of a higher purpose. The unicorn can only be held in the lap of a virgin such as the immaculately conceived Mary, Jesus's mother, and its horn also heals and resurrects, so unsurprisingly it came to symbolize Christ himself. The image of this elusive beast – part creature of flesh and blood, part divine incarnation – weaves together the physical and the metaphysical, truth and fiction, the heavenly and the mundane.

The sophisticated sixteenth century saw the unicorn's star of Bethlehem set; the rise of Protestantism with its distaste for Catholic symbolism eroded its mystical and allegorical standing, leaving it as a metaphor for all that is unbelievable, as in Sebastian's words. At the same time, its medical virtues aroused a new interest. Obviously, one could not consider the unicorn as the symbol of the Saviour while also treating it as a four-legged medicine cabinet. A lively trade in what everybody took for genuine unicorn horns developed among Western royalty and the well-to-do. Martin Frobisher, the privateer, brought back to England a horn whose value was estimated at tens of thousands of pounds. He presented it to Queen Elizabeth I as a gift. Subsequently the horn passed into the ownership of Pope Clemens, who had Benvenuto Cellini himself – the Renaissance super-goldsmith – create a proper reticule for it. Cellini was paid 17,000 ducats, five times the sum Michelangelo received for his work on the Sistine Chapel. Unquestionably the greatest masters of the trade in horns were the Danes, whose royal throne was entirely made from these winding wands of wonder. They religiously kept the secret of the horns' provenance: what they were peddling as horns was in truth ivory – the tusks of the Arctic narwhal – the *Monodon monoceros* or one-toothed unicorn.

A worthy gift to the fairy queen (Paper Fairies, page 161) and the incarnation of ancient warriors (Wonder Women, page 37).

There was hell to pay for that (Moving Heaven and Hell, page 71).

When in the seventeenth century the scam came to light, and people understood that the horns were the actual tooth of some sea creature, belief in the existence of the unicorn as a physical animal plummeted, relegating it to the domain of tales and legends. There, it was allowed to go forth and multiply, usually engaging in a struggle with a lion, its traditional foe. It is a scene that pops up frequently in children's rhymes; in poetry, like Edmund Spenser's *Faerie Queene*; in prose, such as Lewis Carroll's *Through the Looking Glass* and in *Stardust* by Neil Gaiman. While Borges considered the unicorn a precursor of Franz Kafka, Peter S Beagle devoted one of

Fake mermaids survived much longer (Heads or Tails, page 183).

the most beautiful fantasy books ever written to it: *The Last Unicorn*, which was turned into a psychedelic animation film in 1982.

The 1980s were good to unicorns in general. Touched by Lisa Frank's commercial magic wand – she was the woman behind an empire of kitschy pop commodities that bathed the era in neon hues – there were unicorns with radioactively rainbow-coloured horns and tails gracing T-shirts, pencil cases, posters, erasers and diaries. When the 1980s craze subsided, the unicorn was allowed to graze peacefully on the edges of pop culture for a few decades until the millennials dragged it back from its green pastures. Those who wish to interpret their enthusiasm for the unicorn point at Frank as a possible source of this current wave of nostalgia and at the thirst for childlike innocence in an era marked by change, chaos and threat.

Medieval Europeans might have recognized themselves in this escapist yen: for them too, the unicorn served as an escape route from a reality of hardship and chaos. As well as the raging plague, there were changes in climate – leading to food insecurity – and political power struggles escalating into military conflict and farmers' revolts. They pinned their hopes on the unicorn's horn, believing it might save them from their physical and spiritual woes, deliver them from hardship and give them comfort. The belief that the innocence embodied by the virgin, when harnessed in the service of culture and civilization, would overcome wild aggression and calamity as expressed by the unicorn, was turned upside down. In our current "Middle Ages", an interim period full of dangers and strewn with forbidding obstacles we are trying to overcome with our eyes firmly shut, the unicorn represents wide-eyed naivety while human culture itself is the chaotic and cataclysmic danger zone. We no longer want to tempt the unicorn, so we may capture it; now we yearn to set our inner unicorn free. With every one of us perceiving ourselves as the utterly unique snowflake we are, we can all be a unicorn in the great herd of rare animals.

23
HEADS OR TAILS

It was deep at night, when the men of Captain Ahab, their obsessive-compulsive superior, were "startled by a cry so plaintively wild and unearthly – like half-articulated wailings of the ghosts of all Herod's murdered Innocents – that one and all, they started from their reveries … while that wild cry remained within hearing. The Christian or civilized part of the crew believed it was mermaids and shuddered."[1] Herman Melville's vengeful captain with the pegleg was contemptuous of people's vain beliefs in mermaids, elegantly ignoring the fact that he himself was on an epic quest after a partly mythical being. He made it clear to his sailors that what they had heard was simply seals. But on the last watch one of them fell overboard and drowned, as though the sirens who dwell deep in those dark waters had called him to them.

He wasn't the only seafarer aboard the accursed *Pequod* to unite with a mermaid forever. When three friends decided in 1971 to start a shop selling high-quality coffee beans in Seattle's fish market, they chose the name of Captain Ahab's first officer, Starbuck, in an attempt to find one that would go well with the site. They scoured old books containing nautical themes for the shop's logo; it showed an engraving of a bare-breasted, long-haired woman, wearing a crown; the lower part of her body consisted of scaly tail, whose bifurcating parts curved over her head. This served until 1987, when the logo was changed and chastened into a streamlined version with the mermaid's hair covering her cheeky breasts; and in its next and current reincarnation, even her belly button can no longer be seen. When the company planned to bring the initial logo back for a guest appearance as part of its thirtieth-anniversary celebrations, civilized Christians voiced their objection. A spokesman for one devout consumer organization shrieked that the logo, "has a naked woman on it with her legs spread like a prostitute".[2] Conspiracy aficionados claimed that if you turned the logo upside down, with the split tail facing upward, you got the spiralling horns of Baphomet, the infernal goat, the mermaid's breasts turning into his glaring eyes and her crown into his goatee.

> For the Leviathan mentioned in the Bible, which Melville identified with the great whale (Here Be Dragons, page 79).

> And plat du jour in paradise (Moving Heaven and Hell, page 71).

> Of the kind who can prove that the moon landing was filmed in a studio (Man in the Moon, page 115) and that aliens made an unholy alliance with the US government (We Come in Peace, page 123).

Starbucks quickly reverted to its stylized, neutered image. This didn't do the trick, though, for members of the royal house of Saudi Arabia, so to mollify them and ensure coffee sales to their subjects, Starbucks dropped the naughty nymph completely, leaving an orphaned crown floating on the foamy waters their corporate spine seemed to have dissolved into, like Hans Christian Andersen's little mermaid. In his Pulitzer-Prize-winning article, "The Saudi Sellout", Colbert King cites the company's CEO stating, "As a company that is entering many international markets, we are very sensitive to, and highly respectful of, local religious customs, social norms and laws."[3]

Starbucks might well have looked into the local religious customs behind the figure they chose to represent them. Mermaids and various other legendary female water creatures have appeared in many mythologies in geographically diverse places throughout cultural history. At times they are benevolent and generously reward anyone who comes to their aid. But more often they feature as submarine femme-fatales, cold-blooded and heartless, who delight in causing shipwrecks or stirring up storms and floods by a mere wave of their webbed hand, while busying themselves weaving shells into their seaweed-green locks.

The first mermaid on record was Atargatis, chief goddess of northern Syria and patroness of the ancient city of Ascalon. According to some records, she accidentally killed her husband – a not uncommon faux pas – then leapt into the sea from sheer shame, wishing she'd turn into a fish. So great was her beauty that only half of her wish was granted and only the lower part of her body became fish-like. Far out in the Mediterranean, Atargatis encountered another female creature, the siren. First depicted as a combination of a woman and a bird, by the seventh century – and perhaps due to associating with seafarers – the siren's feathers had been replaced by scales and a fish tail. In Greek mythology, the sirens' singing had a reputation for being so enchanting that sailors went mad on hearing it. The sirens "beguile all men whosoever comes to them," warns Homer in the twelfth book of his *Odyssey*. "Whoso in ignorance draws near to them and hears the Sirens' voice, he nevermore returns, that his wife and little children may stand at his side rejoicing, but the Sirens beguile him with their clear-toned song, as they sit in a meadow, and about them is a great heap of bones of mouldering men, and round the bones the skin is

A popular site for supernatural events (Weird Sisterhood, page 25; Here Be Dragons, page 79).

shrivelling." But what is so tempting in the song of the sirens who try to seduce Odysseus (who ties himself to the ship's mast so he may listen to their song without jumping off his ship) is what they are singing about rather than their song itself, "For we know all the toils that in wide Troy the Argives and Trojans endured through the will of the gods, and we know all things that come to pass upon the fruitful earth."[4] Temptation lies not in their actual voice but in *what* they voice – knowledge.

Germany had its own siren, Lorelei the Rhine maiden, who combed her golden hair to the detriment of unfortunate sailors who got so distracted their ships were wrecked on the rocks; while another strand of European folklore featured capricious Melusine, with her snakelike tail that sometimes appeared as two forked fish tails. There were Greek freshwater nymphs, Celtic lake fairies, Arab well spirits, Japanese river deities and more. So intense was the belief in these female water creatures that Blackbeard, the inglorious pirate, made sure he navigated his fleet to steer well clear of them. Christopher Columbus, in a log entry dated 8 June 1493, reported sighting three mermaids near the coast of Rio del Oro in Western Sahara, and added disappointedly: "they were not so beautiful as they are depicted for only after a fashion had human form in their faces."[5] The creatures he saw were probably manatees that looked particularly human.

Other than certain doubtful hoaxes, such as bikini-top wearing manatees adorned with flowers or "The Feejee Mermaid", which appeared in nineteenth-century sideshows and was actually a frightful hybrid made up of a fish tail and a monkey's torso, no warbling women of the waters were anywhere to be found, other than in the realms of fancy or the domains of art, despite the rewards offered to anyone who could come up with a specimen.

But in those regions, they flourished. They were tattooed on bulging, hairy biceps, from kingdoms by the sea to the quays of Nantucket, slippery with whale blood. They sang in operas like Dvorak's *Rusalka* and in music composed to Heine's "Die Lorelei"; they brushed their red tresses in John William Waterhouse's paintings and other dreamlike Pre-Raphaelite works, their tails decoratively stirring the blue expanses on ancient maps.

The person who should take the brunt of responsibility for the sea change in this aquatic goddess's persona, from a beautiful and fatal monster only appeased by human sacrifice to a love-struck

Had he had more accurate maps, he might have been able to avoid his famous ship, *Queen Anne's Revenge*, running aground on 10 June 1718 (The Territory and the Map, page 47).

He also reported seeing Amazons, which casts some doubt on the credibility of his reports (Wonder Women, page 37).

Alongside other imaginary creatures (Here Be Dragons, page 79).

girl willing to sacrifice herself for Prince Charming, was Hans Christian Andersen in his misogynistic tale *The Little Mermaid*. In his version "pride must suffer pain", and a good girl must suffer in silence. His little mermaid is afflicted by a multitude of sins: she is curious about the lives of the land dwellers, covetous of their immortal soul and lusts after the prince. Her trial and punishment, delivered by the sea witch who gives her the legs she craves, is to feel as if she were "treading upon sharp knives, and that the blood must flow",[6] and to lose her tongue and voice.

The little mermaid climbs onto the beach with her new feet, each step unbearably painful, only to find out that princes usually marry princesses rather than mute, love-struck girls. Refusing to save herself by cutting the prince's throat and washing her feet in his blood, she jumps into the sea and dissolves until all there's left of her is foam on the crest of the waves. But do not fear! This is a Christian legend and therefore her ultimate sacrifice endows her with an immortal soul and she is carried off to heaven. The happy ending. Needless to say, this ending did not survive the typical saccharine Disney makeover in the mega-hit musical of the same name. They replaced this Christian sacrificial lamb with dancing lobsters.

Hayao Miyazaki, the great Japanese animator, showed Disney how Andersen's Christian passion can transform into sheer joy without having to add a big dollop of kitsch in his unique version of the story *Ponyo*. In J M Barrie's *Peter Pan* the mermaids are vain and selfish creatures; in *The Chronicles of Narnia* they smile at Lucy Pevensie from down below, in their marine realm, as she passes over them aboard the ship *Dawn Treader*; in doing so they join C S Lewis' mythical menagerie, together with fauns, werewolves, witches, giants, naiads, dryads and a whole host of fantastical beings. In J K Rowling's *Harry Potter* series, the merpeople mourn Dumbledore's death (as do we), their trident-wielding presence Rowling's acknowledgment of Lewis' eclectic tradition. In Tera Lynn Childs' series, which boasts alliterative titles like *Forgive My Fins* and *Fins are Forever*, the heroine is a part-time mermaid who wants to join her high school swimming team and survive the cruel ebbs and flows of adolescence's choppy waters. Jazz Jennings, a 14-year-old transgender girl and cultural icon, explains why, "It's so cool how there's this deep connection with mermaids in the transgender community because they have no genitalia … They

As were also some of the writers who, along with him, created the golden age of British children's literature (Paradise Lost, page 171).

They're a lot less sexual than their wild forefather (Paradise Lost, page 171).

His are described as evil, but not all werewolves are like that (Lupus Est, page 93).

just have this long, beautiful tail to replace that body part that dictates who we are so often."[7] A British foundation that supports transgender children calls itself "Mermaid", and in 2018, *Julian is a Mermaid* was shortlisted for the prestigious Waterstone's Award for Children's Literature, which goes to books that advance LGBTQ+ issues. "There's something about mermaids," said the author, Jessica Love, in an interview, "who knows if that's because they're magical creatures who can live between two realities or because they don't have any genitals, or because they're f***ing great."[8]

Tim Powers' *On Stranger Tides* finally got Blackbeard the pirate to meet mermaids, added a pinch of zombies and mixed all this with a shot of water from the Fountain of Youth to produce a witches' brew that became a rather muddled movie in the *Pirates of the Caribbean* franchise, mostly immortalizing the image of the mermaid as submarine seductress. In *Lady in the Water* by M Night Shyamalan, an aging janitor finds a nymph in his building's pool, who offers him and the other residents what the sirens held out to Odysseus – knowledge. The knowledge in question is that both the janitor and all the other inhabitants of the building are mere figments of the imagination that have taken on flesh and blood.

Who did actually hail from the Caribbean (Head Hunters, page 231).

They can carry blessings, though, if they want to, these mermaids. And thus they are responsible for popularizing the name Madison, following the sensational success of the film *Splash*, a fantasy romantic comedy produced in 1984, starring Tom Hanks in the role of an adorable dork and Daryl Hannah as a not-so-little mermaid, who gets caught up in his fishing nets. The name Madison, which the protagonist picks at random from a street sign, rose meteorically from ranking 216th on the list of America's most popular girls' names that year, to third.

In the home aquarium, too, mermaids swam around busily, especially in TV series dedicated to the supernatural – like *Bewitched* or *Once Upon a Time*, and the Animal Planet channel broadcast a mockumentary about them that was so convincing it prompted a public statement from the US Water Authority to the effect that "no evidence of aquatic humanoids has ever been found."[9] But official statements will never do. The landlocked will go on believing that somewhere out there in the uncharted depths of the element least hospitable to humankind, dwells the ideal, unattainable female creature, eternally virginal due to her imaginary physiology. The embrace of the LGBTQ+ community, monofin swimming classes also known as "mermaiding" and attempts to subdue the seductive nymph and make her suitable for children – it is all to no avail. From the waist up, she has all possible enticements: hypnotic voice, long flowing hair, uncovered breasts; yet from the waist down she is slippery and elusive, sexless, eternally untouchable. No wonder that she can unleash storms and drive sailors out of their minds.

24

THE HUMAN ANIMAL

The midwife who, sometime in the year 1537, lay Mrs Gonzalez' newborn infant into her arms, couldn't help but notice that something about the boy was different. It was hard not to see it. The infant's entire body was covered in down, but unlike the kind that sometimes appears on newborns and gradually disappears during the first few weeks of life, this baby's down only grew thicker. In 1547, the ten-year-old Pedro was dispatched in a cage to the court of Henri II, King of France, as a gift. Henri sent for his court physician to examine the "Wildman", and when the doctor established that the child was no wilder than any other boy his age but just had dense silky hair, soft as sable, covering his entire body except for his lips, the bridge of his nose, his palms and feet, he was set free. Favourably inclined toward the boy, the king had him dressed in splendour and he was educated alongside the children of the nobility. After Henri died, the widowed queen, who was less enthusiastic about Petrus Gonsalvus, as he came to be known, decided to present him with another "gift": curious to find out whether "it" could breed, she brokered a marriage with Lady Catherine, one of her ladies-in-waiting. The queen didn't divulge anything to the bride about the man she was to marry and it is not unlikely that Catherine took fright at first seeing her husband-to-be. However, there is room for hope that the two developed a certain fondness for each other and that Petrus proved himself a true wildman in the bedroom since the couple had seven children, four of whom inherited their father's genetic condition, hypertrichosis (Latin for "too much hair").

Was this story about the marriage of Catherine and Petrus what inspired Gabrielle-Suzanne Barbot de Villeneuve to write *Beauty and the Beast* almost 200 years after Gonsalvus' death? A famous portrait in which Catherine's dainty hand can be seen resting tenderly on her hirsute husband's shoulder may well have served at least as the visual anchor for this tale about a young woman marrying a monster, who becomes fully human thanks to her love. But the narrative frame for Barbot de Villeneuve's tale is much more ancient in origin, with

189

an early version appearing in the stories about Amor and Psyche, which are included in the single Latin novel that has survived intact, written in the second century AD by Lucius Apuleius. Its protagonist, Lucius, accidentally turns himself into an ass – the novel became known as *The Golden Ass* – and in that guise experiences strange adventures and hears many tales, until he reverts to human form. The book's original title, *Metamorphoses*, is in homage to one of the founding texts of the Western canon written by the poet Publius Ovidius Naso (aka Ovid) more than a century earlier, which had already attained classic status by Apuleius' time.

All this unfolded in the reign of Augustus, a passionate defender of the institution of marriage, while he was being slowly poisoned by his wife, Livia. And as the emperor fulminated against the hedonistic decadence pervading Rome and legislated aggressively against promiscuity, Ovid published *The Loves, The Art of Love* and *The Cure for Love*, in which he offers advice to men and women about the advantages of various sexual positions and introduces them to the secret art of seduction. Whether these texts inflamed the emperor or whether Ovid was having an affair with a member of the imperial family – he himself hints at this possibility in one of his poems – is unclear, but in AD 8 he was exiled to some godforsaken corner of the empire, somewhere near the Black Sea. Enraged and in despair, he cast his most important, nearly completed work into the flames. But – luckily for Western culture – not before depositing some copies of the *Metamorphoses* with friends. Edith Hamilton, the great American popularizer of mythology, admitted that "most of the books about the stories of classical mythology depend chiefly upon the Latin poet Ovid."[1] His *Metamorphoses* is the source of some of the most famous myths that made it to our times, such as Apollo's love for Daphne and the tale of Echo and Narcissus. Ovid managed to weave the great wealth of classical and near-eastern myth into a meandering, associative rather than narrative labyrinth, dynamic and multifaceted. The one overarching principle it obeys is change. In the *Metamorphoses* the entire cosmos, as soon as it emerges, is in motion. Everything flows: statues transform into women, men into stones, gods into animals, human beings into forces of nature, young girls become flowers and boys turn into fountains.

These endless transfigurations pose the question of identity and essence. What sets man above animals? Which facets of personality

Among the first erotic handbooks in the Western world (The Pleasure Principle, page 195).

A common expression of despair in writers (Flame and Moth, page 17).

and humanity remain intact when our beloved transforms into a tree, a god turns into rain, a king becomes a wolf? But is this really about mere changes in form? Maybe change affects substance, too? Maybe such transformation of form allows the oppressive inner truth to be set free?

The very prototype of all wolf-men to come (Lupus Est, page 93).

For the gods there are no such questions. When Jupiter wants to seduce young virgins, he may turn into a bull, a swan, a hawk, a quail, a cuckoo or a cloud, but he would always remains the supreme god. His transformations are functional and controlled. Most women, by contrast, change shape as a result of divine interventions such as in order to avoid being raped – like Daphne who turns into a laurel tree to escape Apollo; or like Medusa who, as a result of having been raped by Neptune, god of the seas, is transformed by Minerva as punishment for defiling her temple; or again as punishment by Minerva, who apparently liked the idea of turning women into something horrible, as happened to Arachne, the weaver. During a contest against the virtuous goddess, she had the temerity to immortalize some of the more graphic scenes in which gods change shape as part of their schemes against unsuspecting virgins. Minerva was livid and, devastated by her rage, Arachne tried to hang herself. But death was too good for her for in the eyes of the gods, and only eternal punishment would suffice. So, the goddess turned her into a spider.

Transforming her shining tresses into hissing snakes (Here Be Dragons, page 79).

"... her flowing hair
Fell to the ground, and left her temples bare;
Her usual features vanish'd from their place,
Her body lessen'd all, but most her face.
Her slender fingers, hanging on each side
With many joynts, the use of legs supply'd:
A spider's bag the rest, from which she gives
A thread, and still by constant weaving lives."[2]

In the *Metamorphoses* we witness all the principles and types of transformation that will appear in later narratives: change by force or willingly; transitory or permanent transition; change into a number of figures as opposed to one in particular; transformation for deliverance or, on the contrary, as a penalty.

Many anthropologists agree that humans transforming into animals is one of the most ancient magical practices, part of the ritual trances our ancient forefathers entered when their shamans took on the shape of an animal the tribespeople sought to ensnare by first capturing its totemic spirit. Priest and archeologist Henri Breuil believed that a mysterious, 14,000-year-old painting found in the "Trois Frères" cave in France represented just such a ceremony. "In his drawing of it, reproduced many times over," writes Ronald Hutton in *Witches, Druids, and King Arthur*, "it appears as a dancing male human figure, body in half profile and face turned towards the viewer. It has the eyes of an owl, the tail of a horse, the body of a horse or deer, a long beard, the ears of a deer, animal forepaws, and tall spreading stag's antlers."[3] Breuil named it "The Sorcerer". His controversial find was regarded by the British author and anthropologist Margaret Murray (herself controversial) as the "earliest known representation of a deity"[4] in her 1931 book *The God of the Witches*. Those persecuted as witches, she claimed, were in fact followers of a horned pagan god, who embodied nature and symbolized fertility.

Our ancestors' presumed desire to capture the spirit of the beast they sought to catch resonates in many therianthropic tales where the transformation from human to animal involves an object which, when wielded, has the power to entrap the human–animal in one of its shapes. This is what befalls swan-maidens of various plumage, such as the ones immortalized in Tchaikovsky's best-known ballet, *Swan Lake*. They can be controlled by means of their feather capes (a motif that is absent from the musical version). And it is also what the Valkyries in Norse mythologies endure, as well as Lear's unfortunate children. In the ancient Celtic legend, their jealous stepmother turned them into swans and only Christianity's touch succeeded in restoring their humanity, centuries later, so that they could receive the sacrament and die in the bosom of the Church. The Selkie, the seal wife often found in Celtic legends, sheds her smooth skin, only to be seized by the man who finds it. Hans, the hedgehog in Grimm's fairy tales, has a similar problem. Like Psyche in Apuleius' story, who feared her invisible husband was actually a snake (an image whose phallic-metaphoric force is beyond question), his wife tried to make sure that the man next to her in bed was not some monster. To capture him in his human shape, she cast his quills into the fire.

Fittingly for a narrative strain originating in a myth about Eros (as a male representing love) and Psyche (as a female representing

The Celtic god of the wild, perhaps (Weird Sisterhood, page 25).

In the *Poetic Edda* (Twilight of the Gods, page 65), Wayland the Smith and his brothers encounter three Valkyrie sisters. The name of the first is Hlaðguðr Svanhví, which roughly translates as "Woven-Cap-Battle-Woman-Swan White". The word "woven" may reference the tales of Valkyries using threads in battle to tie up warriors and is associated with many of the deities who determined the fates of mortals and gods alike (Weird Sisterhood, page 25).

The same confusion also occurred with Eve in paradise (Here Be Dragons, page 79).

the soul), therianthropic stories are very often about sexuality. In the *Metamorphoses* the sexual spectrum expands to include a choice of paraphilias as well as a degree of gender fluidity we can only envy today. A female transforms into a male in order to marry a woman, and a man and a woman cling together and meld, becoming a hermaphrodite.

Archaic, prehistoric rituals have undergone metamorphosis and sublimation. The shaman who assumes the shape of the animal whose spirit must be ensnared turns into a man in animal form, seeking to capture a woman. In these narratives, a woman's love is a civilizing, domesticating force, as it was in the world's most ancient epic, that of Gilgamesh. To tame Enkidu – a wild man who feeds on grasses and lives with the beasts, embodying the animalistic, pre-cultural stage of human development – Shamhat, the holy harlot, is sent to tempt him:

> "Shamhat unclutched her bosom, exposed her sex, and he took
>   in her voluptuousness …
> She spread out her robe and he lay upon her,
> she performed for the primitive the task of womankind.
> His lust groaned over her;
> for six days and seven nights Enkidu stayed aroused,
> and had intercourse with the harlot
> until he was sated with her charms.
> But when he turned his attention to his animals,
> the gazelles saw Enkidu and darted off,
> the wild animals distanced themselves from his body."

Once he's done with this erotic high-priestess, Enkidu drinks beer, eats bread, washes, gets dressed, and hey presto! he "turn[s] into a human".[5]

Carnal lust and worldly love in the Middle Ages underwent a process of refinement. Once these transformations no longer constituted a magical practice and had become essentially metaphorical, they and their romantic associations also became legitimate objects of jest, as Shakespeare illustrates in *A Midsummer Night's Dream*. Oberon dispatches Puck to change Bottom's head into that of an ass while enchanting his wife, the queen of fairies. Here's Puck after accomplishing his mission, reporting back to his master, "My mistress with a monster is in love."[6]

A tendency reflected in the tapestries depicting the hunt for the unicorn (The Lady and the Unicorn, page 179).

"And of a king of England too"[a] (Wonder Women, page 37).

Taken from a Freudian perspective the capture or destruction of the swan's wings or the hedgehog's quills are a synecdoche – a part representing the whole – and can be considered an act of castration. In a feminist interpretation this symbolizes the transfer of the phallus, the potency of sexuality, into the capturer's hands. But for Bruno Bettelheim, tales involving the animal-bridegroom represent the stage at which the girl's oedipal desire is transferred from her father to the man she marries, "Only marriage made sex permissible, changed it from something animal-like into a bond sanctified by the sacrament of marriage."[7]

After all, alongside the striking – at times shocking – sexual meanings these therianthropic tales, mythologies and legends reveal, lies another transformation, a theological tectonic shift which began in Ovid's lifetime. He was born one year after Julius Caesar's assassination and flourished during the life of Jesus, the man who himself passed through a complex metamorphosis when his flesh turned into bread and his blood into wine. Ovid's *Metamorphoses* preserve something of that huge swing from polytheism to monotheism, beginning as they do at the moment when a single god creates the universe, and teeming with criticism of the pantheistic pantheon's gods' arbitrariness and cruelty. From Arachne turning into a spider, all the way to that morning when Gregor Samsa awoke and "found himself transformed in his bed into a gigantic insect. He was lying on his hard, as it were armor-plated, back and when he lifted his head a little he could see his domelike brown belly divided into stiff arched segments .... His numerous legs, which were pitifully thin compared to the rest of his bulk, waved helplessly before his eyes."[8] In Franz Kafka's most iconic text, transformation becomes deformation; change, now, is distortion. Unlike in Ovid's *Metamorphoses*, in Kafka's *Metamorphosis* there is neither a vengeful god nor a benevolent goddess, or the other way around. Transformation, here, is inexplicable, an enigma. There is no one to blame and nor is there anyone to turn to in prayer. The transformations of the metamorphic tales also denote how the gods evolve from the totemic animals whose shape is taken on by the shamans into polymorphous beings who can also change our shape, over and beyond changing their own; and from them to a god who has neither body, nor shape nor form. This disembodied, ineffable god enables his followers to undergo the most mysterious transfiguration of all: shedding the chrysalis of this world in favour of becoming a butterfly in the next.

25

THE PLEASURE PRINCIPLE

The baboon wasn't entirely to blame.

The one who took him along to the infamous Hellfire Club, dressed in a cloak with horns attached to his head, was John Wilkes. He was a political activist, militant journalist and short-lived member of the "Medmenham Monks", one of the anarchic clubs that flourished in early-eighteenth-century England. Members dressed up like biblical or mythological characters, joined in parodic versions of satanic or pagan rites, gorged themselves and consumed alcohol – a lot of it. The mood was free and seditious, and since many of the members were aristocrats who also took a more or less active part in the country's governance, the air was often replete with the perfume of sex, the smell of money and the stench of politics.

> The horns were taken off a slain god as befits the member of a club that admits people like him (Number of the Beast, page 79).

When Wilkes released the monkey from the box where he hid it, the baboon went for George Montague, the fourth Earl of Sandwich, a lusty rake and a politician. According to Geoffrey Ashe, author of *The Hell-Fire Clubs: A History of Anti-Morality*, Sandwich was positive that old Harry had come to claim his soul and cried out, "Spare me, gracious Devil, spare a wretch who was never sincerely your servant. I have sinned only from the vanity of being in fashion, never have I been able to commit the thousandth part of the vices which I have boasted of."[1] The baboon escaped and was never heard of again.

A few years before the baboon incident, Wilkes and Thomas Potter, the dejected and wanton son of the Archbishop of Canterbury, had written an erotic parody of the acclaimed poet Alexander Pope's poem "Essay on Man". Potter and Wilkes both detested Sandwich, and this drove them to dedicate the text, which gained the doubtful accolade of "The dirtiest poem in the English language", to Fanny Murray. Murray was one of the great courtesans of her time. The legendary lover Casanova admired her and she was seen in the company – and in the beds – of the country's most illustrious men. She had also become a fashion icon before she began leasing out her favours – exclusively and for a limited period of time only – to the Earl of Sandwich. Wilkes and Potter didn't plan to have the poem published and most definitely not under their own names, but they printed a few copies to circulate discretely among the members of the club. When it fell into Sandwich's hands, he used it as the perfect revenge for the baboon incident. The best show in town opened at the House of Lords on 15 November 1763. The Earl, given permission to speak, started to read aloud. One member nearly fainted:

> "Awake, my Fanny! Leave all meaner things;
> This morn shall prove what rapture swiving brings!
> Let us (since life can little more supply
> Than just a few good fucks, and then we die)
> Expatiate free o'er that loved scene of man,
> A mighty maze, for mighty pricks to scan;
> A wild, where Paphian Thorns promiscuous shoot,
> Where flowers the Monthly Rose, but yields no Fruit.
> O blindness to the future! kindly given,
> That each may enjoy what fucks are marked in Heaven:
> Who sees with equal eye, as God of all,
> The man just mounting, and the virgin's fall,
> Pricks, cunt, and ballocks in convulsions hurled,
> And now a hymen burst, and now a world."[2]

In this performance staged by Sandwich, one of the most renowned lechers of his times, he censored the poem and its authors. It was so hypocritical that even one of Wilkes' enemies commented that he "Never before heard the Devil preach a sermon against sin."[3] In his defence, Wilkes stated that "No man has the right to inquire into my private amusements if they are not prejudicial to society."[4] Which expresses the position of many who came after him when sexuality and its public presentation became a political issue – from John Cleland, whose *Fanny Hill* was also written with Fanny Murray in mind, right up to the scandalous Larry Flynt, publisher of the pornographic *Hustler* magazine, who found himself repeatedly entangled in legal struggles to protect the freedom of expression and the first amendment of the US constitution. But parliament, which despised Wilkes due to his

196

frequent attacks aimed at flaccid politicians and a profligate king, grabbed the opportunity. He was accused of obscenity and profanity (he really shouldn't have used the word "God"), and in spite of public protest (he was rightly considered a defender of individual freedom), he was forced to go into exile in France.

For those interested in political sedition and erotic literature France was the place to aim for. While the seventeenth century and the Enlightenment brought the rise of reason, it also spelled a diminishing in respect for the old institutions like the aristocracy and the Church. In passionate France this led to their increasing ridicule and attack. Sexuality was a perfect battering ram. It fiercely pierced through the fortresses of taboo, doctrine and law, prompting a revolution of desire that encouraged erotic literature to flourish as never before. "The defining paradigm of porn literature in the Enlightenment was the propagation of sexual pleasure as a new religion,"[5] writes Marianna Beck in "The Roots of Western Pornography". Publications such as the 1669 epistolary novel *Les Lettres Portugaises* and *L'École des Filles*, which first appeared in 1655, include two typical features that continued to characterize the genre into the next century. As in *Les Lettres Portugaises* many are set against a religious backdrop, often a convent or a monastery, and while their protagonists are passionate nuns and flirtatious monks, as in *L'École des Filles* they profess to document women's voices and present authentic evidence of their experiences. This was a particularly subversive quality during a time when women had no real social power. "Creating female narrators who were essentially the intellectual equals of men and as capable of, if not eager for, sexual pleasure, was certainly a transgression of expected female roles, and underscored pornography's subversive function."[6] writes Beck. Such subversive acts obviously did not pass unnoticed. The French king and his minions repeatedly attempted to find out who was the author of *L'École des Filles*, but to no avail, and the same was true for the considerable effort invested in preventing its circulation – but the book crossed the Channel nevertheless.

These were merry days in England, too. Eighteen years of puritanical rule had just come to an end; theatres and other sites of entertainment had reopened after long official closures; and the nation was in the grip of a certain unruliness. No one better captured the spirit of those days than Samuel Pepys, the obsessive diarist. Pepys was an extremely sensual man, according to his own writings; we might say he was a constant lecher. When the sermon bored him, he masturbated in Church, and he took the opportunity to check out the intimate parts of his maid when she was combing through his hair for lice. But even he found *L'École des Filles* overly stimulating. In his entry for 9 February 1667 he wrote, "A lewd book, but what doth me no wrong once to read for information sake (but it did *hazer* my prick *para* stand all the while, and *una vez* to *décharger)*; and after I had done it I burned it, that it might not be among my books to my shame, and so at night to supper and to bed."[7] In other words, chiefly the Spanish and French ones highlighted above that Pepys used to cover up his masturbation, he was greatly inspired by the book. Taking the form of an incredibly direct and detailed bawdy dialogue between a young virgin and her experienced, married cousin, the text not only includes descriptions of the male sexual organ and all that can be done with it, but even mentions the clitoris: "the top of the cunt which stands out". In addition, the book offers a wealth of suggestions for a variety of positions, "sometimes my Husband gets upon me, and sometimes I get upon him, sometimes we do it sideways, sometimes kneeling, sometimes crossways, sometimes backwards … sometimes Wheelbarrow, with one leg upon his shoulders, sometimes we do it on our feet, sometimes upon a stool." And there are even references to contemporary condoms, "Some will tye a Pigs Bladder to the Top of their Pricks",[8] and other delights.

The book was also burned in Paris on 9 August 1655, and thus joined a long line of respectable and not-so-respectable works (Flame and Moth, page 17).

Liberated from fiendish contexts (Weird Sisterhood, page 25).

Pepys was not alone in realizing what a powerful effect the erotic word has on the imagination and the body. In her article "The Laws of Eighteenth-Century Sex: Thérèse Philosophe", Jennifer J Davis examines the reflective elements of another French novel, *Thérèse Philosophe*, which "initiates its readers into a community attuned to the physical effects of reading sexually explicit literature […] Texts regularly exhibit power over bodily reactions as the words on the page are transformed in the imagination to affect sensation." So, text and sex create a feedback loop and this is most obvious when the count, who is scheming to become Thérèse's lover, puts her up in a room filled with pornographic art – sculpture, painting and literature – and then gives her the impossible challenge of spending a whole week in the room without seeking release. To his joy and her great pleasure, Thérèse surrenders. Even today, 271 years later, *Thérèse Philosophe* reads like an amazingly progressive and sex-positive book. Catching out little seven-year-old Thérèse as she is stroking the "little man in the boat", her mother ties her hands. Years later, a friendly abbot tells her that these desires are "as natural as those of hunger and thirst [...] when you feel them, there's nothing wrong with using your hand, your finger, to care for this part by agitating it as necessary". When Thérèse eavesdrops on the same abbot having intercourse with his lover, she discovers they use mutual masturbation and withdrawal in order to avoid pregnancy. The lover begs the honourable abbot to come inside her after he has read to her from *Portiers de Chartreux*, "I'm dying of desire and I consent to risk everything"[(9)] but, worried about her future, he refuses – and goes down on her instead. According to Robert Darnton, *Thérèse Philosophe* was the third best-selling book of its time. Tens of thousands of people read it, or were ashamed to confess they did, talked about it or refused to talk about it. It grew so popular and influential that people apparently adopted the contraceptive methods it described, resulting in a significant drop in unwanted pregnancies in eighteenth-century France.

England during those days was less fun than during the initial Restoration revelry, as Wilkes' adventures illustrate. The political unrest in France and the fear that it might spill over and flood the green pastures of Albion led to a moral clampdown.

The most notable literary product of this clampdown was the book that came to be regarded as the first novel in English: *Pamela; or, Virtue Rewarded*. It was published in 1740 by the then printer Samuel Richardson who presented it as authentic "familial letters from a beautiful young damsel to her parents". The heroine, Pamela Andrews, is a 15-year-old maidservant. Her lascivious employer, known only as Mr B, attempts to seduce her, sexually assaults her, slanders her and abducts and imprisons her, while pious Pamela is torn between obedience to her lord and her devotion to the Lord. Her stubborn refusals eventually erode her master's corrupt intentions and he offers her respectable marriage instead.

As a multitude of subsequent novels using the same tropes of class differences, reformed rakes and fallen women proved, this was a winning formula. The book was a huge bestseller and group readings of it were immensely popular.

Some readers saw Richardson as undermining the social order because *Pamela* placed religious virtue above class structure, but

Reading aloud was a common form of entertainment until the middle of the nineteenth century (A Faustian Bargain, page 1).

199

others regarded his work as a show of conformist hypocrisy, since all manner of sins are forgiven as soon as the couple accept the yoke of marriage ordained by the Church. One of the latter was Henry Fielding. In 1741 he published a parody, *An Apology for the Life of Mrs Shamela Andrews*, under the name of Mr Conny Keyber. This time using his own name, a year later he published a picaresque "comic epic poem in prose" as he defined it. Called *Joseph Andrews*, it was a mock-heroic novel about Pamela's brother, his beloved Fanny and their life happily ever after.

But there was no happy ending for Fanny's namesake, the protagonist of the most persecuted and banned novel in the English language, which only became available in the US in 1963 and in the UK in 1970: *Fanny Hill: Memoirs of a Woman of Pleasure*. John Cleland began writing during his many hours of leisure spent in debtors' prison, and the book's first illustrated edition was published in 1748. In spite of its lascivious contents – including orgies, lesbian sex, bisexuality, whippings and so on – this book did not feature explicit language. Cleland, it turned out, was a genius of sexual euphemism, managing to produce about 50 epithets for the penis alone, from "flaming weapon of pleasure",through "stiff horn-hard gristle" to "superb piece of furniture".[10] This was all to no avail when the Bishop of London pointed a finger at him, blaming his immorality for two minor earthquakes that had been felt in the capital, and calling to ban the book. Next in turn, after the author added a homosexual scene to the second edition, it was the lawgivers who were outraged, so Cleland soon found himself in prison again. But the greatest threat of *Fanny Hill* was not the literary representation of sodomy or its ability to rock national institutes. The true groundbreaker was Fanny herself: bright, clever, amusing and easygoing, her totally nonjudgmental attitude to her erotic adventures was utterly remarkable. And to make things worse, not only did she escape paying a price for her wantonness, but in the end she simply became a happy, cheerful housewife right in the middle of the middle class.

Cleland was not the only one to turn his time behind bars into a fruitful and efficient stay. Even those who had grown used to the terrible screams that issued from France's most notorious prison could not stay indifferent on 4 July 1789, when one of the inmates used a makeshift megaphone to beg for help from the people outside at the top of his voice, telling them that the prisoners were being tortured and slaughtered. But ten days later when the Revolution erupted and aid finally arrived, the Bastille only seemed to hold four forgers, two lunatics and one sexual deviant, who was *not* Donatien Alphonse François, better known as the Marquis de Sade. He had been transferred, naked, kicking and screaming to a lunatics' asylum at Charenton. He left behind the manuscript of *The Hundred and Twenty Days of Sodom*, "The most impure tale ever written since the world began", as he deemed it to be.

While until the French Revolution erotic and pornographic literature functioned to expose the aristocracy's or the Church's pudenda, once the craving for Eros was replaced by a desire for Thanatos, and the Jacobins' Reign of Terror drenched the streets of Paris with blood, it was no longer the time for frivolous flirtation but for nihilism and anarchy. Sade's work does not direct itself only at the old, irrelevant foes – the orders of state and Church – but against any order as such, opening a door to the realm of chaos in which pleasure and pain are one and the same and the body is simultaneously a tool of destruction and an object to be destroyed. For Sade, women are not equal partners and their voices are inaudible except for when they shout out in pain or cry for help. Nothing of Fanny's cheerfulness remains, nor Thérèse's curiosity, nor indeed these ladies' relative autonomy over their bodies. This state of being is what led the sexologist and psychiatrist Richard von Krafft-Ebing to name the sexual perversion defined as deriving pleasure from causing pain to another after the marquis.

But while the men in Sade's writings enjoy enslaving, humiliating and physically and emotionally punishing women, the other writer who entered Krafft-Ebing's dictionary of sexual pathologies was Leopold von Sacher-Masoch, who was active a century after Sade and described the sexual gratification derived from the experience of pain and the pleasure of total surrender. The protagonist of Sacher-Masoch's novel *Venus in Furs*, published in 1870, seeks to be enslaved and punished by the cruel woman he admires. The book was to a considerable extent based on his own life and on the regime his mistress Fanny von Pistor imposed on their relationship.

The gothic novel of the late eighteenth century merged the sensual sensibility with romantic sentiment. To allow for the suspension of disbelief and for prudence's sake, it relegated its sensational plot to exotic provinces like the Pyrenees and the

Howling at the moon (Man in the Moon, page 115).

Unlike Sade and Cleland, who spent their days in prison indulging in erotic fantasies, there were those who took advantage of their time behind bars to dream of ancient aliens (We Come in Peace, page 123) or kings of old (King of Cups, page 153).

De Sade believed his magnum opus had been lost forever. Having had little warning that he was to be moved, the Marquis hid the 12m-long (36ft) and 11cm-wide (4in) scroll, inscribed on both sides in tiny handwriting, behind some loose bricks in the wall of his cell and asked his long-suffering wife to retrieve it. But it was too late. Revolution had broken out. He claimed he wept *larmes de sang* (tears of blood) over its loss. He went to his grave without knowing that the manuscript was found, kept hidden, sold and eventually published in 1904, escaping the fate that befell many works lost forever (Flame and Moth, page 17).

And sexy Catholics reign supreme (Fear Itself, page 237).

Byron himself was an infamous seducer of women. His questionable morality caused Westminster Abbey to deny him burial there. He was laid to rest in the Church of St Mary Magdalene, only to have his coffin opened, like that of a vampire (Blood Lust, page 93) in 1938 by the Reverend Canon Barber who wanted to make sure that the illustrious dead poet in the crypt was indeed Byron. His body, it was reported, was preserved in excellent condition, revealing the fact that the deceased was prodigiously endowed (The Body Electric, page 221).

Apennines, where Radcliffe situated *The Mysteries of Udolpho* in 1794, or to Italy, where the blood is warm.

The famous fictional libertine and seducer of women, Lord Byron's philandering *Don Juan* (1819–1824), hails from Spain. The poem was "taboo from the first", writes Ernest Hartley Coleridge in his 1903 introduction to the work. "The earlier issues of the first five cantos were doubly anonymous. Neither author nor publisher subscribed their names on the title page. The book was a monster, and, as its maker had foreseen, 'all the world' shuddered."[11]

But by the nineteenth century things began to change. Although, like Wilkes, Byron used his satirical epic to take a thinly veiled swing at some of the notables of his time, including a stab at poet laureate Robert Southey, and despite Wordsworth announcing in 1820, "I am convinced that Don Juan will do more harm to the English character, than anything of our time",[12] the inexplicit escapades of Don Juan and his lovers pale by comparison to those of his predecessors, though the poetry is sublime. And for Byron's contemporaries, sublime was what it was all about. The Romantic movement sought to infuse lust with feeling, thus elevating pleasure to the heights of ecstatic and aesthetic exhilaration. And while its male poets won critical acclaim, it was the female authors of the day who won hearts.

From the trio of Eliza Haywood, Delarivier Manley and Aphra Behn, dubbed "The fair triumvirate of wit", who dominated the literary milieu of the eighteenth century and the bestselling author of the nineteenth century, Marie Corelli, whose book *Murder of Delicia* sold 52,000 copies in its first year of publication; to Elizabeth Gaskell, the female answer to Charles Dickens, and Harriet Beecher Stowe, the woman who, according to Lincoln, wrote the book that started the great Civil War; to the Gothic author Ann Radcliffe, one of the most popular writers of her time, women began taking their narratives into their own hands.

And then it was time to assert dominion over the body. Following centuries of erotic educational stories written by men pretending to speak for women, in 1954 a book that sent shockwaves through France's bourgeoisie was published – *Story of O*. Its protagonist seems to have stepped out of Sade's tales. A woman is taken by her lover to an isolated castle, where she is chastised, sexually dominated, humiliated, branded, exploited and in every possible manner turned into an object of desire for the castle's residents. O has no name, her entire being is reduced to a gaping hole suggested by the symbol that represents her, and from the book's publication it has continued to generate heated debate. There are those who feel that the text – like Sade's work – humiliates and devalues women, and others who think that the heroine's ready and willing subjection, the conscious control she retains even when dominated and her consent to everything done to and with her, is tantamount to a declaration of women's liberation from men's oppression. The story lends a voice to its protagonist even though she is forbidden to speak, but many years passed before the book's author claimed hers. The pseudonym of Pauline Réage sparked much speculation and some believed only a man could have written such an obscene text about control over a helpless woman. But when the secret was exposed, 40 years after the book's first publication and four years before the death of its author Anne Desclos, it confirmed what was largely known to the seventeenth- and eighteenth-century authors of erotic literature and later confirmed by modern studies – that women have sexual fantasies matching, if not outdoing, men's in both variety and intensity, and that domination often plays an important role in their erotic fantasies. As the feminist debate flared up and opinions about prostitution and pornography polarized in the early 1980s, different types of women authors appropriated the genre of erotic writing, which had been men's exclusive domain for centuries.

One way into feminine fantasy, chosen by two of the most prominent new women authors of erotic works, was through collective fantasy or folklore with all its pent-up aggression. Angela Carter, who wrote *The Sadeian Woman and the Ideology of Pornography*, published *The Bloody Chamber* in 1979, a collection of stories full of dark sexuality based on fairy tales like "Beauty and the Beast", "Snow White" and "Sleeping Beauty". Anne Rice, who wrote *Interview with the Vampire*, took the implied necrophilia – of the prince kissing the princess' cold lips – one step further. In her extremely explicit quartet, which was published under a pseudonym, the heroine wakes from sleep only after her virginity has been taken and endures a series of painstakingly detailed and graphic agonies in the company of three captive princes. "I wanted to create a book where you didn't have to mark the hot pages,"[13] Rice explained when in the 1990s she eventually

Which may have been based on a real story (The Human Animal, page 189).

A creature whose sexuality had been an integral part of his allure since the nineteenth century (Blood Lust, page 93).

identified herself as the writer of *The Claiming of Sleeping Beauty*. At the end, as always in a fairy tale, they lived happily ever after.

Erotic literature lived alongside romantic literature until eventually the two genres began to rub up against each other. The one was looking for physical pleasure and passion, and the other was intent on finding love and marriage. And when they finally went to bed, they begat a new genre dominated by women. Extremely successful and turning over huge sales revenues, romance novels are second only – and by a small margin – to thrillers. With annual sales of over a billion dollars in the US alone (as of 2013) the genre occupied about a fifth of the entire publishing trade.

The internet opened up the new horizon of "retelling": fan fiction, and especially amateur erotica or as it is better known, "slash porn". This was the breeding ground for the enormously popular phenomenon, *Fifty Shades of Grey*. E L James' book almost singlehandedly launched a new genre of its own: the BDSM romance, the vanilla version of *Story of O*, suburban sadomasochism that good women may safely enjoy without having to worry they will end up like poor Emma Bovary after leafing through Sade's *Justine; or the Misfortunes of Virtue*.

For reading erotic literature has always come with a degree of risk, if not to the reader, then to the social order and its beneficiaries. From the wild, liminal cultural territory it has taken over, it mounts an assault on the mainstream. At its best this genre is equally occupied with undergarments and undermining, seeking not to subserve but to subvert. The majority of the genre's output may perpetuate patriarchal positions and reaffirm gender power relations, but there are those who use it to infiltrate the status quo and circulate alternative approaches to sexuality, to feed the erotic imagination stimulating simulations that free desire from morality and conventions.

26
VALLEY OF THE DOLLS

One year before he died, René Descartes accepted an invitation from Christina, Queen of Sweden, to be her personal tutor. He boarded a ship sailing for Stockholm, taking along a young woman whom he introduced as his daughter, Francine. Since no one saw her again throughout the voyage, the rugged sailors strong on superstitions grew so suspicious that they broke into the famous philosopher's cabin to see her with their own eyes. What they found was a full-size doll, made of leather and metal, who looked so much like a real girl that they took fright and threw it overboard. Anthony Ferguson, who recounts this anecdote in *The Sex Doll: A History* admits its apocryphal nature, but Descartes was well known for the automata he made and even though he never married, he did have a daughter. Her name was Francine and she had passed away aged five, nine years before this incident. There's no way of knowing what this man of reason planned to do with his doll, but the sailors who dumped it into the sea were familiar with at least one use. The French called dolls of this kind *dames de voyage* (travel ladies). In the seventeenth century, the age of great exploration when vessels capable of crossing oceans undertook ever more ambitious journeys, seafarers would take along an early specimen – a "speci-woman" – of our latter-day inflatable doll. It was a contraption in the shape of a human female, put together from cloth wound around a bamboo frame and wearing a dress, ready to gratify the sailors' lusts. Seamen from the Low Countries produced the same type of dolls from cane covered with leather. In the course of their trade negotiations with the Japanese empire in the eighteenth century, they left some of these dolls behind and along with them the notion of the "Dutch wives", which became a byword for low-grade sex dolls. But the mythic and poetic origins of these artificial wives go back much further. According to Ovid's *Metamorphoses* the relationship between the Cypriot sculptor Pygmalion and Galatea, the perfect female he carved from ivory, was far from platonic. Having lost hope in his perennially disappointing relations with women:

The first were designed and produced by a god (Ex Machina, page 213).

So ambitious in fact that sometimes they defied belief (The Territory and the Map, page 47).

Compared to the other transformations recorded in this work, a sculpture that comes to life is relatively benign (The Human Animal, page 189).

"Pygmalion loathing their lascivious life,
Abhorr'd all womankind, but most a wife:"
he decided to make his own helpmeet.
"And carv'd in iv'ry such a maid, so fair,
As Nature could not with his art compare ...
He knows 'tis madness, yet he must adore,
And still the more he knows it, loves the more:
The flesh, or what so seems, he touches oft,
Which feels so smooth, that he believes it soft.
Fir'd with this thought, at once he strain'd the breast,
And on the lips a burning kiss impress'd."

And when Venus, answering his plea, breathes life into the sculpture, Pygmalion "kisses her white lips, renews the bliss,
And looks, and thinks they redden at the kiss;
He thought them warm before: nor longer stays,
But next his hand on her hard bosom lays:
Hard as it was, beginning to relent,
It seem'd, the breast beneath his fingers bent."[1]

But not everybody can count on divine intervention, and technology can come in handy. The protagonist of E T A Hoffman's story "The Sandman" is a young student, Nathanael, who is hounded by the memory of his father's violent death at the hands of a man he calls the Sandman, a legendary figure who gouges out children's eyes. Nathanael encounters Olympia, the daughter of his teacher, "A very tall and slender lady, extremely well-proportioned and most splendidly attired ... there was something fixed about her eyes as if, I might almost say, she had no power of sight. It seemed to me that she was sleeping with her eyes open." Nathanael, whose melancholic artistic tendencies are not appreciated by his fiancée Clara, falls head over heels in love with Olympia. "He sat by Olympia with her hand in his and, in a high state of inspiration, told her his passion, in words which neither he nor Olympia understood. Yet perhaps she did; for she looked steadfastly into his face and sighed several times, 'Ah, ah!' Upon this, Nathanael said, 'Oh splendid, heavenly lady! Ray from the promised land of love – deep soul in whom all my being is reflected!'" Siegmund, his friend, tries to understand what is so attractive about this silent woman, "How a sensible fellow like you could possibly lose your head over that wax face, over that

As befitting a romantic soul (Fear Itself, page 237).

wooden doll ... Her pace is strangely regular, every movement seems to depend on some wound-up clockwork." Olympia scares him and Nathanael's other friends: "We find your Olympia quite uncanny, and prefer to have nothing to do with her," he tells him. Nathanael is infuriated, but it turns out his friend was right. Nathanael witnesses Olympia's "father" Professor Spallanzani and Coppola, a dealer in optical apparatus whom Nathanael recognizes as Coppelius, the Sandman from his childhood, fighting over her and sees her fall apart in their hands, revealing herself as "a lifeless doll".[2]

Hoffmann, an outstanding representative of German Romantic literature, and a product of the *Sturm und Drang* movement, published "The Sandman" in 1816. In 1870 Léo Delibes composed the music for *Coppélia*, a comic ballet with libretto by Charles-Louis-Etienne Nuitter, which was loosely based on "The Sandman", and in 1881 Jacques Offenbach wrote the opera *The Tales of Hoffmann*, also based on this story and two other texts by Hoffmann. The author himself, who died in 1822 from the syphilis he contracted in his youth, never saw this *Gesamtkunstwerk*. The German psychiatrist Ernst Jentsch referred to "The Sandman" in a short article he published in 1906: "Zur Psychologie des Unheimlichen" – or "On the Psychology of the Uncanny". The *unheimlich* – literally "un-homelike" – or the uncanny, refers to the way in which something familiar and recognizable may come to appear or to be experienced as unfamiliar and unrecognizable. The notion points at the anxiety we feel, for example, when we "doubt as to whether an apparently living being really is animate and, conversely, doubt as to whether a lifeless object may not in fact be animate".[3] Inspired by Jentsch, Freud further probed this feeling, also in its relation to Hoffmann's tale, which he virtually took to pieces in the process, leading to his famous article "The Uncanny". He argued that it is not Olympia the doll who is responsible for arousing Nathanael's anxiety, but the recurring mentions of Sandman's quest for gouged-out eyes that litter the story, embodying the Oedipus complex and the castration anxiety it is associated with. And this is what interferes with Nathanael's ability to have a full and healthy relationship with a real, flesh and blood woman like Clara; it is also what sends him into the mechanical arms of Olympia, who is a perfect object of desire, an immaculate reflection, a smooth screen onto

This is the source of some of our fear of the living dead (Head Hunters, page 231).

Of the kind vampires don't have (Blood Lust, page 93).

207

which Nathanael can project his desires without having to fear rejection, refusal or castration.

Eager entrepreneurs had already found a bolder and less circuitous approach than psychoanalysis to deal with castration anxiety. A French catalogue from 1904 boasts dolls for which there is "no fear of blackmail, jealousy, argument, or disease."[4] Iwan Bloch, in his 1908 book *The Sexual Life of Our Time* elaborates on these "fornication dolls" made by "clever mechanics who, from rubber and other plastic materials, prepare entire male or female bodies," with genital organs "represented in a manner true to nature. Even the secretion of Bartholin's glands is imitated, by means of a 'pneumatic tube' filled with oil."[5] We don't know whether the puppet ordered by the Czech-Austrian writer and artist Oskar Kokoschka in 1915 was equipped with all these novelties, but unlike with Alma Mahler, widow of the famous composer and Kokoschka's capricious lover, there were no angry discussions and jealous scenes with the puppet. He ordered the doll to be shaped like Alma, and he went so far as having her clothes – all the different layers including her underwear – made by Mahler's own dressmaker. He took the doll to the opera (did they attend *The Tales of Hoffmann?*) and for rides in his carriage. Her end, though, was like Olympia's. She was decapitated and destroyed in the course of a drunken brawl. Freud might have been aware of the scandal, and if so, perhaps thought of it while writing his article. After all, he did treat Mahler, who was trying to cope with his wife's extra-marital relations. Someone who definitely knew about Kokoschka's doll and was inspired by it was the German Surrealist Hans Bellmer. Like Kokoschka, Bellmer opposed the rising force of Nazism, both in his daily life and in his art. Disturbing, erotic, broken and somehow put together again, these dolls, which he began to make in 1933, were shaped by this resistance, as their distorted form was a mockery of the Aryan worship of the perfect body. They were also influenced by an (apparently unconsummated) attraction to his 15-year-old cousin.

Anthony Ferguson considers Bellmer the father of the modern inflatable doll. "The uncanny, eroticized models created by Bellmer in the 1930s differed from the functional sex doll only in that they lacked the necessary orifices for penetration,"[6] he explained. The evolution of these orifices took off in earnest after World War II. There are claims that it was Hitler who instigated

You could just as well live in a utopia (Best of All Possible Worlds, page 247).

Who literally wrote the book on the Marquis de Sade (The Pleasure Principle, page 195).

the production of these dolls, in an attempt to offer the Aryan soldier an alternative method for sexual release avoiding real-life encounters with inferior races, but these claims are unreliable. Unreliability was also the problem with the early vinyl inflatables: they were of inferior quality and tended to explode or otherwise deflate upon more vigorous use. Finally, a durable dummy for sexual gratification became possible with the introduction of latex and silicone.

In Hitler's utopia, as in many other dictatorships, the sex drive was a problem to be solved (Best of All Possible Worlds, page 247).

Like the vampiric Jews (Blood Lust, page 93).

The dedicated effort to develop sex dolls that are simulacra of men's fantasies of the ever available, obedient, amply endowed, smooth-skinned, young and immortal female represents the total objectification of women, and pornography is as usual in the forefront. The porn industry rushes to incorporate, adapt and prostitute any technological advance, dragging the "real doll" industry into a kind of "Pygmalion project" aiming for the perfect product. In addition to moving autonomously, this doll will register and react to motion, and open its mouth over and beyond the more obvious uses, to produce words, creating a convincing effect of life and even of will. There are those, here and now, who spend their sexual and emotional life in the company of such puppets, treating them way beyond mere sexual appliances, as objects of love and devotion. David Levy, artificial intelligence scholar and author of *Love and Sex with Robots*, believes that "there are millions of people in this world, who for one reason or another cannot make good relationships themselves with other human beings … I think when they've got the option of having relationships with very sophisticated robots, that will for many of them fill a big void in their lives and make them much happier."[7]

One of these millions was David Mills, the happy owner of a sex doll, who states that "I truly like women; however I don't prefer to associate with people."[8] Still, his first encounter with his doll was traumatic. He opened the box, his heart pounding, tore the plastic cover, and … screamed in terror. The scaringly realistic doll was staring at him with dead and glassy eyes. Mills' doll was made by RealDoll, a company conceived by an art student called Matt McMullen and produced by the engineers of his suggestively named company – Abyss.

According to novelist Ann Radcliffe, "Terror expands the soul, and awakens the faculties to a high degree of life"[a] (Fear Itself, page 237).

But what McMullen and his competitors must somehow cross in their effort to make the perfect sex-bot, is not an abyss but rather a valley – the so-called "uncanny valley". In the 1970s, when pornographic technologies were limited to film, Japanese computer science professor Masahiro Mori was developing a hypothesis about how, on contact with near-perfect human simulacra, we tend to have an uncanny experience of the kind that made Mills scream at the sight of his sex doll's vacant look, or what Siegmund, Nathanael's friend, registered in Olympia's presence. Mori argued that when a robot is nothing at all like a human, we have no difficulty interacting with it and when it is a perfect imitation, the same applies. But anything in between triggers the sensation Jentsch described in his article and which Hoffmann captured in "The Sandman" – a dread of something that is neither dead nor alive. It is precisely this threatening sense of alienation, this distorted strangeness that experts in the fields of robotics, computer animation and artificial intelligence are trying so hard to overcome on their way to the holy grail of their profession, which in 1950 Alan Turing defined as an artificial mechanism that will be able to make us believe it's alive. These days, unlike in Turing's times, it seems that a series of printed replies will not convince us of a computer's "humanity". It must also come wrapped in an equally persuasive voice and body. Still, a female sex-bot may have it easier passing Turing's test – all it takes is for it to spread its legs.

Will it fall to sex dolls to serve as the bridge over uncanny valley? Or will they be the embodiment of the abyss? Is it easier to set aside our revulsion at their pseudo-human shape because they serve a sexual purpose? This might be true – for at least half of humanity. The fact that the majority of sex dolls come in the form of hypersexualized females intended for men – marketed for men and acquired by men – is not just a reflection of women's different biology and psychology, and the different ways they achieve sexual satisfaction and release, but is also a result of the way they react to the uncanny. Research into gender bias regarding the integration of androids into the human sphere indicated that women were more sensitive to uncanny phenomena, responded more negatively to them and were both quicker and more apt at identifying artificial human features. These differences have yet to be studied and explained, but they – like the phenomenon of the uncanny valley – are likely to have archaic biological roots. Claude Draude, head of an interdisciplinary, international work group of gender/diversity in informatics systems at Kassel University, believes that the reason might be to do with how we

This is the source of some of our fear of vampires (Blood Lust, page 93).

Which, according to legend, can also bestow eternal life, like those potentially enjoyed by artificial beings (King of Cups, page 153).

He called this test "The Imitation Game", after a popular parlour game (Ex Machina, page 213).

As expressed by countless romance novels (The Pleasure Principle, page 195).

Like the fact women have an easier time at identifying snakes during the luteal stage of their ovulation cycle (Here Be Dragons, page 79).

define the uncanny. She wonders whether, since the home is commonly perceived as the cultural-sociological female domain par excellence, the "un-homelike" which threatens the very existence of that home, is antithetical to the feminine.

These same gender differences are reflected, too, in the way popular culture represents intimate relations with sex dolls or robots. Whether we are looking at drama or romantic comedy like *Lars and the Real Girl* or *Her*; the weird Japanese porn "inflatable doll"; the film noir *Blade Runner*; *Westworld*'s western; *The Stepford Wives* horror; or the parody of *Austin Powers* – the sex doll is always well endowed with female sex features, like protruding breasts and a velvety voice, or has a traditional female role like that of the perfect housewife, the dedicated housekeeper, the French maid or the damsel in distress. Most of these imaginary relations are with men – in love with, yearning for, exploiting or dominating ersatz figures of femininity. Male sex-robots are a lot rarer to come by, and in contrast with their wanton sisters, they flaunt their moral clout. Isaac Asimov's *The Naked Sun* has a male robot who has sex with his owner out of compunction, because hurting her feelings would be in breach of one of the three laws of robotics. The Android officer Data in *Star Trek: The Next Generation* uses sex with his comrade in arms Tasha Yar as a way to discover new worlds of human emotion.

Isaac Asimov created the three laws due to an aversion to plots in which human thirst for knowledge causes robots to "turn stupidly on [their] creator for no purpose but to demonstrate, for one more weary time, the crime and punishment of Faust."[b] (A Faustian Bargain, page 1). But the bigger sin was that of Victor Frankenstein (The Body Electric, page 221).

"By around 2050," predicts David Levy in his book, "robots will be hugely attractive to humans."[9] But until this happens, if ever it does, the real dolls provoke enthusiastic support on the one hand and ethical and moral questions on the other. Admirers consider them an answer to a range of sexual and emotional maladies and discomforts, like those expressed by the growing and troubling incel (an abbreviation of "involuntary celibate") online subculture whose members define themselves as unable to obtain a romantic partner or sustain a sexual relationship; and a solution – as one sex-doll manufacturer explained – for residents of homes for the elderly, the disabled and so on. The faithful preach that an army of advanced, sensual female robots will take care of prostitution, sex trafficking, rape and even paedophilia. Opponents, at the same time, believe that their existence and growing popularity will unleash an even more intense objectification of women's minds and bodies, encourage increased detachment and alienation between the genders and inspire dangerous levels of escapism.

They regard those who support this rise of the sex machines as capitulating to a whole bunch of paraphilias, from necrophilia and somnophilia (being aroused by having sex with, respectively, the dead or the sleeping), to agalmatophilia (a special proclivity for sculptures). But then there are those who simply admit to being "robosexuals", claiming that their preference inflicts no damage on either women or men. They achieve release in the embrace of technology.

Like Sleeping Beauty (The Pleasure Principle, page 195).

The cautionary tale of Hoffmann's "The Sandman" is more relevant now than ever. Even though Nathanael appears to get over losing Olympia upon discovering her true nature and manages to return to Clara and resume his old life, the reverberations of his trauma eventually take him to the brink of insanity and death. Infatuation with what is neither alive nor dead will always be sterile, one-sided and partial, and once the object of desire manifests itself in its full, artificial splendour, the resulting loneliness is more ferocious and forbidding than ever. The price of giving in to anxiety – of castration, intimacy, the relationship, the gaze (and blindness) of the other – together with turning away from the human-all-too-human such anxiety involves, is the loss of self.

27

EX MACHINA

In the beginning humans brought god forth out of the machine. There was chaos on stage. But at the end of Euripides' play, a chariot appeared, drawn by dragons – an automaton, some believe, powered by steam – dragging along Medea, who had murdered her children. The *deus ex machina* was only one of the dramatic concepts developed by this great Greek playwright, along with the "prologue", which is still in use to this very day. However, from the moment the automaton first surfaced in Greek tragedy, the dramatic ploy of using it met with much animosity. In his play *Women at the Festival* Aristophanes mocked Euripides by making him seem to pop out of one of his own much-beloved machines in the final act. And Aristotle hated the sudden appearance of a supreme (or infernal) force that resolves the intricacies of plot in a way that doesn't flow naturally: "Within the action there must be nothing irrational. If the irrational cannot be excluded, it should be outside the scope of the tragedy."[1]

The very first automata – Greek for "able to move of their own accord" – were the animated creations of a god, Hephaestus, the lame blacksmith. In his *Iliad*, Homer describes "Golden handmaids also who worked for him, and were like real young women, with sense and reason, voice also and strength, and all the learning of the immortals."[2] Automatons were made to entertain the masses as well, like Heron of Alexandria's mechanical puppet theatre, which worked on the basis of a primitive computer system consisting of ropes and knots. Sometimes they came to entertain the aristocracy, as in the case of the medieval programmable band of the prolific Ismail al-Jazari, who constructed a boat with two drummers, a harpist and a flautist that floated on a lake for the pleasure and delight of illustrious guests at royal drinking parties. Through the centuries notable automatons have included Da Vinci's Magnetic Knight, Jacques de Vaucanson's Digesting Duck and Baron Wolfgang von Kempelen's chess-player, The Turk. Following a century of wins over international celebrities like Napoleon Bonaparte (he was a tireless cheat), The Turk turned out

According to literature, only a few are deserving enough to ride on their backs (Here Be Dragons, page 79).

Achievements the porn and computing industries can only dream of (Valley of the Dolls, page 205).

Who also invented a drinks dispenser – as did Johannes Kepler (We Come in Peace, page 123).

to be a clever sham; instead of an automaton, it was a contraption operated by a chess master hiding inside. For decades The Turk astonished and confused astute observers. Many of them – for example, Edgar Allen Poe – were sure there was a person hiding in the machine but couldn't figure how and where. The Turk became an icon of popular culture and has since featured in guest roles in literature and science fiction series like *Doctor Who* and *Terminator: The Sarah Connor Chronicles*, which features software named "The Turk" that evolves into the artificial intelligence network "Skynet" and subsequently aims to destroy humanity.

Automatons were generally met with ambivalence, and this is illustrated in the ancient Chinese legend about King Mu of Zhou, who was presented with a young man made out of fabric, paper and lacquer who could sing, move and even wink at the ladies of the court. In a fury, "the king tried the effect of taking away the heart, and found that the mouth could no longer speak; he took away the liver and the eyes could no longer see; he took away the kidneys and the legs lost their power of locomotion. The king was delighted."[3] What was it about these human-like creatures? Were they mechanical gods? Programmed servants? Entertainment machines? Or something a lot more baffling, close to life itself, an imitation whose power, beauty and skills outdid its origin?

"The life-sized machines that perform complicated tasks, blow trumpets, dance and so forth, very easily give one a feeling of unease,"[4] wrote Ernst Jentsch in his article "On the Psychology of the Uncanny" (1906), and Sigmund Freud, following him in 1919 wrote about the "singularly stiff and soulless",[5] mechanical doll Olympia, in E T A Hoffmann's "The Sandman", swirling in the arms of the unfortunate Nathanael.

Had Freud waited another year before publishing the article he might have included a reference to a new play by the Czech writer Karel Čapek, which was all the rage in the capitals of Europe. *R U R* introduced the world to automatons' direct descendants and christened them with a name that has stuck to them ever since: "robot". Čapek's brother came up with the word "robota" which means "serf labour" in the Czech language, to denote Karel's synthesized and artificial creatures that looked frighteningly like humans. According to the play's plot, they are produced in a factory, and they revolt against their makers. In their manifesto, which calls all robots of the world to unite, these humanoid slaves "proclaim

Who knew well how to use the tools of pure logic (*Fear Itself*, page 237).

Like the babies in Aldous Huxley's *Brave New World* (*Best of All Possible Worlds*, page 247).

man our enemy, and an outlaw in the universe", adding: "Robots throughout the world, we command you to kill all mankind. Spare no man. Spare no woman. ... Then return to work. Work must not be stopped."[6]

Above the heads of Čapek's unbridled robots hovered the spirit of a mystical automaton, which – according to modern folklore – was created in the city where Čapek lived and died, a few months before the Nazis marched into Prague. Čapek, due to his pacifist views, was on their hit list even before they invaded, and since the rumour of his death did not reach them, they mistakenly arrested his brother, Joseph. He finally died in Bergen-Belsen, in 1945, a few days before the end of the war in which millions of the people who created that famous automaton, the Golem, lost their lives.

Formed of clay or earth, endowed with super-human strength but devoid of free will or consciousness, the Golem could be animated in one of two ways (don't try this at home): by inserting a piece of paper containing one of God's names into its mouth or by etching the Hebrew word *emet* – "truth" – onto its forehead. To switch it off, you just remove the piece of paper or strike out the first letter, thus changing the inscription to *met*, Hebrew for "dead".

It is said that Solomon ibn Gabirol, the Andalusian philosopher and poet of the twelfth century, created a golem housekeeper. Thirteenth-century German Kabbalist Eleazer of Worms left a mystical text giving detailed instructions on how to create a golem, and a fifteenth-century manuscript tells of the creation of a beautiful and silent female golem, made for love. But the most famous golem of all was allegedly and apocryphally vitalized by Rabbi Judah Loew of Prague in the sixteenth century.

It was, as it is so often, the best and worst of times. It was an age of immense scientific discoveries: it was the season of starlight, of Galileo, Kepler, Brahe; and the epoch of great art: of Michelangelo, Cervantes, Shakespeare and da Vinci. It was also the age of ferocious witch trials, a season of religious wars, an epoch of blood libel.

The latter was what prompted the Jewish need for a strong protector. After all, it was the century that saw the establishment of the first ghetto. According to legend, the rise of anti-Semitism throughout Europe brought Rabbi Loew to create a golem that would defend his community against attacks. The Golem fulfilled its tasks, from collecting firewood to clubbing aggressors – and as

Today we would define him as "robosexual" (Valley of the Dolls, page 205).

One of the inspirations for Milton's Satan (Number of the Beast, page 79).

The writer of one of the earliest works of science fiction, *Somnium* (Man in the Moon, page 115).

Who may have provided inspiration for the tragedy of Hamlet, Prince of Denmark (We Come in Peace, page 123).

Who also wrote his lost play during that period (Flame and Moth, page 17).

Most of which took place in Europe (Weird Sisterhood, page 25).

Accusations of using the blood of Christians in Jewish ceremonies had far-reaching consequences (Blood Lust, page 93).

befits a Jewish automaton, rested on the Sabbath – but it all went awry when the rabbi lost control over his creation. The Golem ran amok and had to be deactivated, then to be laid to rest in the attic of Prague's Old–New Synagogue, where supposedly it continues to rest to this day.

One of the earliest horror movies ever made is the 1920 silent German Expressionist film *Der Golem, wie er in die Welt kam,* (*The Golem: How He Came into the World*). Based on a novel of the same name by Gustav Meyrink and published in 1915, it expresses the primal German fear of Jews and their mystical powers. These fears and fascinations come to the fore in Michael Chabon's *The Amazing Adventures of Kavalier & Clay*. In the novel, Joe Kavalier escapes the Nazi occupation of Czechoslovakia that took Joseph Čapek's life by hiding in a coffin with the inert body of the Golem, which was smuggled out of the country so it would not fall into the hands of Nazi occultists. He later became one of America's most prominent comic book artists. The cover art of the novel portrays "The Escapist", Kavalier & Clay's superhero, punching Adolf Hitler and referencing Captain America's first issue, which showed him doing just that a year before his country joined the war. Fulfilling the wishes of its Jewish creators, Jack Kirby (born Jacob Kurzberg) and Joe Simon (born Hymie Simon), Captain America battled anti-Semitism both at home and on the front lines, thus following in the shuffling footsteps of the Golem, which can be read as a precursor of the modern superhero.

However, in the 2018 film *The Golem*, which was the first cinematic adaptation of the story since 1951, the Golem is created by a woman, a bereaved mother who seeks to protect her community from destruction. This golem is not a hulking and powerful figure of a man or a vaguely humanoid lump of clay, but a child. This choice highlights another threatening and seldom mentioned experience reflected with all automatons: parental anxiety. This is expressed in horror works like *Rosemary's Baby*, which lay bare our fears for, and also of, those we created – our offspring.

Čapek's play sparked the imagination of many contemporaries including George Bernard Shaw and C K Chesterton. But the vision Čapek held out resonated with every humanmade monster that ever turned on its maker, from the automata the mythological craftsman Daedalus constructed and about whom Plato recounts that they had to be restrained from going wild, all the way to

Something Victor Frankenstein also tried to tackle (The Body Electric, page 221).

Rumour has it that during World War II, and as part of the Reich's mystical treasure hunt, a Nazi official died under suspicious circumstances after entering the synagogue's attic (Twilight of the Gods, page 65).

There were quite a few superheroes who volunteered for the mission (No Man's Island, page 57).

After finishing the Minotaur's prison labyrinth (A Rat in a Maze, page 147).

Victor Frankenstein's murderous and heartrending monster. The underlying, common terrors were the fear of the human potential to arouse slumbering technological giants that might lead to the end of humanity itself; the shudder every slave inspires in their owner with the realization that the Other is far more like us than we would like to believe; and the deep psychological dread of the uncanny, the near-human, whose likeness might expose our strangeness to ourselves.

Masahiro Mori, who laid out the topology of "the uncanny valley", draws a distinction between the humanoid robot – the android – and the one that is clearly mechanical and does not pretend to evoke the human shape. The humanoid robot awakens our archaic fear of death, which is communicated through the robot's un-living body and a deep concern of being replaced by more successful and improved copies of ourselves, our offspring and our mortality reflected in them. This apprehension is wonderfully conveyed in Ray Bradbury's story "Marionettes Inc." and is the origin of a whole panoply of psychological, biological, hormonal, religious and ethical anxieties that we suffer.

The magic spell that will defuse these fears and subdue the mechanical slaves was invented by an outspoken critic of *R U R*: "Čapek's play is, in my own opinion, a terribly bad one," wrote Isaac Asimov, not exactly known for his gentle approach, "but it is immortal for that one word. It contributed the word 'robot' not only to the English but, through English, to all the languages in which science fiction is now written."[7] In order to make sure these slaves would not revolt against their masters, Asimov, one of the founding fathers of science fiction, elaborated the three laws of robotics, a marvel of psycho-robotic conditioning:

1. A robot may not injure a human being or, through inaction, allow a human being to come to harm.
2. A robot must obey the orders given it by human beings except where such orders would conflict with the First Law.
3. A robot must protect its own existence as long as such protection does not conflict with the First or Second Law.

This also holds when the robot in question is expected to supply sexual services (Valley of the Dolls, page 205).

Most of Asimov's stories about robots deal with interpretations and possible infringements of these laws. For observing them first of all requires understanding hard-to-define notions such as "human", "robot" and "harm". This led Jack Williamson to develop the "humanoids" using Asimov's laws. In his book robots take this logic to its extreme, protecting humankind from anything that might possibly harm them, including sadness and loss, heartbreak and misery and, ineluctably, people themselves.

However, not all authors in the genre were willing to take Asimov's laws on board, hence not all their writings are shaped by them. In the sinister world Philip K Dick created, androids are made to do humans' dirty work in space colonies, from mining to prostitution, "Either as body servants or tireless field hands, the custom-tailored humanoid robot [is] designed specifically for YOUR UNIQUE NEEDS, FOR YOU AND YOU ALONE – given to you on your arrival absolutely free." But things can go wrong, and the "loyal, trouble-free companions"[8] rise up against their enslavers. The hero of Dick's classic *Do Androids Dream of Electric Sheep?* is a member of a special police force organized to stop these machines, which can be told apart from real humans only by their inability to feel empathy. This human quality that they lack is measured by means of the "Voight-Kampff" test.

In 2010, Amy Harmon, a *New York Times* reporter, interviewed Bina48, a female android who was designed to look like and have the memories of Bina Rothblatt, wife of trans entrepreneur Martine Rothblatt. With a nod toward Dick, one of the first questions Harmon asked Bina48 was "Do androids dream?" The android paused and her rubber face, which was programmed to display 64 expressions, appeared puzzled, and then she replied, "Sure. But it's so chaotic and strange that it just seems like noise to me."[9] Harmon's interview served as a kind of Turing test aimed at distinguishing between a thinking person and a calculating machine, and Bina48 didn't pass. In 2017, in another interview, software called "Eugene" managed to convince 33 per cent of the scientists who had a five-minute conversation with it, that they had been talking to a 13-year-old Ukrainian boy.

In 1950, Alan Turing, the man who laid the foundations for modern computer science and was a genius code breaker and persecuted homosexual, published an article entitled "The Imitation Game", after a popular party game. The original game "is played with three people, a man (A), a woman (B) and an interrogator (C) who may be of either sex. The interrogator stays in a room apart from the other two. The object of the game for the

Terraforming is hard work (We Come in Peace, page 123).

interrogator is to determine which of the other two is the man and which is the woman."[10]

What would happen, Turing wondered in his article, if the man would be replaced by a computer. Would the interrogator be able to identify he was not facing a person but an artificial intelligence?

But Turing's test poses more fundamental questions. Is it possible to replace a human with a computer? Is it possible to design and program a computer that is not only "human" but also "masculine", so as to deceive the interrogator? Turing's hypothetical proposal, written years before the first computer was built, examines not only the complexity of the computer but the humanity of the interrogator. This is a test that not only the computer but also its creator must pass, and it focuses on our early expectations and assumptions about what we perceive as "man" and "woman", "human" and "machine".

What would happen if "Eugene" was situated inside the body of a 13-year-old boy who looks like an actual boy in every possible way, a cybernetic Pinocchio capable of expressions of human feeling? This is what Brian Aldiss' short and sad story "Supertoys Last All Summer Long", and Steven Spielberg's film "AI" are about. Both look at the world through the eyes of a machine and find humans wanting. It is humankind itself that fails the empathy test, because while androids dream of love, humans will, maybe forever, consider them mere electric sheep, mechanisms that can be switched on and off according to our physical or emotional needs.

Whether the androids are out to annihilate humanity – as they are in the *Terminator* films and the TV series *Battlestar Galactica* – or in a search for personal freedom, as in Ridley Scott's *Bladerunner*, the postmodern film noir made on the basis of Philip K Dick's above-mentioned novel, they all point a finger in our direction.

When these mechanical sheep show their unwillingness to go obediently to their own slaughter, they face us with a terrifying vision of permanent revolution in which the means of production rises up against the producer, the agents of hubris whom the ancient Greek playwrights described so well – violent gods rising up against us from the machines we made ourselves.

28

THE BODY ELECTRIC

Just a bit before four in the afternoon, on a cold Saturday early in December 1803, Mrs Foster left her home, taking along her young daughter. They were never seen alive again. After three days of searching, their bodies were found in Paddington Canal. The husband was led before the judges at the Old Bailey and claimed innocence. All evidence was circumstantial and, even though some people reported that his wife had shown suicidal tendencies and had more than once expressed her wish to die together with her little girl, the court sentenced Foster to death by hanging. In the days leading up to his execution, Foster recanted and confessed to the killing. He stopped eating and grew so weak that the prison guards had to support him on his way to the gallows: he was wearing the same brown coat and red waistcoat he had been sentenced in. The officer at Newgate prison, who documented the event, observed that Foster was a "decent looking young man," and added, "he died very easy."[1]

This ease, however, did not last long.

Foster's lifeless body was cut free from the rope and taken to a nearby building, where Giovanni Aldini was ready to hook it up to an electric current. With the cables in place "the jaws of the deceased criminal began to quiver, and the adjoining muscles were horribly contorted, and one eye was actually opened ... The right hand was raised and clenched, and the legs and thighs were set in motion." The sight was so gruesome that the beadle, a Mr Pass, "was so alarmed that he died of fright soon after his return home," the newspaper reported and "some of the uninformed bystanders thought that the wretched man was on the eve of being restored to life."[2]

For his experiment Aldini employed one of the earliest versions of the battery – a container in which zinc and copper plates were stacked alternatingly. Ironically, the inventor of this device was Alessandro Volta, the rival (and friend) of Luigi Galvani, who happened to be Aldini's uncle and was known among his fellow Bolognese as "the frog's dancing master". Apparently by a fluke, in the autumn of 1786 Galvani made the legs of a dead frog move when he inadvertently touched it with a metal scalpel that had picked up an electric charge. He believed he had discovered the animal electricity stored by the body. Volta, on the other hand, thought that the electricity was released through a chemical reaction between metals. Younger and better connected, Volta gained the patronage of Napoleon Bonaparte and Galvani had to resort to dispatching his young nephew to drum up supporters for his method.

Not everybody was blown away by Aldini's experiment. The media described it as "prostitution of galvanism". Aldini himself, though, was adamant that what he was doing was not "only employed to cause sudden gestures, and to convulse the remains of human bodies; as a mechanic deceives the common people by moving an automaton by the aid of springs and other contrivances",[3] but to find out how to use electricity to transfer the spark of life to a dead body. However, the sensational press reports helped turn his demonstrations into the latest fad. The crown prince offered patronage and the crème de la crème from all over the world, including the French ambassador, the Ottoman consul and the British aristocracy, flocked to witness these events where Aldini made a dog's severed head wag its tongue. The watchdogs of democracy, in response, stuck out theirs – as the following ode by Thomas G Fessenden, writing under the pseudonym Dr Christopher Caustic, illustrates:

> Not only mechanics toyed with such automatons, but also playwrights (Ex Machina, page 213).

> "For he ('tis told in public papers),
> Can make dead people cut droll capers,
> And shuffling off death's iron trammels,
> To kick and hop like dancing camels.
> To raise a dead dog he was able,
> Though laid in quarters on a table,
> And led him, yelping, round the town,
> With two legs up, and two legs down.
> And this most comical magician
> Will soon in public exhibition,
> Perform a feat he's often boasted,
> And animate a dead pig-roasted.
> With powers of these metallic tractors,
> He can revive dead malefactors;
> And is re-animating daily,
> Rogues that were hung once, at Old Bailey!"[4]

For some, though, galvanism was much more than some macabre parlour game. Charles Wilkinson, author of *Elements of Galvanism*, who assisted Aldini in his experiments, was one of those who considered it "an energising principle, which forms the line of distinction between matter and spirit, constituting in the great chain of the creation, the intervening link between corporeal substance and the essence of vitality".[5] For them, the discussion of (and dabbling with) these invisible forces, involved the divine and innate forces of nature. Vitalism, one of the most important strains in the philosophical–scientific discourse of the eighteenth century, sought to determine how we tell the difference between what is alive and what isn't. What is there in the living body that there isn't in the dead one? For the chemical contents and mass are identical. Whatever it is, where does it come from? Benjamin Franklin, of the famed experiment with the kite, argued that electricity might be God's way of contacting the world – lightning communicates His word, crossing the chasm between mind and matter, with the spark passing between the one and the other.

Here's a tip. If it tries to drink your blood (Blood Lust, page 93) or to eat your brain (Head Hunters, page 231) – it isn't.

There was another god who used thunder (Twilight of the Gods, page 65).

Such a momentous phenomenon with such far-reaching implications could not possibly be the object of scientific study alone. In this era of miracles and wonders, when human reason began to lift nature's veil of mystery by discovering its deepest secrets, codes and terrors, science itself was an amalgam of philosophy, politics, theology and poetry. If you wanted to be a scientist you had to be a poet too – and if you wanted to be a poet, you had to be something of a scientist. Vitalism, at this point in time, wasn't just the province of electrochemists like Humphry Davy or William Nicholson who were among the discoverers of electrolysis, but was also the realm of naturalists like Erasmus Darwin, who put down his innovative thinking about the origins of life, which had a great impact on his grandson Charles, in rhyme in a long poem called *The Loves of the Plants*. From the correspondence between Davy and the major Romantic poet Samuel Taylor Coleridge, we can observe the great interest the poet had in galvanism. Nicholson and Davy liked to spend time in the company of the radical political power couple of the late eighteenth century: the anarchist philosopher William Godwin and his wife, the proto-feminist and author of *A Vindication of the Rights of Women*, Mary Wollstonecraft.

Which awarded him entry into the *Index Librorum Prohibitorum* (Ex Libris, page 9).

They were brilliant, sharp-witted and well matched. Their relationship was burning bright but their love, which unfolded in mind and matter simultaneously, was short-lived. Only ten days after giving birth to their daughter – ten days during which Mary hemorrhaged from the torn placenta caused by the physician who delivered the infant, and got septicemia – she died. To his friend Thomas Holcroft, a heartbroken Godwin wrote, "I firmly believe there does not exist her equal in the world. I know from experience we were formed to make each other happy. I have not the least expectation that I can now ever know happiness again,"[6] and he gave the baby girl the name of the beloved mother.

Fifteen years later Mary Godwin was visiting her mother's grave when she met a man sitting there, writing poetry. He was six years her senior, an acolyte of her father and his wife was carrying their second child. His name was Percy Bysshe Shelley. It was in many ways a perfect fit. A gifted and well-educated young woman, the offspring of the loving union between two of the greatest intellectuals of their time, and a talented, passionate and poetic young man, a free spirit and member of the hottest literary set in the country. Godwin did not think so. Mary's loving father disowned her and broke his ties with Shelley, who abandoned his pregnant wife and son to be with Mary. The two eloped to Europe but had to return to England when they ran out of money and Mary found herself pregnant. She gave birth to a daughter two months prematurely, when she herself was 18 years old. "Nurse the baby, read," she wrote in her diary, every day, over the course of ten days. Until, on the eleventh day, "I awoke in the night to give it suck it appeared to be sleeping so quietly that I would not awake it." But the baby girl never woke again. "Find my baby dead," she noted down in the morning. Mary, her breasts swollen and painfully infected, her sleep fitful, fell into a profound depression. "Dream that my little baby came to life again; that it had only been cold, and that we rubbed it before the fire, and it lived," she wrote in her diary, "awake and find no baby."[7]

A year later Mary had a son, William, and after a few months they travelled abroad for a holiday, which they spent together with Shelley's friend George Gordon, Lord Byron, who was also the lover of Claire Clairmont, Mary's step-sister from her father's second marriage. His famous and infamous lordship was at that time staying at Villa Diodati on Lake Geneva in the company of his private physician, Dr John William Polidori. Bright young things that they were, they did what bright young things do: they read, wrote, debated and made love. As for the latter: mainly Byron with Claire. Back in England they were called the "League of Incest" but two of them would eventually become the most prominent of the Romantic poets, and two gained fame as the progenitors of phantoms.

It was a cold stormy summer. A year earlier, a volcano on one of Indonesia's islands erupted, causing 92,000 deaths and filling the atmosphere with huge quantities of volcanic ash. The effects were felt far beyond the archipelago. It was the coldest year since the fifteenth century and extreme climate changes were felt on a global scale. Black clouds blotted out the sun, farmlands suffered a cold spell leading to lost harvests; there were snowstorms in June and hail in July. It was 1816, "the year without summer", and the guests stayed put at the villa, whiling their time away with parlour games. Taking his clue from a collection of German supernatural horror stories, Byron decided to stage a competition in which each of them had to write a scary story. Mary was worried, "'Have you thought of a story?' I was asked each morning, and each morning I was forced to reply with a mortifying negative." One evening the conversation reached the subject of vitalism. Mary, who at the time was reading *Elements of Chemical Philosophy* by Davy, her father's friend, recorded in her diary, "Perhaps a corpse would be re-animated. Galvanism had given token of such things; perhaps the component parts for a creature might be manufactured, brought together, and endued with vital warmth." It was past midnight, but she couldn't sleep. Then she had a kind of vision, in which she saw "the pale student ... kneeling beside the thing he had put together. I saw the hideous phantasm of a man stretched out, and then, on the working of some powerful engine, show signs of life and stir with an uneasy, half-vital motion. Frightful must it be, for supremely frightful would be the effect of any human endeavour to mock the stupendous mechanism of the Creator of the world."[8] Mary won the competition.

A motion that surely puts him inside the "uncanny valley" (Valley of the Dolls, page 205).

Shelley didn't come up with anything, Byron kept himself busy scribbling a "Fragment of a Novel" which he never completed, and Polidori, taking his inspiration from his disreputable patient, worked hard at a novella he called *The Vampyre*. Mary Shelley's *Frankenstein; or, the Modern Prometheus*, was published in 1818.

Which he never intended to publish (Blood Lust, page 93).

Even though the book doesn't mention electricity in any direct way, for Mary Shelley's contemporaries immersed in the jerking limbs of an executed murderer, dancing dead frogs and chopped off, lolling dogs' heads, Frankenstein's story didn't stray all that far from reality. "It was on a dready night of November that I beheld the accomplishment of my toils," recounts Victor Frankenstein, the student, "I collected the instruments of life around me, that I might infuse a spark of being into the lifeless thing that lay at my feet." He goes on with a description that could easily have been taken from a newspaper report about Aldini's experiments, 15 years earlier, "I saw the dull yellow eye of the creature open; it breathed hard, and a convulsive motion agitated its limbs."[9]

Shelley's book wasn't merely meant as a cautionary tale about the dangers of science, a romantic narrative of creation, death and obsession, and a sophisticated epistolary work. In addition to all that, it was a family novel.

A form that was very popular in the eighteenth and nineteenth centuries, and gave a seal of authenticity to two of the most fantastical genres (The Pleasure Principle, page 195; Fear Itself, page 237.).

Before her husband's premature death, Mary had already lost three out of four children and endured a miscarriage that resulted in such heavy bleeding that Shelley had to get her to sit on a block of ice to stem it. She thoroughly understood how death could lead to the creation of life. She was haunted by her cold, dead babies and her mother who had died so shortly after giving birth to her. "You, my creator, detest and spurn me, thy creature, to whom thou art bound by ties only dissoluble by the annihilation of one of us," says the monster to Frankenstein, and Mary to her deceased mother. "Have I not suffered enough, that you seek to increase my misery?" the creature asks the man who created him, and Mary lashes out at the father who blamed her for her mother's death, "Remember that I am thy creature; I ought to be thy Adam, but I am rather the fallen angel, whom thou drivest from joy for no misdeed."[10] The

The Prodigal Son (Number of the Beast, page 79).

monster that Mary dug up from the howling depths of her soul – the true hero of the story – is nameless. Moreover, Mary published the book anonymously, abandoning her given name, the one that belonged to her mother; and forsaking her last name, the one that belonged to her estranged father; even forfeiting Shelley's name though by then they were already married. Both the creator and her creation have no names of their own.

From the moment *Frankenstein* was published, it occupied a place of growing importance in a culture that was becoming more and more modern (the word *Modern* was an integral part of its title) and more and more anxious. For socialists, it represented the revolt of workers against their masters; for psychoanalysts it

As Karl Ĉapek admirably summarizes it (Ex Machina, page 213).

presented a new Oedipus, a story of the son seeking to destroy his father; for theologians, an atheist parable about Lucifer's struggle against God; feminists saw it as a story about an unnatural pregnancy – a man who seeks to take away women's singular ability to produce life; for scientists it was a novel about humankind's terror of the mighty natural forces it had just begun to harness, its fears that these forces might escape our control and take control over us; and finally, it questioned progress, in the form of two of the formative archetypes of the industrial and mechanized era: the monster made by humans and the mad scientist.

There are much more direct and brutal ways to achieve this goal (Best of All Possible Worlds, page 247).

Which may haunt his descendants for many generations to come (Remember to Forget, page 139).

Unsurprisingly, electricity gave Frankenstein's monster not just life, but immortality. What the doctor tried to achieve in his laboratory, cinema managed to do on the screen. The first motion picture starring Frankenstein was shown to a terrified audience in 1910, and it was filmed by the wizard of Menlo Park, the inventor of the electric light bulb, and one of the founders of the art of cinema – Thomas Alva Edison. Like all the other characters in this silent film, the monster was mute, but once the "talkies" began he remained voiceless, unlike the others. While Mary Shelley's Frankenstein was an articulate autodidact whose reading list included the Romantics' all-time top ten, such as John Milton's *Paradise Lost* and Goethe's *The Sorrows of Young Werther*, as well as Ovid's *Metamorphoses* and Plutarch's *Lives*, he was replaced by a coarse lumbering hulk only capable of grunts, the part Boris Karloff enacted in the 1931 version, with his square haircut and the signal bolt sticking halfway out of his neck.

If Mary Shelley was this creature's mother, then surely cinema was its father – an abusive one, however, who humiliated his son, made him deformed and robbed him of his dignity, intelligence and voice. Still, the film industry also gave him a bride, as well as a broad and flourishing social circle that included Dracula, Abbott and Costello and others. Hammer, the production company known for its taste for monster trash, produced many Frankenstein-based horror movies, and the grotesque creature also inspired comic musicals like *The Rocky Horror Show*, or parodies like Mel Brooks' *Young Frankenstein*. However, it wasn't Bobby Pickett's "Monster Mash" that caused Mary Shelley's creature to rise to its iconic and terrifying stature. Nor the hundreds of articles proffering analysis of the science behind the novel, or of the circumstances in which it was written. From *The Stress of Her Regard,* Tim Powers' secret history of the mythic and mystical events that formed the background to the writing competition from which modern fantasy and science fiction took off, to Ken Russell's *Gothic* about the League of Incest's debauchery, many have tried to unearth the dark secret of Villa Diodati during that "wet ungenial summer",[11] as Mary Shelley described it, and to make sense of the terror this staggering monster evokes.

Mary Shelley remained the last keeper of that secret. In the same year that *Frankenstein* was published, Fanny, her half-sister, committed suicide; and in 1816 Harriet, Shelley's abandoned wife, took her own life too, as did Polidori in 1821. Byron fell ill and died in Greece in 1824. His heart was removed, interred under a tree in Missolonghi and later sent to England to be buried with the rest of his body. Shelley himself drowned in 1822. Due to quarantine regulations he had to be cremated on the shore at the site of the accident, but his heart resisted the flames (contemporary scholarship attributes this fact to possible calcification of the organ due to tuberculosis). His friend Edward Trelawny removed Shelley's heart, which was eventually given to Mary who carried it with her in a box until the day she died. In 1852, a year after her death, it was found in her desk wrapped in the pages of "Adonais", one of its previous owner's last poems. The heart was eventually laid to rest with the body of their son Percy Florence Shelley when he died in 1889.

"The last relic of a beloved race," is how Mary referred to herself, "my companions, extinct before me."[12] Lionel Verney, the protagonist of *The Last Man*, the book she published eight years after *Frankenstein*, suffers the same fate. The novel takes place in the late twenty-first century, a future in which climate disasters together with an epidemic join to destroy all of humanity except for Verney himself.

Frankenstein scares us not only because of the monsters we might create and unleash, but also because of the monsters we may become if we cross the lines of morality, if we make light of our responsibility, if we allow ourselves to be guided by hubris. This is the warning engraved deep in the novel's genome. The most striking manifestation of this is the fact (critics already remarked on it as early as 1908) that many tend to confuse the names of maker and monster. If we read the novel from the "familial" perspective, that is not so strange. Victor is the "father" and progenitor of the creature, and so it is only reasonable for the two of them to share the same family name. Danny Boyle's stage version of the novel capitalized on this monstrous aspect of both main characters, by swapping the roles of Frankenstein and the monster every night between the two leading actors. The TV series *Penny Dreadful* suggests a similar idea when its version of the monstrous creature reverts to being the educated, troubled, miserable and merciless one of Mary Shelley's original text. But if knowledge is knowing Frankenstein isn't the monster, then wisdom is knowing Frankenstein is the monster. Frankenstein's repulsion at and rejection of the living being he's brought into the world turns him into a monster. Turns them both into monsters. Their punishment is to lose everyone they loved or wanted to love. The loneliness of the creature and its creator lost on the icy plains, the loneliness that is awaiting all of us, is the final horror Mary Shelley holds out to us. It is a horror she knew all too well.

29
HEAD HUNTERS

On the evening of 18 May 2011, the server of the CDC – the US Centers for Disease Control and Prevention – crashed, as tens of thousands of citizens were trying to get information about a new life-threatening catastrophe: the zombie apocalypse. "Plan your evacuation route," the experts advised, "When zombies are hungry, they won't stop until they get food (i.e. brains), which means you need to get out of town fast!"[1]

Given its usual weekly rate of visits of around 2,000, the site couldn't cope with 30,000 in the space of only a few hours and had to shut down. But not for long. Like any zombie worth its name, it quickly returned to life to give useful advice to anyone preparing for the dawn of the living dead. The advice came under the heading "Preparedness 101" and it was an instant internet sensation. "Preparedness" was consciously and amusingly applying the image of the zombie in order to provide vital public information about what to do in cases of humanmade emergency or natural disaster.

The zombies themselves, it is fair to assume, remained indifferent: they were made to be used, just like the slaves who were instrumental in creating the religion that allowed their very existence – Vodou.

The Santo Domingo slave corrals in the eighteenth century were darker than death or night. Half of the slaves – members of various African tribes – died of fatigue, hunger and exposure within a few years of forced labour to gratify their masters' insatiable appetite for sugar. This created a constant craving for fresh bodies. Perhaps it's not surprising then that the horrifying possibility of everlasting toil, even after death, arose within Vodou.

The Vodou religion was born out of both physical and metaphysical distress, for the white man never settled for the body if the soul too could be possessed. And so, the slaves were forced to abandon their heathen ways to embrace the charitable faith that justified the superiority of their enslavers – Christianity – and incorporated Catholic elements that served to camouflage

One of whom somehow made her way to a small town in Massachusetts, Salem (Weird Sisterhood, page 25).

The word became synonymous with any wild, puzzling and scary religious practice (A Rat in a Maze, page 147).

The slaves revolted in 1801, much like their mechanized representations (Ex Machina, page 213).

the rituals worshippers had brought with them from West Africa. Vodou's supreme creator, Bondyé (from the French, *bon dieu*) refrains from mundane interventions on behalf of his suffering faithful. It is the *Lwa*, the spirits, who are responsible for human lives, and any intercourse between humans and them requires the mediation of the great Papa Legba. Some spirits are benevolent, others not so. The Bokor or Vodou sorcerer invokes these spirits. He may, if he wants, put an evil spell on the dead body, which then is resurrected but devoid of free will; now it must serve the one who raised it from the grave. This enslaved, resurrected body is called a zombie, and the fear it initially engendered did not arise from the possibility of the zombie coming for you but of you becoming one.

Black magic in general, and zombies in particular, were never an important component of Vodou. The modern zombie is a hybrid that is the outcome of a collusion between ancient beliefs and modern technology – moving pictures. Its first cinematic portrayals were directly linked to its slavery heritage. The first zombie movie, *White Zombie*, was a 1932 horror film starring Bela Lugosi, fresh from the grave of Dracula, whom he portrayed a year earlier. The script, set in a sugarcane plantation in Haiti, tells the story of a man who longs for another's fiancée and agrees to allow a Vodou master to turn her into a zombie so he can have her. It ends badly for all involved. The salient details were based on the book credited with the popularization of the word "zombie" in the English-speaking world, *The Magic Island*, published in 1929.

Its author, William Seabrook, was an American occultist, explorer, journalist and, at least once in his life, cannibal. Seabrook, who had a keen interest in Haitian Vodou, had this to say about the apparition: "while the zombie came from the grave, it was neither a ghost, nor yet a person raised like Lazarus from the dead. The zombie is ... endowed by sorcery with a mechanical semblance of life ... People who have the power to do this go to a fresh grave, dig up the body before it has had time to rot, galvanize it into movement, and then make of it a servant or slave ... setting it dull heavy tasks, and beating it like a dumb beast if it slackens."[2]

The 1943 horror film *I Walked with a Zombie*, based on an article of the same title by Inez Wallace, draws its inspiration from Charlotte Brontë's Victorian masterpiece *Jane Eyre* while echoing the slavery narrative by placing the plot in a sugarcane plantation, but this time located on the Caribbean island of Saint Sebastian

In an authorized adaptation of Bram Stoker's novel (Blood Lust, page 93).

And an acquaintance of Aleister Crowley (King of Cups, page 153).

It is not the only monster driven by Galvanism (The Body Electric, page 221).

where the madwoman in the attic turns out to be the owner's zombie wife.

In spite of a plethora of truly bizarre B-movies, from zombie-wielding Nazis in the 1943 *Revenge of the Zombies*, to alien zombies in Ed Wood's 1957 so-bad-it's-good cult movie *Plan 9 from Outer Space*, zombies had to wait until the Swinging Sixties to get their grave groove. It was in horror director George A Romero's infamous 1968 *Night of the Living Dead* that the creature we recognize as a zombie (Romero referred to it as a "ghoul") took its first slow, uncertain and terrifying steps. Here, for the first time, the menacing Other was not a mad Nazi scientist or a mindless, murderous slave, but ourselves, our neighbours and children. The movie tapped into the growing sense of civil unrest and paranoia that swept the United States against the backdrop of the mounting resistance to the US military presence in Vietnam. The fact that the last man standing, the only surviving member of the group that barricaded itself in a remote farmhouse for fear of the living dead, was the one played by African-American actor Duane Jones, and that he was shot by an armed posse who considered him to be a threat, seemed especially poignant in light of Reverend Martin Luther King's assassination earlier that year.

"[Romero] bred the zombie with the vampire," writes James Twitchell in *Dreadful Pleasures: An Anatomy of Modern Horror*, "and what he got was the hybrid vigour of a ghoulish plague monster."[3]

And indeed, the roots of the terror zombies arouse in us can be traced back to a medieval cautionary tale, which emerged in the wake of the apocalyptic shadow cast by the Black Death, immortalized on church frescoes all across Europe. In *The Three Living and the Three Dead*, a poem of that period, three kings encounter three walking corpses, maggot-infested and worm-eaten, adorned with crowns. "Such shall you be," the dead warn the living. The zombie is a memento mori who shuffles in our direction, his hands held out before him, threatening to grab us. It is a horrifying reminder of what awaits us in the dust to which we will return. Maybe his slow pace allows us to get out of the zombie's way, but never for long because death always catches up with us, whether snatched by the rotting teeth of the living dead or by the grinding jaws of time.

Romero's films spawned a whole genre, and the cinematic zombie developed into something more sophisticated. Horror

After linking them to any other type of occult activity (No Man's Island, page 57).

Our sworn and constant enemy, in all its guises (Fear Itself, page 237).

Like the one that fuelled the alien conspiracy (We Come in Peace, page 123).

Which led to a belief that Satan was the ruler of the world (Number of the Beast, page 79).

films in the 1980s improved the typical, rather simple zombie diet of human flesh, which evolved into a more delicate dish of human brains. After years of having been respectfully dumped into the twilight zone of culture's nightmares, zombies are now on the verge of global domination of the mainstream. Works featuring zombies have been proliferating over the past decades, spreading like an epidemic: computer games (*The Enemy Within* and its diverse follow-ups); parodies (*Shaun of the Dead*); post-apocalyptic horror (*28 Days Later*); rom-coms (*Warm Bodies*); war movies (*World War Z*); TV series (*The Walking Dead*, *The Santa Clarita Diet*); literary gestures (*Pride, Prejudice and Zombies*); and more.

This is true, at least, for the period following its fashionable makeover of the nineteenth century (Blood Lust, page 93).

This particular mode of death in the midst of life lacks the glamour and intimate seduction of the vampire. No refined sip of blood, no smooth and slender throats of yielding virgins in flowing satin robes, no faint Transylvanian lilt. If the vampire is also Eros, then the zombie is only Thanatos, death at its most abject. In their current shape zombies consort with the taboo on cannibalism and this turns them into the ideal threat to our civilization. Zombies are the mindless, maddened masses coming literally to devour us; they are pure unadulterated consumption run amok.

It is no coincidence that the zombie aims for the brain, the seat of sound reason, because it seeks to ruin human judgment. And victory is ensured. Each victim is a potential recruit, a soldier in the predatory swarm of former humans who have transformed into humanity's absolute antithesis. For the dead shall always, always outnumber the living.

Echoes of this can be found even in the world's oldest written narrative, *The Epic of Gilgamesh*. After rudely rejecting the advances of the goddess Ishtar, the offended deity asks her father, Anu, god of the heavens, to help her secure Gilgamesh's downfall, or else:

"I will knock down the Gates of the Netherworld …
and will let the dead go up to eat the living!"[4]

Who maintains his wits at least part of the time (Lupus Est, page 93).

Unlike other monsters in the West, as the aforementioned vampire, the werewolf and other Others, the zombie is a cultural immigrant. He does not exist in folk tales, he has no canonical literary work to his name like Bram Stoker's *Dracula* or a great artist who will tell us his story in compelling prose, as Mary Shelley did for *Frankenstein*. The lack of this established tradition enabled the lightning-fast evolution of the zombies from remote-controlled slaves (a cautionary tale for colonials), through genetic experiments gone awry (a lesson in human hubris), to plague bringers (a reminder of nature's supreme powers), and they continue to adapt in order to survive. This ever-mutating monster is the *poltergeist* of the *zeitgeist*, a ghost that haunts the spirit of the times. Zombies are the poster boys of global panic in the 2000s, the awful embodiment of what is dead and buried but returns to feast on the flesh of the world's most glutted nations.

30
FEAR ITSELF

On an autumnal morning in 2000, Captain James Miclon peeped through the filthy window of Bryan Smith's mobile home. His brother had not heard from him for the past three days. Smith was dead on his bed, apparently after taking an overdose of painkillers. It was 21 September. And by creepy coincidence it was also the 53th birthday of the man whom Smith had hit with his car a year earlier. When one of the dogs in the backseat went wild and distracted Smith, his car ran into a pedestrian, who was walking deep in thought on the roadside. The pedestrian was severely injured: one lung was punctured; his pelvis and four ribs were broken; his spine and skull were cracked; and his right leg was crushed and barely saved from amputation.

Smith was charged with dangerous driving, his licence was revoked and his mental state went into rapid decline. Smith's lawyers argued that he could hardly expect a fair trial in a town where the ballpark, the ambulance service and the public library had all been largely provided by the man he almost ran over. The generous benefactor he had hit was author Stephen King, emperor of horror, king of fear, the most successful American writer in the world with more than 50 books and almost 200 short stories to his name.

King's father had given him his first whiff of the addictive drug of fear. One day he left home, mumbling, "Just going to get some cigarettes", never to return, leaving his wife behind to deal with their two sons. King was two years old. Seven years later, when rummaging in the loft through some of his disappeared father's things he found a tattered paperback, on whose cover a yellow-eyed monster peeped out from under a tombstone. It was a collection of stories by H P Lovecraft from the early twentieth century.

"Lovecraft ... opened the way for me," writes King, "as he had done for others before me ... it is his shadow, so long and gaunt, and his eyes, so dark and puritanical, which overlie almost all of the important horror fiction that has come since."[1] Like

Don't blame
it on the moonlight
(Man in the Moon,
page 115).

It was probably
similar to the one in
which Charles Conan
Doyle ended his life.
His son also became
one of the founders
of a new genre (Paper
Fairies, page 161).

Which is also
what Christopher
Robin's mother liked
to do (Paradise Lost,
page 171).

Whose
uncanny visions were
frightening in their
own right (Valley of
the Dolls, page 205).

Author of one
of the most influential
fantasy books of the
twentieth century
(Paper Fairies,
page 161).

Unlike other
authors Lovecraft
did not believe in
self-censorship and
a re-examination of
his works reveals his
demonstrable racism
(Flame and Moth,
page 17).

him, Howard Philips Lovecraft was fated to grow up fatherless. He was born in August 1890 in Providence, Rhode Island, and he was only one year older than King when his father vanished into a lunatic asylum after a psychotic episode brought on after contracting syphilis. He died there five years later. Howard stayed under his unstable mother's tender care: "His mother did tell him that he was 'grotesque' and that he should not go out at daytime for fear of scaring the neighbours,"[2] writes R Alain Everts in his essay "Howard Phillips Lovecraft and Sex: or The Sex Life of a Gentleman". She preferred to let him grow his hair, made him wear dresses and spoke to and about him in the feminine rather than do something about his frequent nightmares. Lovecraft spent the next years in the loft reading anything he could lay his hands on, for example the *Iliad* and the *Odyssey*, works by E T A Hoffmann and Lord Dunsany, and more. He had a severe mental breakdown aged 18, which prevented him from graduating from high school and subsequently taking up academic studies. Instead, he retreated ever further into his inner world and, inspired by his prodigious reading, started to write and slowly build up an entire pantheon, including a complex hierarchy of gods of atrocity and decay – the product of his own seething mind.

Probably prey to almost every known type of phobia (including, for example, a fear of water, animals, women, crowds and darkness), Lovecraft inserted descriptions of vague anxieties into his many stories, creating exceptionally extreme sensations of fear, his depictions of psychotic, man-eating and child-molesting ghouls often prompting the journals that accepted his stories to cut and mercilessly censure them. After his mother ended her life in the same institution his father had died in, Lovecraft married Sonia Green, a Jewish woman who accepted his suit in spite of his anti-Semitism and "although both were not enthusiastic in any sexual sense of the word, both were able to sustain satisfying sexual relations,"[3] writes Everts. But their marriage did not last very long and after their separation Lovecraft returned to New England where he lived until his death in 1937, finally fulfilling his mother's prophecy and scaring the neighbours.

In the last decade of his life, Lovecraft developed the narrative cycle of Cthulhu, which brought him long-awaited recognition and a lasting ghoulish glory. Cthulhu is a monstrous octopus-like god who dwells deep below the seas, an evil muse for poets in the grip of madness and terror-crazed authors to whom he sent nightmares, which they then reproduced in their writings. In the Cthulhu stories, like in many of Lovecraft's other works, the central theme is the dangerous nature of knowledge. For Lovecraft, curiosity killed not only the cat – man's deeply ingrained drive for knowledge roused archaic, dark forces from their slumbers.

The same thirst that drove Faust to make a pact with the Devil (Number of the Beast, page 79).

His complex cosmology projects humankind as an insignificant speck in a vast universe abuzz with horrors beyond human understanding. Here the earth is, at best, a toy in the hands of malevolent forces and in a worst-case scenario, a meaningless crumb. Humans' efforts to grasp what is beyond them to gain control of their fate always results in death, atrocity and insanity. "The most merciful thing in the world, I think, is the inability of the human mind to correlate all its contents," he wrote in "The Call of Cthulhu". "We live on a placid island of ignorance in the midst of black seas of infinity, and it was not meant that we should voyage far."[4]

Lovecraft, a contemporary of Jung and Freud, was entranced by the broad expanses of the unconscious and by the Jungian notion of the collective unconscious and the symbolic system of the archetypes. Later in life, as he developed his cosmology, which became increasingly based in archeology, mysticism, anthropology and simple paranoia about the paranormal, Lovecraft began to believe that many of his texts were based on glimpses into the hidden worlds surrounding us. In his huge correspondence (close to 100,000 letters), he encouraged other authors to creatively venture into the universes he constructed and to go on developing his mythologies. Even in his lifetime a sect of believers emerged who considered the pseudo-sources he referenced, like the *Necronomicon*, to be authentic existing writings revealing all that is hidden. Theosophists and Cabalists referred to the etymology of his monsters and their characteristics as signs and portents of creatures that existed before humankind. They compared Cthulhu to Yam, the Lord of the Seas in the Judaeo-Christian mythologies inherited from the Canaanite pantheon and crowned him the prophet who managed to see behind the veil into the true order of things.

And thus gave his permission to an early form of fanfiction (The Pleasure Principle, page 195).

Which is usually referred to as a sea serpent or a dragon, or both (Here Be Dragons, page 79).

A particularly extreme version of the mad scientist archetype (The Body Electric, page 221).

The film industry made much use of his work for horror films and B movies based on the stories like "Herbert West – Reanimator". Death metal bands used texts taken from his books and one psychedelic band simply called itself "H P Lovecraft".

During his lifetime, his stories were published only in magazines and failed to make it into the literary mainstream or even into fiction of the genre. Nowadays some of the greatest artists in these genres owe him their respectful dues – from H R Geiger to Stephen King, from William S Burroughs to Neil Gaiman. Lovecraft's ability to create nightmarish worlds from anything that came his way, while consistently keeping the image of terror deliberately obscure is what made him one of the most original, terrifying and fascinating authors in the field. "The oldest and strongest emotion of humankind is fear," he wrote in one of his articles, "and the oldest and strongest kind of fear is fear of the unknown."[5]

Whose lost books are safely preserved in the library of everything (Ex Libris, page 9).

Dread, of course, had always lingered in the recesses of the human mind, whether it is in the ghost stories of the first century written by Tacitus, or the Roman historian and his friend, Pliny the Younger. The latter established some of the genre's key elements, like the ones in the story he tells of the philosopher Athenodorus Cananites, who was surprised by the low price asked for a house he wished to buy. But being a stoic, he went ahead and paid. Late at night, as he laboured over his writings, the spirit of an old man bound in chains appeared before him. The ghost beckoned him to follow, pointed at a spot in the yard and disappeared. Athenodorus began to dig, unearthing the skeleton of a chained man. He gave it a proper burial, and the spirit did not return to visit him or the house he had obtained at a bargain price.

In other folkloric traditions improper burial leads to the creation of vampires (Blood Lust, page 93).

Who liked to make sure the punishment fitted the crime (Moving Heaven and Hell, page 71).

Terror is also abundant in the visions of their fourteenth-century compatriot Dante, and it might have been the spirit of these ancients that inhabited the British writer Horace Walpole who, in 1764, wrote the first Gothic novel *The Castle of Otranto*, situating the action in the secret, dusty and haunted passages of a half-ruined Italian castle, and whose origins he attributes to a Latin manuscript of a thirteenth-century monk. The protagonist of Matthew Gregory Lewis' 1796 scandalous novel *The Monk* is a clergyman who sells his soul to the Devil, has sex with witches and gets entangled in a plot involving violent murder, incest and all manner of dire straits, all taking place in Spain. The imagination of Ann Radcliffe, his great contemporary bestseller writer, took

Clergymen were very popular in the erotic literature of those days (The Pleasure Principle, page 195).

her all the way to the Pyrenees and the Apennines as the backdrop to the excrescences of *The Mysteries of Udolpho*, which she published in 1794. Jane Austen stabbed Radcliffe's books with her sharp pen in *Northanger Abbey*, whose title mocked her contemporaries' fashionable penchant for intangible intrigues, walking dead and picturesque ruins.

But it would take a while until actual zombies emigrated to the West (Head Hunters, page 231).

It was Radcliffe too, who suggested a basic typology of terrors in one of the first steps toward a theory of the genre. Terror or dread is a sense of anxiety of what is to come, while horror is the nausea and repulsion that the event itself arouses. "Terror", writes Radcliffe, "expands the soul, and awakens the faculties to a high degree of life", while horror "freezes, and nearly annihilates them".[6] The Romantics longed for this awakening of the faculties. For them, supernatural horror offered an experience beyond mere shudders, giving them access to the transcendent, summoning a powerful reverence or the "numinous", as Rudolf Otto, the scholar of religions called it in *The Idea of the Holy*. This is the fear and trepidation instilled by the sublime. The sense of the numinous, which precedes and exceeds the rational, is the awesome sense of facing "a great God, mighty and a terrible",[7] a bolt of lightning in his fist, irate and wrathful, as depicted in the Bible as well as in many mythologies and religions. The *numen* is the absolute Other who exceeds the limits of the human, an alien who cannot be known. The numinous arouses the *mysterium tremendum* (the tremendous mystery) in us. The authors of British Gothic novels had ample reason to locate their narratives in the dramatic, foreign scenery of Europe and the ritual spaces of its monasteries. This allowed them to create a simultaneous experience of alienation on both the physical and the religious levels, taking the reader out of the quiet verdant landscapes of their home, from Protestant aridity into the sublime mystery of the towering mountains, ancient castles and the juicier rites of Catholicism.

In the 1960s our piercing fear of aliens gained an iconic form (We Come in Peace, page 123).

But it was not only British writers who were drawn to these locales. Influenced by Walpole's *The Castle of Otranto*, Edgar Allan Poe placed Prince Prospero, the protagonist of his story "The Masque of the Red Death", in a fortified abbey where he and his guests seek refuge from the raging plague outside, like the characters of Boccaccio's *Decameron*. But there is no escape, "Darkness and Decay and the Red Death held illimitable dominion over all."[8] Darkness and decay awaited Poe as well. On 3 October 1849, a Baltimore printer by the name of Joseph W Walker sent the following urgent note to Dr Joseph E Snodgrass, "Dear Sir, There is a gentleman, rather the worse for wear, at Ryan's 4th ward polls, who goes under the cognomen of Edgar A Poe, and who appears in great distress, & he says he is acquainted with you, and I assure you, he is in need of immediate assistance."[9]

When the doctor finally arrived, he found the gothic poet, the father of detective fiction and the master of metaphysical horror, with his hair filthy, his face dirty and his clothes tattered. His eyes were glazed and he was hallucinating. Poe had been on his way to New York a week earlier. No one knows how he got to Baltimore or what he did during that lost week. He died four days later. Possible causes of his condition include alcohol poisoning, rabies, meningitis, syphilis, epilepsy, a suicide bid and even attempted murder. The true cause of death remains unknown to this day, a mystery that marks the end of this enigmatic writer's life.

One possible source of the vampire myth (Blood Lust, page 93).

Poe was buried in a simple wooden casket. Only eight people were in the procession and the funeral lasted exactly three minutes. Reverend W T D Clemm gave a perfunctory ceremony due to the sparse attendance and the inauspicious weather, "a dark gloomy day, not raining but just kind of raw and threatening,"[10] as the Sexton George W Spence defined it. "Edgar has seen so much of sorrow," wrote his cousin Neilson, "that, to him, the change can scarcely be a misfortune."[11] It seems that the macabre qualities Poe attracted in life continued to cling to him even after his death. The marble tombstone ordered was destroyed in a freak train accident, while the simple slab set in its place only carried the inscription "No. 80". Poe's bones were not allowed to rest and in 1873, a quarter of a century after his death, his grave was moved to a new and more dignified location and a new tombstone was erected above it. But the second ceremony was again fraught with mishaps. The undertakers initially exhumed the wrong body and then the tombstone was positioned facing the wrong way. In 2009, 160 years after his death, yet another funeral was held for him, attended by dozens of people in Victorian garb. This was a result of the growing popularity Poe had gained, mainly after his death, as befits a writer who was fascinated by malignant memory and gnawing guilt, which he captured with unparalleled precision.

Poe's writing took two seemingly diverging paths. On the one hand, he wrote dozens of stories of supernatural horror, pieces of all-encompassing anxiety such as "The Pit and the Pendulum" and "The Fall of the House of Usher", which were revered by metaphysical poets like Charles Baudelaire and Stéphane Mallarmé; and on the other, three short works featuring the protagonist Auguste Dupin, which established one of the most popular genres of the last two centuries – detective fiction.

This pendulum, moving between the possible and the impossible, from logic to madness, permeated Poe's art through the hardships of his life. He knew what he was saying when he declared that "the death of a beautiful woman is, unquestionably, the most poetical topic in the world."[12] His mother died of consumption when he was three years old, and his child bride, his 14-year-old cousin Virginia, also contracted it. One evening, while singing to him, she started vomiting blood. As Poe wrote to George W Eveleth, he loved her "as no man ever loved before", and he was devastated. "Her life was despaired of. I took leave of her forever." But a simple death was not on the cards for Poe and his beloved. "She recovered partially and I again hoped. At the end of a year the vessel broke again – I went through precisely the same scene. Again, in about a year afterward. Then again – again – again & even once again at varying intervals. Each time I felt all the agonies of her death – and at each accession of the disorder I loved her more dearly & clung to her life with more desperate pertinacity … I became insane, with long intervals of horrible sanity." The nightmare ended only six years later, during which time Poe wrote his great poem, "The Raven". "I had indeed, nearly abandoned all hope of a permanent cure," he confessed to Eveleth, "when I found one in the *death* of my wife. This I can & do endure as becomes a man – it was the horrible never-ending oscillation between hope & despair which I could no longer have endured without the total loss of reason. In the death of what was my life, then, I receive a new but – oh God! how melancholy an existence."[13] Thus, Poe rooted his work in what tormented him most of all, the same cruel pendulum, the same terrible oscillation that gives his writing its tremendous momentum, a perpetuum mobile of sublime beauty and bottomless pain.

Filmmakers from D W Griffith to Roger Corman, from Dario Argento to Jan Švankmajer adapted his work, but more than that, Poe himself appeared as a character in dozens of works of literature, comics, TV and film. He loitered on the cover of *Sgt Pepper's Lonely Hearts Club Band* and joined Batman in solving crimes. Ray

Some scholars have speculated that the couple's marriage was never consummated. Similar hypotheses have also arisen regarding the marital relations of James Matthew Barrie (Paradise Lost, page 171).

The Exiles is set in the year 2120, when a spaceship bound for the red planet (We Come in Peace, page 123) carries the last surviving copies of works by Poe, Shakespeare and Dickens, now outlawed and burned on earth (Best of All Possible Worlds, page 247).

While pornography has remained a negligible literary genre in scope, its relatively respectable and sensual sister, erotica, is now enjoying an unprecedented flourish thanks to romance fiction (The Pleasure Principle, page 195).

Who is seen as the iconic oppressor and oppressed simultaneously (Blood Lust, page 93).

Created by slaves (Head Hunters, page 231).

Bradbury imagined Poe living on Mars, Angela Carter traced the Freudian connection between him and his actress mother in "The Cabinet of Edgar Allan Poe", and Sigmund Freud himself wrote the preface to Marie Bonaparte's analytical biography of his life and works.

The iconic status of Edgar Allan Poe, the creeping influence of H P Lovecraft, the tremendous success of Stephen King and the continuing and growing popularity of the horror genre, raise the fundamental question of fear as entertainment, horror as a consumer experience. Why the hell do we want them to scare us? What draws us toward a genre that presents us with everything we dread and abhor: death, violence, unknowing, pain? Because of horror's huge popularity, mainly on TV and in film, scholars tried to decipher the secret of its chilling attraction, and in 2010 a peer-reviewed academic journal dedicated only to "Horror Studies" was launched. Robin Wood was among the pioneers of this discipline, taking the genre out of the coffin where it had been buried next to other supposedly pulp genres – such as science fiction and pornography – in order to stimulate theoretical discussion. In his article "An Introduction to the American Horror Film", he relies on a psychoanalytic reading of horror, suggesting that the genre offers an opening for our repression and oppression. The monster – a serial killer, vampire, zombie – always represents political or sexual subversion, the marginal, the suppressed and denied, the return of the repressed in its most terrifying shape. For sociologists, the monster that terrifies us refers to the society that produced it at a specific and threatening point in time. A good illustration of this is the Oscar-winning horror comedy *Get Out* by the African-American director Jordan Peele, which examines US relations between blacks and whites through the genre's polarizing lens. Another example is the horror drama TV series *Lovecraft Country*, based on 2016 novel of the same name by Matt Ruff, examining segregation in the 1950s with a healthy dollop of unholy terror in the form of Lovecraftian monsters representing inherent bigotry and violence toward African Americans.

"If movies are the dreams of the mass culture," said Stephen King, "horror movies are the nightmares."[14] It is in nightmares, argues the brain and cognitive scientist Antti Revonsuo, that we will find the answer. Though controversial, his theory of "threat simulation" is supported by some empirical evidence. He believes that dreams are the "fire drill" of the brain, a way to expose ourselves to high-risk situations without actual being in physical danger and allowing us to train our inborn "fight or flight" responses. Of all the emotions we experience while dreaming, "fear [is] the most common," he says, "and anger the next most common."[15] Not so surprising, if we remember that research has shown our dreams present us time and again with situations where we find ourselves falling or drowning; experiencing loss, escape, embarrassment, failure; or naked in public. A study carried out in 2017 with people who talk in their sleep found that 46 per cent of what participants said had negative contents; 10 per cent included the word "no", and another 10 per cent the word "fuck" in all its various declensions, even though the same people only used the word in 0.003 per cent of their waking-life expressions. This theory holds that exposing ourselves to threatening and repulsive subject matter during our waking hours – when we are usually polite, in control of our impulses and don't give free rein to our violent needs and liminal desires – is likely to be another instance of threat simulation. So that once we do bump into a vampire or a zombie, we know straightaway what to do.

Whether the blood and guts in certain works of the horror genre express an atavistic yearning for the imagined moment of our birth or refer to some infantile state prior to when we were told not to get ourselves dirty; whether they show that we are monsters or actually enable us to define ourselves by means of the monstrous; or whether they simply give us a chance to contact the sublime through dread – all works of horror are frightening, each in its own way. Each of us, after all, has their different anxieties, and what scares one person is not necessarily frightening to another. Social conventions, our cultural sensitivities, gender, ethnic origin, age, education – they all make a difference to the way a horror novel or a scary movie affects us. What they share, however, is the *mysterium* – the unknown and unknowable. The horror genre does not necessarily offer us a cathartic happy end. It has sufficient presence in the cultural canon and has reached far enough into the mainstream for us to know that even if the book or film in question ends with the downfall of whatever formed the threat, the odds are that evil will return to blight our lives. For though the monsters may change, dread is eternal: a crack through which we may witness the abyss of our soul, a door leading into chaos.

The moment when we were expelled from paradise (Moving Heaven and Hell, page 71).

31

BEST OF ALL POSSIBLE WORLDS

On a hot summer morning in 2009, some owners of Amazon Kindles awoke to a brave new world. Their account displayed a refund for a total of 99 cents, while all traces of a book they had purchased on the website had been erased. The long arm of the law had reached into their homes, to devices lying peacefully by beds, tossed on desks or snoozing in bags, wiping them clean of one of the most influential novels of the twentieth century: *1984* by George Orwell. The watchful eye of the big brothers at Amazon had noticed the book appeared on the site in breach of copyright, and with a blink of that same eye they erased it. Thus, in a display of unconscious irony, Amazon applied methods taken directly from the work they deleted, a work that deals with erasing, concealing, rewriting reality, reprogramming the individual by those in power, creating a terrifying vision of a world where "who controls the past controls the future: who controls the present controls the past".[1]

Kindle owners, for their part, reacted angrily to what they defined as a "digital book burning", thus alerting the world to the danger inherent in the name the company chose for the device.

But its hard plastic casing did not save the e-paper from catching fire – not even virtually – in a process the deleted novel itself excelled at describing: "It was an automatic action to lift the flap of the nearest memory hole and drop it in, whereupon it would be whirled away on a current of warm air to the enormous furnaces."[2]

Throughout history, dictators and sovereigns have all too well known the deep truth of the slogan that Orwell put in the mouth of his totalitarian Party: "Ignorance is Strength".[3] And what can be stronger than fire to put between us and knowledge? A paradise of fools is heaven for the rulers, and the best way to get rid of texts that threaten the rulers is simply to burn them.

Ray Bradbury was only 13 years old when he read about the Nazis' great book-burnings in the news, but the flaming pyres were etched in his memory. In the preface to the 1967 edition of

Not recommended, especially if you copy a witch's spell book (Weird Sisterhood, page 25) or a map (The Territory and the Map, page 47).

Such as emperor Shih Huang Ti (Ex Libris, page 9).

As did Jehoiakim, the king of Judah (Flame and Moth, page 17).

247

Like the one expressed by the bonfires lit on 30 April on Walpurgis Night, a Christian celebration that coincides with the Viking beginning of spring holiday (Twilight of the Gods, page 65). In Germany it is also called *Hexennacht*, when the witches go out for their revelry (Weird Sisterhood, page 25). Some of the terrifying happenings in the short story "Dracula's Guest" by Bram Stoker, occur on that night (Blood Lust, page 93).

The Nazis saw themselves as creatures akin to these natural forces (Lupus Est, page 93).

Who sought to base his right to the throne – among other things – on an ancient connection to Arthur, the king who was and will be (King of Cups, page 153).

Intended initially to serve as a warning, not as a model (No Man's Island, page 57).

Fahrenheit 451 he wrote, "When Hitler burned a book I felt it as keenly, please forgive me, as his killing a human, for in the long sum of history they are one and the same flesh."[4] From the burning of the Reichstag, through the Olympic torch in Berlin, to the crematorium in Auschwitz, Nazism made political, allegorical and practical use of fire, and worshipped its pagan might and elemental power. It was the perfect medium to change the old tradition from then onward, as Hitler's great rival from the east, Stalin, did. From the smoky remnants of these old traditions, they both aspired to forge the foundations of a new society.

The birth of such a society is always accompanied by utopian, messianic passions. "A politics which wishes to change the system radically will be designated as utopia," writes Marxist theorist Frederick Jameson, "any attempt to change it will be accompanied by violence … efforts to maintain the changes will require dictatorship."[5] The seeds of the notion of an inevitable closeness between utopia and dictatorship, between the total realization of an ideal and the reality of ideological totalitarianism, were sown in Plato's *Politeia*, which Karl Popper in his book, *The Open Society and Its Enemies* mentions as laying the foundations of fascism. The same seeds also spring out of the work that gave the utopian genre its name. Thomas More was a lawyer, theologian, philosopher and the right-hand man of Henry VIII. This *little, true book, not less beneficial than enjoyable, about how things should be in a state and about the new island Utopia*, which he published in 1516, took its island's name from the Greek: *ou* ("not") and *tópos* ("place"), which translates as "no-place". But More himself was positively aware of the similarity to "Eutopia": *ef* ("good" or "well") and *tópos* ("place"), pulling the idea in the direction of "good place". The island is divided into households whose members lead agrarian and proto-socialist lives and hold all property communally. But life on this wondrous island comes at a price. Freedom of movement is restricted. Passage requires permits. Like the slaves on the island bound by gold chains, the people of Utopia are also limited by boundless abundance. Yet the utopian ideal continued to strike a chord throughout the centuries, even as its components changed. There were utopias with dazzling technology and inconceivable progress, like Francis Bacon's *New Atlantis*, whose people enjoy flying machines, submarines and a form of wireless communication, but are governed by a secretive group of philosopher-scientists. Some mainly stood out for their descriptions of social change, like one of the first American utopias, *Looking Backward* by Edward Bellamy, which was written in 1888. In his vision of Boston in the year 2000 all industry is nationalized, food is communal, there is enough work for all and there are no banks, famine, wars or police. Those who oppose all this goodness are treated as lunatics. The book was hugely successful, almost as popular as *Uncle Tom's Cabin* or *Ben Hur: A Tale of the Christ*, the bestsellers of the time. In Bellamy's 1897 sequel *Equality*, women are equal to men and wear trousers, population is strictly controlled and, most importantly, no one writes or reads books anymore.

A crime punishable by death (Wonder Women, page 37).

As the writers of utopias knew, literature has the power to generate change. But utopias themselves do not need changing. They are the very antithesis of it, for they are perfect just as they are. But change is an inalienable part of life itself and therefore, if utopia is indeed heaven, to enter it one must be dead. This death is stylistically reflected in utopian literature from More onward, by the flatness of the genre's characters, its static plot, and righteous, black-and-white didactics. There are no real protagonists or antagonists in utopia, only wide-eyed strangers who marvel at the multitude of cheerful, faceless people. "The citizens of utopia are grasped as a statistical population," Jameson argues, "there are no individuals any longer ... this effect of anonymity and of depersonalization is a very fundamental part of what utopia is and how it functions."[6] In utopia individual freedom is not possible, and the individual as such must cease to exist. To create the perfect society for all, utopian politics breaks down the indivisible and, like the splitting of the atom, this action also requires the application of brute force to the smallest unit in society – the individual.

Or unborn (Moving Heaven and Hell, page 71).

To use brute force, a powerful government is needed and to maintain stasis, a regime that does not allow any change. And so to describe the effects of such a government and regime, we also required a new literary form – dystopia, or anti-utopia.

The word "dystopia" was used as an antonym for utopia by adding the Greek prefix δυσ ("bad") to *tópos* ("place") and was first mentioned in a speech delivered by economist and philosopher John Stuart Mill to the British House of Commons in 1868. "What is commonly called utopian", he said as a critique of his government's Irish policy, "is something too good to be practicable, but what

Like Mary Wollstonecraft before him, Mill was emphatically opposed to the subjection of women (The Body Electric, page 221).

they appear to favour is too bad to be practicable."[7] Though Mill was (and perhaps *because* he was) a visionary who supported goals radical for his time, such as women's rights, the abolition of slavery and environmental awareness, he truly understood the lie behind the utopian passion and how it might turn paradise into purgatory in the process of its realization.

From those early days, dystopias have become one of the most popular genres, especially – and perhaps unsurprisingly – among young adults. Books turned into major TV series and movies, such as Suzanne Collins's *The Hunger Games*, Veronica Roth's *Divergent* and James Dashner's *The Maze Runner* to name but a few, express current economic, climatic and political concerns and fears about the world we are bequeathing them, the good earth we wished to leave them and in our greed and thoughtlessness turned into a planet in peril.

But the genesis of these contemporary prophets of doom occurred in the early twentieth century. Europe had celebrated 100 years of relative peace and the US was whirling in industrial gaiety. It was too good to be true. Too good to last. The 100 years' peace went up in flames in 1914 and the industrial merry-go-round ground to a halt in the great economic depression. An entire European generation was lost in the war. Pessimism took the place of the roaring optimism of the 1920s. Utopian visions turned into enormous social experiments in Russia, Spain, Italy and Germany, unimaginable atrocities were committed in the name of justice and the individual was sacrificed on the altar of the greater good. The first half of the bloodiest century in human history saw the emergence of the first literary dystopias, novels that looked at the terrible present and saw before them an even more horrible future: utopia stripped of the plump flesh of democracy to reveal the bare bones of tyranny. The first, arguably, was Jack London's *The Iron Heel* published in 1908. Constructed as a manuscript (complete with scholarly footnotes) discovered in AD 2600, which had been hidden for centuries, it tells the story of a socialist mass movement gaining strength in America and the subsequent conservative backlash. This results in a seizure of power and the establishment of a dictatorship, the titular "Iron Heel". But mass socialist movements themselves could be fraught with danger, as Russian author Yevgeny Zamyatin learned all too well. Prolific writer and lapsed Bolshevik, his 1921 novel *We* had the dubious honour of becoming the first book banned by the Soviet censorship board.

The novel is set centuries after the United State has brought the world to its knees. It is a glass megalopolis, a panopticon whose citizens are under constant surveillance by the Bureau of Guardians. These citizens have no names, only designations. The protagonist, D-503, is chief engineer of a spaceship under construction, whose mission will be to conquer the final frontier, to seek out strange new worlds, new life and new civilizations, and to boldly vanquish them, bringing its message of pure reason and logic. But love is not reasonable and passion is not logical. D-503 meets femme fatale I-330. She drinks, she smokes, she is a member of the resistance and he can't resist her. But since this is a dystopia, the end is ultimately a bitter one. D-503 is subjected to the Great Operation and reprogrammed. Now, devoid of all emotion or imagination, he betrays his beloved and reports on her execution with absolute detachment.

After the book was banned, Zamyatin arranged for the manuscript to be smuggled out of the Soviet Union. Copies made their way back to the USSR and began circulating in secret. When it was discovered, Zamyatin lost his job. No publishing house or magazine would work with him and his friends, colleagues and family were persecuted. "I Am Afraid", he declared in an essay published the same year that *We* came out, demonstrating once again his astonishing foresight, "True literature can exist only where it is created, not by diligent and trustworthy officials, but by madmen, hermits, heretics, dreamers, rebels and skeptics."[8]

Desperate and demoralized, Zamyatin appealed to Joseph Stalin in 1931, requesting to leave the USSR, citing "the death sentence that has been pronounced upon me as a writer here at home"[9] as the reason for his request. By 1932 he and his wife were in Paris.

The same year across the channel, writer and philosopher Aldous Huxley published *Brave New World*. Set in 2540 or 632 AF (After Ford, that is Henry Ford, the American industrial tycoon who became a god-like figure in the novel). This is a future where people are biologically engineered and psychologically conditioned to be happy consumers and satisfied workers; "mother" is a dirty word; food is plentiful and "soma", an engineered drug with no side effects, is the population's bread and butter. There is no more

That's nothing to be ashamed of. Some of the best literature in the world was banned (Flame and Moth, page 17).

In Fritz Lang's 1927 dystopia *Metropolis*, which takes place in 2026, a mesmerizing female robot incites the workers to riot (Valley of the Dolls, page 205).

The question of how to behave toward other life forms on alien planets continues to haunt humanity (We Come in Peace, page 123).

Among other things, Aldous Huxley was the godfather of the psychedelic counterculture. In his famous essay *The Doors of Perception* (1953), a name he took from the work of English poet, painter, and printmaker, William Blake, he describes and analyzes his experiences with mescaline, a hallucinogenic drug naturally occurring in some species of cacti. But it is possible that the one who introduced him to transcendental experiences via drug use was the superstar of occultism, Aleister Crowley, with whom he had a series of meetings in Berlin in 1930 (King of Cups, page 153).

monogamy, parenting or art; but nor is there any war, crime, disease or religion. Into this wondrous world comes John "the Savage", a young man raised on a reservation outside the World State with only the complete works of Shakespeare to keep him company. He despises the superficiality, is disgusted by the permissiveness and is terrified of the emptiness he sees all around him. Like Leibniz, the eighteenth-century philosopher who argued that "an imperfection in the part may be required for a greater perfection in the whole",[10] John protests "I don't want comfort. I want God, I want poetry, I want real danger, I want freedom, I want goodness. I want sin ... I'm claiming the right to be unhappy."[11]

Eric Arthur Blair also claimed the right to be unhappy and, while Huxley was writing his book, set out to experience life with all its dangers and sins. The result was *Down and Out in Paris and London*, published in 1933, in which he first used the pen name George Orwell. Under this name Orwell wrote literary reviews for a living, such as the one in which he compared Zamyatin's *We* to Huxley's *Brave New World* and pointed out many similarities between the two, "though Huxley's book shows less political awareness and is more influenced by recent biological and psychological theories".[12] In 1949 it was Huxley's turn to write of Orwell's "most important" book and perhaps the most terrifying vision of the future yet written – *1984*. In contrast with Huxley's novel, whose population lives in a utopia experienced as a dystopia only from an outsider's point of view by the character John and the reader, *1984* is a dystopia that insists it is a utopia, the best of all possible worlds. "The fabulous statistics continued to pour out of the telescreen. As compared with last year there was more food, more clothes, more houses, more furniture ... more of everything except disease, crime, and insanity," the party inform the people of Oceania. They seemingly "lived longer, worked shorter hours, were bigger, healthier, stronger, happier, more intelligent, better educated".[13] But in practice they all lived in a state of constant wretchedness, constant terror, constant hatred. "In our world there will be no emotions except fear, rage, triumph and self-abasement," pontificates O'Brien, the Inquisitor, to Winston Smith, the man who dared to love, "there will be no art, no literature."[14] Orwell's Party deemed "Various writers, such as Shakespeare, Milton, Swift, Byron, Dickens, and some others"[15] worthy of being translated into Newspeak, the artificial language created by the Party in order to abolish "thoughtcrime" – the mere contemplation of autonomy, free will and self-determination. "When the task had been completed, their original writings, with all else that survived of the literature of the past, would be destroyed."[16]

Huxley didn't need such measures to prevent the inhabitants of his utopia from reading. Pavlovian conditioning techniques applied in infancy ensured that children "grow up with what the psychologists used to call an 'instinctive' hatred of books and flowers ... They'll be safe from books and botany all their lives."[17] However, the World Controller, Mustapha Mond, owns a secret library containing old and forbidden books, including the Bible, and "A whole collection of pornographic old books. God in the safe and Ford on the shelves."[18] In Zamyatin's United State, no one reads the "idiotic books of the ancients",[19] and state-sanctioned sonnets are read aloud during public executions.

> Pornographic and erotic literature itself, as a genre, has a long reckoning with God and His representatives on earth (The Pleasure Principle, page 195).

In Bradbury's *Fahrenheit 451*, humanity uses the gift of fire Prometheus stole for us to burn books and eradicate knowledge. Books are not only banned and abhorrent, as in Huxley's *Brave New World*, or rewritten and erased like in Orwell's *1984*. The punishment for keeping them is hospitalization or execution, and the books themselves are burned by the firemen, once saviours of lives and now destroyers of culture, the vanguard of a disguised dystopia, an alienated society amusing itself to death. "A book is a loaded gun in the house next door,"[20] Captain Beatty in *Fahrenheit 451* warns Guy Montag, the protagonist and a fireman with a forbidden penchant for books.

> There are historical precedents, "Those who concealed books were branded by a red-hot iron and condemned to build the outrageous wall until the day of their death," [a] writes Jorge Luis Borges in "The Wall and the Books" (Ex Libris, page 9).

After all, books are dangerous things. "There are books of the same chemical composition as dynamite," Zamyatin wrote, "the only difference is that a piece of dynamite explodes once, whereas a book explodes a thousand times."[21] Literature is as dangerous to dystopia as it is to utopia, since they are two sides of the same coin. One is not the opposite of the other, but an integral part of it, since one person's utopia is inevitably another's dystopia.

> As books are a wonderful tool for the purpose of creating the individual (A Faustian Bargain, page 1).

Bradbury's book was written in the wake of Senator Joe McCarthy's communist witch-hunt, his attempt to preserve American utopia and protect it from the red peril of Soviet dystopia. But in 1985, the year after Orwell's dire prophecy was supposed to have been fulfilled, Canadian author Margaret Atwood published a book dedicated to a victim of the historic witch-hunt itself: Mary Webster, also known as "Half-Hanged

> Whose sentence was passed a few years before the famous Salem witch trials (Weird Sisterhood, page 25).

Mary". Whether Webster was indeed related to Atwood is unclear, "Some days, my grandmother would say we were related to her and on other days, she would deny the whole thing because it wasn't very respectable," Atwood says, but she chose to dedicate *The Handmaid's Tale* to her "because she is an example of a female person wrongly accused … a symbol of hope because they didn't actually manage to kill her. She made it through."

For Atwood, writing her dystopia was not a matter of considering the future or observing the present, but rather of looking back into the past. "There's a precedent in real life for everything in the book," says Atwood, knowing all too well that one woman's dystopia is another woman's reality, "I decided not to put anything in that somebody somewhere hadn't already done."[22] And one of those things was prohibiting women to read, "Reading? No, that's only a hand cut off, on the third conviction,"[23] recalls her protagonist and narrator, Offred. A manuscript discovered in the tradition of London's *Iron Heel*, *The Handmaid's Tale* was one of several feminist works of dystopian science fiction in the 1980s, like those of writer and linguist Suzette Haden Elgin. *Native Tongue*, which came out in 1984, is her first book of a trilogy taking place in the twenty-second century, generations after the repeal of the 19th Amendment, citing the natural limitations of women, "No female citizen of the United States shall be allowed to serve in any elected or appointed office, to participate in any capacity (official or unofficial) in the scholarly or scientific professions, to hold employment outside the home without the written permission of her husband."[24]

In Elgin's future, various alien races frequent the earth, and the need to communicate with them allows for the dominance of linguists, but only those of the right gender – men. The sexes occupy two wholly different spheres, men are from Mars and women are from Venus. In hiding, as an act of defiance and alliance, they create Láadan, a new language for women, one that will allow them to say what they had no words for.

Native Tongue was an attempt to artistically illustrate the assertion of postmodern feminist Hélène Cixous, that "women must … invent the impregnable language that will wreck partitions, classes, and rhetorics, regulations and codes … In one another we will never be lacking."[25] But Elgin's novel and the language she invented for it, deals not only with the autonomy that women try

Lest they become rebellious (A Faustian Bargain, page 1) or overexcited (The Pleasure Principle, page 195)

Named after the Roman god of war (We Come in Peace, page 123).

Actually, it is the Moon that is more frequently associated with the feminine in ancient mythologies (Man in the Moon, page 115).

to carve out for themselves, but also with what legally deprived them of their liberty – patriarchy.

Feminism also had its own utopia, which solved the problem of patriarchy by creating a place without it – *Herland*, written by feminist Charlotte Perkins Gilman and published in monthly installments during 1915. *Herland* is an all-feminine utopia relying on asexual reproduction, which is invaded by three ragged male adventurers. The book focuses on gender roles and whether they are inherent or a result of social construction, on female individuality and on non-possessive motherhood.

In Atwood's dystopia, and throughout history, procreation and having children was very much on the regime's mind. Atwood's Republic of Gilead officially expropriates women's bodies and confiscates their offspring, severing all connection between sexuality, reproduction and romance alike.

For Huxley, conditioning abolished the nuclear family. "The world was full of fathers – was therefore full of misery; full of mothers – therefore of every kind of perversion from sadism to chastity; full of brothers, sisters, uncles, aunts – full of madness and suicide ... There were also monogamy and romance," but none of that was needed now, for "everyone belongs to everyone else."[26]

Big Brother strives to achieve the same result through coercion and oppression: "We have cut the links between child and parent ... in the future there will be no wives and no friends. Children will be taken from their mothers at birth, as one takes eggs from a hen."[27] In *Brave New World* children are factory-produced, in the best tradition of Henry Ford's production lines, while in *We* women must be approved by the United State before they are allowed to conceive, and the protagonist's licensed lover O-90 risks her life to have a child.

> Like the ones where the machines that were made for us can be made – until they too will rise up and rebel against us (Ex Machina, page 213).

In *Fahrenheit 451* there is no need for coercion, conditioning or certification. Montag's wife is not interested in children and her friend declares, "No one in his right mind, the Good Lord knows, would have children!"[28]

"The sexlessness of utopians is a constant in the anti-utopian tradition,"[29] Jameson writes. The context-free sex on offer in *Brave New World* is a sport that people must practice as part of a healthy life. Sexual ecstasy can only be reached in a warm embryonic darkness, everyone singing the monotonous anthem "Orgy-Porgy" together.

In *We* sex is perfunctory. At regular intervals the citizens of the United State are allowed a "sex hour" and "The rest is only a matter of technique. You are carefully examined in the laboratory of the Sexual Department ... Then you file an application to enjoy the services of Number so and so, or Numbers so and so. You get for that purpose a check-book (pink). That is all." This practice has been in place for "three hundred years since our great historic Lex Sexualis was promulgated" and its implications are that "there is no more reason for envy or jealousy."[30]

In *The Handmaid's Tale* the sexual act is a fertility ritual, "Her legs are apart, I lie between them, my head on her stomach, her pubic bone under the base of my skull, her thighs on either side of me. She too is fully clothed. My arms are raised; she holds my hands, each of mine in each of hers. This is supposed to signify that we are one flesh, one being ... My red skirt is hitched up to my waist, though no higher. Below it the Commander is fucking."[31]

However, the ultimate goal of Orwell's Party is to do away with all of that: "The sex instinct will be eradicated ... We shall abolish the orgasm."[32] To that end, there is the Anti-Sex League, and to that end there is the Two Minutes Hate, which Winston uses to entertain masochistic musings. In *Fahrenheit 451* there is no intercourse or intimacy, but there is no organized disapproval of them either. What awakens the fireman Montag to a new awareness of his world is the innocence of one dreamy girl.

Huxley infantilized passion, Zamyatin turned it into bureaucracy, Atwood into an unholy religious rite, while Orwell tied together sex and pain and Bradbury romanticized it. Passion and love thus become the axis on which revelation and revolt revolves in these works.

> Literature dealing with passion has been subversive from its inception (The Pleasure Principle, page 195).

It is a revelation that leads to John's suicide at the end of *Brave New World*, to Winston's and D-503's betrayal and surrender, but also to Offred's possible escape and to Montag's redemption. Atwood allows her protagonist to "step up, into the darkness within; or else the light"[33] and alludes to the possibility that she manages to regain her freedom, while Bradbury creates a cruel yet comforting *Bildungsroman* whose end is nothing but a beginning, a sliver of hope for the salvation of the individual. The teachers Montag meets by the rusting train tracks are guardians of the ember of knowledge who transform it from written text to oral tradition. Its bearers are living books. Not paper birds that go up in flames deceptively easily, but memory, the phoenix rising from the ashes of the ruined cities. The physical object, the book itself, is transient. As Zamyatin's countryman and contemporary Mikhail Bulgakov well knew, a book does not even have to be written – or printed – in order to exist. A book is an idea. "Manuscripts do not burn."[34]

Memory may be our salvation, but it may also be our doom (Remember to Forget, page 139).

Instead, they set us aglow.

NOTES

1. A Faustian Bargain

1. Hirasuna, Delphine. The Curse of "The Great Omar". *The Journal of Business and Design*. 30 November 2016.
2. Khayyam, Omar. *Rubaiayat* (translated by Edward Fitzgerald). University of Minnesota. 1937 [translation 1859]. p. 31.
3. Sagan, Carl. *Cosmos*. Ballantine Books. 2013 [1980]. p. 295.
4. Tuchman, Barbara W. *The March of Folly: From Troy to Vietnam*. Ballantine Books. 1985. pp. 114–15.
5. Ibid., p. 107.
6. de Montaigne, Michel. *The Complete Essays* (translated by M A Screech). Penguin Classics. 1993 [1570–1592].

2. Ex Libris

1. Moran, Lee. Library Sends Police Officer to Collect Overdue Books ... from a Five-Year-Old Girl. *Mail Online*. 3 January 2012. https://www.dailymail.co.uk/news/article-2081591/Library-sends-police-officer-collect-overdue-books-year-old-girl.html.
2. Lebowitz Rossi, Holly. Police Sent to 5-Year Old's Home to Collect Overdue Library Books. *Parents.com*. 4 January 2012. https://www.parents.com/health/parents-news-now/police-sent-to-5-year-olds-home-to-collect-overdue-library-books/.
3. Frying Pans, Forks and Fever: Medieval Book Curses. *Medieval manuscripts blog*. The British Library. 23 May 2017. https://blogs.bl.uk/digitisedmanuscripts/2017/05/frying-pans-forks-and-fever-medieval-book-curses.html.
4. Greenblatt, Stephen. *The Swerve: How the World Became Modern*. W W Norton & Company. 2011. p. 43.
5. Ibid., pp. 29–30.
6. Drogin, Marc. *Anathema!: Medieval Scribes and the History of Book Curses*. A Schram. 1983. pp. 52–3.
7. Marcellinus, Ammianus. *The Roman History of Ammianus Marcellinus During the Reigns of the Emperors Constantius, Julian, Jovianus, Valentinian, and Valens* (translated by C D Yonge). G. Bell & Sons. 1902. p. 18.
8. Pratchet, Terry. *Guards! Guards!* HarperCollins. 2001. p. 8.
9. Borges, Jorge Luis. The Library of Babel. *Collected Fictions* (translated by Andrew Hurley). Penguin Books. 1998. p. 115.
10. Lasswitz, Kurd. The Universal Library (translated by Erik Born). *Mithila Review*. 2017. https://mithilareview.com/lasswitz_09_17.
11. Borges, Jorge Luis. *Seven Nights* (translated by Eliot Weinberger). New Directions. 1984. p. 110.
12. Borges, Jorge Luis. *The Wall and the Books* (translated by Gaither Stewart). https://southerncrossreview.org/54/borges-muralla.htm.
13. Borges, Jorge Luis. Poem of the Gifts (translated by Alastair Reid). *Seven Nights*. New Directions. 1984. p. 110.
14. Klineberg, Eric. *Palaces for the People: How Social Infrastructure Can Help Fight Inequality, Polarization, and the Decline of Civic Life*. Crown. 2018. p. 240.
15. Carnegie, Andrew. Carnegie Corporation of New York. https://www.carnegie.org/interactives/foundersstory.
16. Angelou, Maya. *Speech in the Schomburg Center for Research in Black Culture, New York Public Library*. October 2010. https://www.youtube.com/watch?v=udESQF1bdxg.

3. Flame and Moth

1. *King James Bible*, Jeremiah, 36:23.
2. Putz, Wilhelm. *Handbook of Medieval Geography and History* (translated by R. B. Paul). D. Appleton & Company. 1850. p. 37.

3. Heinrich Heine, quoted in Gallo, Antonio. Where They Burn Books, They Will Ultimately Burn People Also. *Medium*. 13 December 2019. https://medium.com/la-mia-biblioteca/where-they-burn-books-they-will-ultimately-burn-people-also-34b835d13b7d.

4. Lord Cosmo Lang of Lambeth. Preservation of Historical and Art Treasures. *Hansard*. 16 February 1944.

5. Eisenhower, Dwight. Preservation of Historical Monuments (letter). 26 May 1944. https://www.eisenhowerlibrary.gov/sites/default/files/research/online-documents/monuments-men/033-006.pdf.

6. Marshall, George. Protection: Artistic Historic Monuments in Italy (letter). 1944. https://www.eisenhowerlibrary.gov/sites/default/files/research/online-documents/monuments-men/033-019.pdf.

7. Streitfeld, David. Book Report. *Washington Post*. 24 August 1997.

8. Greenblatt, Stephen. *The Swerve: How the World Became Modern*. W W Norton & Company. 2011. p. 7.

9. Kelly, Stuart. *The Book of Lost Books: An Incomplete History of All the Great Books You'll Never Read*. Polygon. 2010. p. xxi.

10. Ibid., p. xvii.

4. Weird Sisterhood

1. Homer. *The Iliad* (book 19) (translated by A T Murray). William Heinemann Ltd. 1924.

2. Neumann, Erich. *The Fear of the Feminine and Other Essays on Feminine Psychology*. Princeton University Press. 1994. p. 171.

3. Shakespeare, William. *Macbeth*. Act I Scene III.

4. Ibid., Act IV, Scene I.

5. Ibid., Act I, Scene V.

6. Ibid., Act V, Scene I.

7. Russell, Jeffrey and Brooks, Alexander. *A History of Witchcraft: Sorcerers, Heretics and Pagans*. Thames & Hudson. 2007. p. 73.

8. Sprenger, Jakob, Heinrich Kramer and Henricus Institoris. *Malleus Maleficarum* (translated by M Summers). Dover Publications Inc. 1978 [1486].

9. Purkiss, Diane. *The Witch in History: Early Modern and Twentieth-Century Representations*. Routledge. 2013. p. 134.

10. Ibid., p. 137.

11. Ewan, C L'Estrange (ed.). *Witch Hunting and Witch Trials: The Indictments for Witchcraft from the Records of 1373 Assizes Held for the Home Circuit AD 1559–1736*. Routledge. 1929. p. 274.

12. Sprenger, Jakob, Heinrich Kramer and Henricus Institoris. *Malleus Maleficarum* (translated by M Summers). Dover Publications Inc. 1978 [1486].

13. Borman, Tracy. *Witches: A Tale of Sorcery, Scandal and Seduction*. Jonathan Cape. 2013. p. 165.

14. *King James Bible*, Exodus, 22:18.

15. *King James Bible*, Samuel, 28:7.

16. Boyer, Paul and Nissenbaum, Stephen (eds). SWP No. 125. Tituba. *The Salem Witchcraft Papers: Verbatim Transcriptions of the Court Records*. De Cappo Press. 1977.

17. Shakespeare, William. *Macbeth*. Act I, Scene I.

18. Bobel, Chris. *New Blood: Third-Wave Feminism and the Politics of Menstruation*. Rutgers University Press. 2010. p. 124.

19. WITCH manifesto. 1968. https://media.contemporaryartlibrary.org/store/doc/7993/docfile/original-cb2cae449b3d481603957db824e1da11.pdf.

5. Wonder Women

1. 111th US Congress. *Public Law 94: Joint Resolution: Proclaiming Casimir Pulaski to be an Honorary Citizen of the United States Posthumously*. 6 November 2009.

2. "The Skeleton Looked Very Female": Casimir Pulaski, Dubbed the "Father" of the American Cavalry, Was Most Likely Intersex. *HeadTopics Canada*. 4 August 2019.

3. *The Ballad of Mulan* (translated by Jack Yuan). c. sixth century AD. https://en.wikisource.org/wiki/Translation:Ballad_of_Mulan.

4. Licata, Salvatore J and Petersen, Robert P. *The Gay Past: A Collection of Historical Essays*. Routledge. 2014 [1985]. p. 31.

5. *King James Bible*, Deuteronomy, 22:5.
6. St Thomas Aquinas. *Summa Theologiae* (translated by Fathers of English Dominican Province). 1265?–1274. https://en.wikisource.org/wiki/Summa_Theologiae?fbclid=IwAR0cTlPzTB4DZtCV_ffyR0aBU7zjpd0zL3gWvXHGc-HPdcKDuOQ5nR0HELs.
7–8. *The Trial of Jeanne D'Arc* (translated by W P Barrett). Gotham House, Inc. 1932.
9. Queen Elizabeth I. *Speech to the Troops at Tilbury*. 9 August 1588. https://www.rmg.co.uk/stories/topics/queen-elizabeth-speech-troops-tilbury.
10. Murphy, Arthur (ed.). *The Works of Cornelius Tacitus, Vol 3*. Luke White. 1794 [c. first–second centuries AD].
11. Cassius Dio. *Roman History*. Volume VIII of the Loeb Classical Library edition. 1925.
12. Saxo Grammaticus. *The Danish History*, Books I–IX. c. thirteenth century AD. https://www.gutenberg.org/ebooks/1150.
13. Tolkien, J R R. *The Return of the King: Being the Third Part of the Lord of the Rings*. Houghton Mifflin. 1994 [1955]. p. 944.
14. Ibid., p. 823.
15. Burton, Richard Francis. *A Mission to Gelele, King of Dahome* (second edition). Tinsley Brothers. 1864.
16. Adams, Maeve. The Amazon Warrior Women and the De/construction of Gendered Imperial Authority in Nineteenth-Century Colonial Literature. *Nineteenth-Century Gender Studies*, vol. 6, no.1. Spring 2010.
17–18. Marston, William Moulton. Why 100,000,000 Americans Read Comics. *The American Scholar*, vol. 13, no. 1. Winter 1943–44.
19. Gloria Steinam, quoted in Pace, Eric. Lovely and Wise Heroine Summoned to Help the Feminist Cause. *New York Times*. 19 October 1972.
20. Thorbecke, Catherine. UN Decision to Appoint Wonder Woman as Female Empowerment Ambassador Sparks Outrage. *ABC News*. 21 October 2016.
21. Hurley, Kameron. "We Have Always Fought": Challenging the "Women, Cattle and Slaves" Narrative. *A Dribble of Ink*. 20 May 2013.
a. *The Trial of Jeanne D'Arc* (translated by W P Barrett). Gotham House, Inc. 1932.

6. The Territory and the Map

1. Jacobs, Frank. The Fabulous (and Indeed False) Mountains of Kong. *Big Think*. 23 August 2016.
2. Jim Naughten, quoted in Mallonee, Laura. The Fake Mountain Range that Appeared on Maps for a Century. *Wired*. 12 September 2017.
3. Swift, Jonathan. On Poetry: A Rapsody. *The Poems of Jonathan Swift D. D., Vol 1*. J Huggonson. 1733.
4. Wynne Jones, Diana. *The Tough Guide to Fantasyland: The Essential Guide to Fantasy Travel*. Daw Books. 1996. p. 9.
5. Carpenter, Humphrey (ed.). *The Letters of J. R. R. Tolkien*. Houghton Mifflin. 1981.
6. Baldwin, Thomas. *Airopaidia*. J Fletcher. 1786.
7. Henrikson, Alan K. The Map as an "Idea": The Role of Cartographic Imagery During the Second World War. *The American Cartographer*, vol. 2, no. 1. 1975.
8. Welcome to Argleton. January 2010. https://web.archive.org/web/20100109182500/http://www.argleton-village.co.uk.
9. Carroll, Lewis. *Sylvie and Bruno*. Dover Publications. 1988 [1889].
10. Borges, Jorge Luis. On Exactitude in Science. *Collected Fictions* (translated by Andrew Hurley). Penguin Books. 1998. p. 325.
a. Wilde, Oscar. *The Soul of Man under Socialism*. Arthur L Humpreys. 1990 [1891].

7. No Man's Island

1. Merlin Burrows Twitter account. https://twitter.com/BruceMerlinB
2. Plato. Critias. In *The Dialogues of Plato* (translated by Benjamin Jowett). Random House. 1937 [1892, trans] [360 BC].
3. Manguel, Alberto and Guadalupi, Gianni. *The Dictionary of Imaginary Places*. Macmillan. 1980. p. 24.
4. Feder, Kenneth L. *Encyclopedia of Dubious Archeology: From Atlantis to the Walam Olum*. ABC-CLIO. 2010. p. 31.

5. Rosenberg, Alfred. *The Myth of the Twentieth Century: An Evaluation of the Spiritual Intellectual Confrontations of our Age* (translated by James Whisker). Black Kite Publishing. 2010.
6. Pringle, Heather. *The Master Plan: Himmler's Scholars and the Holocaust.* Hyperion. 2006. p. 5.
7. Kurlander, Eric. *Hitler's Monsters: A Supernatural History of the Third Reich.* Yale University Press. 2017.
8. Goodrick-Clarke, Nicholas. *The Occult Roots of Nazism: Secret Aryan Cults and Their Influence on Nazi Ideology.* New York University Press. 1993.
9. HLS Nuremberg Trials Project. HLSL Seq. No. 11635. 19 August 1947. http://nuremberg.law.harvard.edu/transcripts/1-transcript-for-nmt-1-medical-case?seq=11635.
10. Tal, Uriel. *Religion, Politics and Ideology in the Third Reich.* Routledge. 2004.
   a. Voltaire. *Candide.* Boni and Liveright Inc. 1918 [1759].

8. Twilight of the Gods

1. Frank, Roberta. The Invention of the Viking Horned Helmet. *International Scandinavian and Medieval Studies in Memory of Gerd Wolfgang Weber.* 2000. pp. 199–208.
2. Ahmed Ibn Fahdlan, quoted in Eyewitness to the Vikings. *Sky History.* https://www.history.co.uk/shows/the-real-vikings/articles/eyewitness-to-the-vikings.
3. Letter from Alcuin of York to Ethelred, King of Northumbria. 8 June 793. https://www.bbc.co.uk/history/trail/conquest/viking/loot_01.shtml.
4. Young, Bryan. How the Mighty Thor Busted into Comic Books and the Big Screen. *HowStuffWorks.* https://entertainment.howstuffworks.com/arts/comic-books/mighty-thor-busted-into-comic-books-and-big-screen.htm.
5. Beller, Steven. Herzl's Tannhäuser: The Redemption of the Artist as Politician. *Austrians and Jews in the Twentieth Century: From Franz Joseph to Waldheim* (edited by Robert S. Wistrich). Palgrave Macmillan. 1992. pp. 38–57.

9. Moving Heaven and Hell

1. Pope Paul III. Quoted in Love, Idalis. 4 Artists Who Openly Hated their Clients (And Why it's Amazing). *The Collector.* 14 November 2020. https://www.thecollector.com/artists-who-hated-their-clients/.
2. Dante Alighieri. *The Divine Comedy* (translated by Henry Wadsworth Longfellow). Ticknor and Fields. 1867 [c. 1320]. Canto 3.
3. Ibid., Canto 1.
4. Shelley, Percy Bysshe. A Defence of Poetry. *A Defence of Poetry and Other Essays.* The Bobbs-Merrill Company. 1904 [1821]. p. 61.
5–6. Dante Alighieri. *The Divine Comedy* (translated by Henry Wadsworth Longfellow). Ticknor and Fields. 1867 [c. 1320]. Canto 34.
7. Scarry, Elaine. *The Body in Pain: The Making and Unmaking of the World.* Oxford University Press. 1987. p. 4.
8. *King James Bible,* Kings 2, 23:10.
9. *King James Bible,* Ecclesiastes, 9:5.
10. Milton, John. *Paradise Lost* (Book I). Oxford University Press. 1998 [1667]. p. 8.
11. Shakespeare, William. *The Tempest.* Act I Scene II.
12. Sartre, Jean-Paul. No Exit. *No Exit and Three Other Plays* (translated by Lionel Abel). Vintage. 1989 [1944]. p. 47.

10. Number of the Beast

1. *King James Bible,* Isaiah, 45:7.
2. Ibid., 14:12.
3. Gregory I. Letter to Abbot Mellitus. Epsitola 76, PL 77. 1215–1216. https://sourcebooks.fordham.edu/source/greg1-mellitus.txt.
4. Kaufmann, Walter. Introduction. *Goethe's Faust: Part One and Sections of Part Two.* Doubleday. 1963. p. 47.
5. *The Koran,* surah Al-Hijr, verse 26.
6. Blake, William. *The Marriage of Heaven and Hell.* University of Miami Press. 1963 [c. 1793]. p. 49.
7. Pullella, Philip. Pope Blames Devil for Church Divisions, Scandals, Seeks Angel's Help. *Reuters.* 8 October 2018.

8. Reilly, Nick. "Hail Christian!": The Church of Satan Salutes Christian Bale's Golden Globe Victory. *NME*. 7 January 2019.

9–10. Burwick, Kevin. Church of Satan Doesn't Care About Satanic Temple's Sabrina Netflix Lawsuit. *TV-Web*. 11 November 2018.

11. Milton, John. *Paradise Lost*. 1667. Oxford University Press. 1998 [1667]. p. 8.

11. Here Be Dragons

1. *King James Bible*, Isaiah, 27:1.
2. *King James Bible*, Revelations, 12:3.
3. Ibid., 12:7.
4. Ibid., 12:9.
5. Homer. *The Iliad* (translated by A T Murray). William Heinemann Ltd. 1924.
6. Ovid. *Metamorphoses* (translated by Sir Samuel Garth and John Dryden). Printed by S Powell for G Risk, G Ewing and W Smith. 1727 [c. 8 AD].
7. Isbell, Lynne A. The Fruit, the Tree and the Serpent: Why We See So Well. *The Montreal Review*. October 2011.
8. *King James Bible*, Genesis, 3:15.

12. Blood Lust

1. Bishop Nicholas of Modrus. In Cazacu, Matei. *Dracula*. Brill. 2017. p. 167.
2. Summers, Montague. *The Vampire, His Kith and Kin*. K. Paul Trench, Trubner. 1928. p. 32.
3. Le Fanu, Joseph Sheridan. *Carmilla*. The Dark Blue. 1872. p. 592.
4. McConnell Stott, Andrew. The Poet, the Physician and the Birth of the Modern Vampire. *The Public Domain Review*. 2014. https://publicdomainreview.org/essay/the-poet-the-physician-and-the-birth-of-the-modern-vampire.
5–7. Polidori, John William. *The Diary of Dr. John William Polidori / Letters* (edited by William Michael Rossetti). 1816.
8. McConnell Stott, Andrew. The Poet, the Physician and the Birth of the Modern Vampire. *The Public Domain Review*. 2014.
9. Polidori, John William. *The Vampyre; A Tale*. Sherwood, Neely, and Jones. 1819.
10. McConnell Stott, Andrew. The Poet, the Physician and the Birth of the Modern Vampire. *The Public Domain Review*. 2014.
11. Dumas [père], Alexandre. *The Count of Monte Cristo*. George Routledge and Sons. 1888.
12. McConnell Stott, Andrew. The Poet, the Physician and the Birth of the Modern Vampire. *The Public Domain Review*. 2014.
13. Hitler, Adolf. *Mein Kampf* (translated by James Murphy). Elite Minds Inc. 2010 [1939]. p. 266.
14. Marcus, Jacob. *The Jew in the Medieval World: A Sourcebook, 315–1791*. JPS. 1938. p. 121.
15. Stoker, Bram. *Dracula*. Archibald Constable and Company. 1897.
16–17. Bresheeth, Haim. The Vampire Genre: Labelling the Other through Blood. In Bresheeth, Haim, Sand, Shlomo, and Zimmerman, Moshe (eds). *Cinema and Memory: A Dangerous Relationship*. The Zalman Shazar Center for Jewish History. 2004. pp. 153–67.
18–21. Stoker, Bram. *Dracula*. Archibald Constable and Company. 1897.
22. Dumas [père], Alexandre. The Vampire of the Carpathian Mountains. In *The Best Vampire Stories 1800–1849: A Classic Vampire Anthology (Book 4)*. Bottletree Books. 2020 [1848].
23. *Book of Wisdom*, 7: 26. Good News Translation.
24. Freud, Sigmund. *New Introductory Lectures on Psychoanalysis* (translated by James Strachey). Norton. 1964 [1933]. p. 73.
25. Ibid., p. 74.

13. Lupus Est

1. Boren, George. *The Damnable Life and Death of Stubbe Peeter*. 1590.
2. Soniak, Matt. A Brief History of Real Life "Werewolves". *Mental Floss*. 31 October 2014. https://www.mentalfloss.com/article/59824/brief-history-real-life-werewolves.

3. Eisler, Robert. *Man into Wolf: An Anthropological Interpretation of Sadism, Masochism, and Lycanthropy*. Routledge and Kegan Paul. 1951. p. xxiii.

4. Ovid. *Metamorphoses* (translated by Sir Samuel Garth and John Dryden.) Printed by S Powell for G Risk, G Ewing and W Smith. 1727 [c. 8 AD].

5. *King James Bible*, Daniel 4:33.

6. *The Epic of Gilgamesh* (translated by Maureen Gallery Kovacs). Stanford University Press. 1989. p. 6.

7. Sprenger, Jakob, Heinrich Kramer and Henricus Institoris. *Malleus Maleficarum* (translated by M. Summers) Dover Publications Inc. 1978 [1486].

8. Tyson, Donald (trans.). *The Demonology of King James I*. Llewellyn Publications. 2011 [1597]. p. 153.

9. *The Lays of Marie de France* (translated by David R. Slavitt). Athabasca University Press. 2013. p. 47.

10. Zipes, Jack. *The Trials and Tribulations of Little Red Riding Hood: Versions of the Text in Sociocultural Context*. Bergin & Garvey. 1983. p. 5.

11. Perrault, Charles. Little Red Riding Hood. *The Blue Fairy Book* (translated and edited by Andrew Lang). Longmans, Green, and Company. 1891. pp. 51–3.

12. Stevenson, Robert Louis. *Travels with a Donkey in the Cévennes*. Penguin Books. 2005 [1878].

14. Man in the Moon

1. Heinlein, Robert. The Man who Sold the Moon. *The Past through Tomorrow: Future History Stories*. Science Fiction Book Club. 1987 [1949]. p. 183.

2. Kennedy, John F. Address at Rice University on the Nation's Space Effort. 12 September 1962. https://er.jsc.nasa.gov/seh/ricetalk.htm.

3. Shesol, Jeff. Lyndon Johnson's Unsung Role in Sending Americans to the Moon. *The New Yorker*. 20 July 2019.

4. Johnson, Lyndon B. Vice President's Memorandum for the President, "Evaluation of Space Program". *NASA Historical Refernce Collection*. 28 April 1961.

5. Shayler, David J and Moule, Ian. *Women in Space: Following Valentina*. Springer. 2005. p. 44.

6. Ibid., p. xxviii.

7. Berger, Eric. Netflix Film Examines Why NASA Shunned Women Astronauts in Early Days. *ArsTechnica*. 20 April 2018. https://arstechnica.com/science/2018/04/netflix-film-examines-why-nasa-shunned-women-astronauts-in-early-days.

8. Giggy, Sean. She Could've Been the First Woman in Space; 60 Years Later, She's About to Go. *WFAA*. 26 July 2019. https://www.wfaa.com/article/features/she-couldve-been-the-first-woman-in-space-60-years-later-shes-about-to-go/287-2da981f2-befe-4f19-8e16-b7c64405561f.

9. Leibach, Julie. The "Bunny Girl" on the Moon. *Science Friday*. 6 December 2013. https://www.sciencefriday.com/articles/the-bunny-girl-on-the-moon.

10. Rubio, Marco. Twitter, 31 August 2018. https://twitter.com/marcorubio/status/1035502827131613184.

15. We Come in Peace

1. Welles, Orson. War of the Worlds. *The Mercury Theatre of Air*. 30 October 1938.

2. The War of the Worlds: Myth or Legend? *ABC Radio National*. 24 August 2014.

3. Caspar, Max. *Kepler* (translated and edited by C. Doris Hellman). Dover Publications. 1993 [1959]. p. 130.

4. Achenbach, Joel. Biosphere 2: Bogus New World. *Washington Post*. 8 January 1992.

16. Force Majeure

1. Carter, Helen. Jedi Religion Founder Accuses Tesco of Discrimination Over Rules on Hoods. *The Guardian*. 18 September 2009.

2. Capon, Felicity. Thousands of Turkish Students Demand Jedi Temples on Campus. *Newsweek*. 7 April 2015.

3. Rakowitz, Michael. *The worst condition is to pass under a sword which is not one's own*. Tate Modern. 22 January – 12 May 2010.

a. Patell, Cyrus R K. *Cosmopolitanism and the Literary Imagination*. Palgrave MacMillan. 2015.

b. Padel, O J. The Nature of Arthur. *Cambrian Medieval Celtic Studies*, vol. 27. 1994.

17. Remember to Forget

1. Potter, Dan. *Ancient Egyptian Tomb Warnings, Curses and Ghosts*. National Museums Scotland. https://blog.nms.ac.uk/2017/06/23/ancient-egyptian-tomb-warnings-curses-and-ghosts.
2. Madsen, Michael (director). *Into Eternity* (film). 2010.
3. Sandia National Laboratories Report. Expert Judgement on Markers to Deter Inadvertent Human Intrusion into the Waste Isolation Pilot Plant. November 1993.
4. Human Interference Task Force. Technical Report: Reducing the Likelihood of Future Human Activities that Could Affect Geologic High-Level Waste Repositories. May 1984.
5. Musch, Sebastian. The Atomic Priesthood and Nuclear Waste Management: Religion, Sci-Fi Literature and the End of our Civilization. *Zygon, Journal of religion and science*, vol. 51, no. 3. September 2016.
6. *The Song Celestial, or Bhagavad-Gita* (From the Mahabharata) (translated by Sir Edwin Arnold). Truslove, Hanson & Comba, Ltd. 1900.
7. Oppenheimer, Robert. Security Hearing – 1954. *Atomic Heritage Foundation website*. https://www.atomicheritage.org/history/oppenheimer-security-hearing.
8. Oppenheimer, Robert. On the Trinity Test (video). *Atomic Archive*. 1945. https://www.atomicarchive.com/media/videos/oppenheimer.html
9. Oppenheimer, Robert. On the Trinity Test. *Atomic Archive*. 19 July 1945. https://www.atomicarchive.com/media/photographs/trinity/index.html.

18. A Rat in a Maze

1. The Great 1980s Dungeons and Dragons Panic. *BBC News*. 11 April 2014.
2. Schnoebelen, William. Straight Talk on Dungeons and Dragons. *Chick Publications*. https://www.chick.com/Information/article?id=Straight-Talk-On-Dungeons-and-Dragons.
3. Borges, Jorge Luis. The House of Asterion. *Collected Fictions* (translated by Andrew Hurley). Penguin books. 1998. p. 21.
4. Jerome, Jerome K. *Three Men in a Boat (To Say Nothing of the Dog)*. Dover Publications. 2018 [1889]. p. 40.

19. King of Cups

1. White, Alan. A Man "Confessed To Killing His Housemate" After A Tarot Card Reader Turned Over a "Death" Card. *BuzzFeed News*. 21 October 2015. https://www.buzzfeed.com/alanwhite/a-man-confessed-to-killing-his-housemate-after-a-tarot-card.
2. Eliot, T.S. *The Waste Land*. Faber & Faber. 1972 [1922]. p. 23.
3. Sutin, Lawrence. *Do What Thou Wilt: A Life of Aleister Crowley*. St Martin's Press. 2002. p. 372.
4–5. Eliot, T.S. *The Waste Land*. Faber & Faber. 1972 [1922]. p. 24.
6. Carl Gustav Jung, quoted in Greer, Mary K. Carl Jung and Tarot. *Mary K. Greer's Tarot Blog*. 31 March 2008. https://marykgreer.com/2008/03/31/carl-jung-and-tarot.
7. Steinbeck, John. *The Acts of King Arthur and His Noble Knights*. Farrar, Straus and Giroux. 1993. p. xi.
8. Twain, Mark. *Mark Twain's Notebooks and Journals*. https://twain.lib.virginia.edu/yankee/cycomphp.html.
9. Tolkein, J R R. Letter 131 to Milton Waldman. c. 1951. https://www.tolkienestate.com/en/writing/letters/letter-milton-waldman.html.

20. Paper Fairies

1. Miller, Russell. *The Adventures of Arthur Conan Doyle: A Biography*. Thomas Dunne Books. 2008. p. 394.
2–3. Conan Doyle, Arthur. *The Coming of the Fairies*. Hodder & Stoughton Ltd. 1922.
4. Losure, Mary. Sir Arthur and the Fairies. *The Public Domain Review*. June 12, 2013. https://publicdomainreview.org/essay/sir-arthur-and-the-fairies.
5. Sontag, Susan. *On Photography*. Dell Publishing. 1977. p. 9.
6. Lord Tennyson, Alfred. *The Princess*. Macmillan Company. 1917 [1847]. p. 57.

7. Tolkien, J R R. *The Lord of the Rings: The Fellowship of the Ring*. HarperCollins. 2012 [1954]. p. 336.
8. Ibid., p. 315.
9. Tolkien, J R R. *On Fairy-Stories. Tree and Leaf*. Houghton Mifflin Company. 1965. p. 5.
10. Allingham, William. "The Fairies", in *Poems*. Henry Holt and Co. 1989 [1850]. p. 23.
11. Sharp, William and Ernest Rhys. Oisin in Tirnanoge, or The Last of the Feni. In Warner, C D et al (eds). *The Library of the World's Best Literature, Volume VIII*. 1917. https://www.gutenberg.org/ebooks/33385.
12. Tolkien, J R R. *On Fairy-Stories. Tree and Leaf*. Houghton Mifflin Company. 1965. p. 10.
13. Ibid., p. 43.
14. Barrie, J M. *Peter Pan; or, the Boy Who Wouldn't Grow Up*. Borders Classics. 2006 [1911]. p. 22.
a. Conan Doyle, Arthur. The Adventure of the Sussex Vampire. *The Casebook of Sherlock Holmes*. Viking. 2011 [1924]. p. 114.

21. Paradise Lost

1. Lewis, C S. *The Chronicles of Narnia: The Last Battle*. Enrich Spot. 2016 [1956]. p. 114.
2. Barrie, J M. *Peter Pan; or, the Boy Who Wouldn't Grow Up*. Borders Classics. 2006 [1911]. p. 125.
3. *King James Bible*, Isaiah 11:6.
4. Christopher Milne, quoted in Ruggeri, Amanda. A A Milne and the Curse of Pooh Bear. *BBC Culture*. 28 January 2016.
5. Christopher Milne, quoted in Oliver, Mark. The Heartbreaking True Story of the Real Boy Behind Christopher Robin. *All That's Interesting*. 20 January 2019. https://allthatsinteresting.com/christopher-robin-milne.
6. Milne, Christopher. *The Enchanted Places*. Eyre Methuen. 1974. p. 77.
7. Windling, Terri. J. M. Barrie and Peter Pan. *Endicott Studio*. 2004. https://web.archive.org/web/20100426103530/http://www.endicott-studio.com/rdrm/rrPeterPan1.html.
8. Briggs, Julia. *A Woman of Passion: The Life of E. Nesbit*. New Amsterdam Books. 1987. p. 115.
9. Lawrence, Ben. Five Children and a Philandering Husband: E Nesbit's Private Life. *The Telegraph*. 2 April 2020.
10. MacCarthy, Fiona. *Eric Gill*. Faber and Faber. 1989. p. 239.

22. The Lady and the Unicorn

1. Stronk, Jan P. *Ctesias' Persian History: Part 1*. Wellem Verlag. 2010. p. 101.
2. Pliny the Elder. *Natural History* (translated by John F. Healy). Penguin Books. 1991 [c. AD 77].
3. Borges, Jorge Luis and Guerrero, Margarita. *The Book of Imaginary Beings* (translated by Norman Thomas di Giovanni). Avon Books. 1969. p. 239.
4. Isidore of Seville. *Thy Etymologies* (translated by Stephen A Barney, W J Lewis, J A Beach, and O Berghof). Cambridge University Press. 2010 [c. 600–625].
·5. Shakespeare, William. *The Tempest*. Act III Scene III.

23. Heads or Tails

1. Melville, Herman. *Moby-Dick; or, The Whale*. Harper and Brothers. 1851. p. 577.
2. Walsh, Paul. Group Finds Starbucks Logo Too Hot to Handle. *StarTribune*. 16 May 2008.
3. King, Colbert I. The Saudi Sellout. *The Washington Post*. 26 January 2002.
4. Homer. *The Odyssey* (translated by A T Murray). William Heinemann Ltd. 1919.
5. Sullivan, Blair and Symcox, Geoffrey. *Christopher Columbus and the Enterprise of the Indies: A Brief History with Documents*. Palgrave Macmillan, 2005. p. 83.
6. Andersen, Hans Christian. The Little Mermaid. *The Fairy Tales of Hans Christian Andersen*. Lippincott. 1899. p. 134.

7. Jazz Jennings Reveals the Reason Behind Her Love of Mermaids. *The List.* https://www.thelist.com/269036/jazz-jennings-reveals-the-reason-behind-her-love-of-mermaids.

8. St John, Sofia. Boys Can be Mermaids, Too. *Medium.* 14 January 2020. https://medium.com/@sstjohn96/review-of-julian-is-a-mermaid-e68ae27d8166.

9. Are Mermaids Real? *National Ocean Service.* https://oceanservice.noaa.gov/facts/mermaids.html.

24. The Human Animal

1. Hamilton, Edith. *Mythology.* Little, Brown and Company. 1942. p. 21.

2. Ovid. *Metamorphoses* (translated by Sir Samuel Garth and John Dryden). Printed by S Powell for G Risk, G Ewing and W Smith. 1727 [c. 8 AD].

3. Hutton, Ronald. *Witches, Druids, and King Arthur.* Bloomsbury Academic. 2006. p. 33.

4. Murray, Margaret. *The God of the Witches.* Oxford University Press. 1981 [1931]. p. 23.

5. *The Epic of Gilgamesh* (translated by Maureen Gallery Kovacs). Stanford University Press. 1989. p. 9.

6. Shakespeare, William. *A Midsummer Night's Dream.* Act III Scene II.

7. Bettelheim, Bruno. *The Uses of Enchantment: The Meaning and Importance of Fairy Tales.* Vintage Books. 2010 [1975]. p. 83.

8. Kafka, Franz. *The Metamorphosis* (translated by David Wyllie). Borders Classics. 2007 [1915]. p. 3.

a. Queen Elizabeth I. *Speech to the Troops at Tilbury.* August 9, 1588. https://www.rmg.co.uk/stories/topics/queen-elizabeth-speech-troops-tilbury.

25. The Pleasure Principle

1. Lord, Evelyn. *The Hell-Fire Clubs: Sex, Satanism and Secret Societies.* Yale University Press. 2008. p. 105.

2. Potter, Thomas and Wilkes, John. *An Essay on Women.* c. 1755. http://keithblayney.com/Blayney/Essay.html.

3. Cash, Arthur. *John Wilkes: The Scandalous Father of Civil Liberty.* Yale University Press. 2008. p. 152.

4. Thomas, Peter D G. *John Wilkes: A Friend to Liberty.* Oxford University Press. 1996. p. 66.

5–6. Beck, Marianna. The Roots of Western Pornography: The French Enlightenment Takes on Sex. *Libido: The Journal of Sex and Sensibility.* December 2003.

7. Pepys, Samuel. *Diary of Samuel Pepys.* George Bell & Sons. 1893 [1668]. 10 February 1668.

8. Anon. *The School of Venus, or the Ladies Delight, Reduced Into Rules of Practice*, translated from the French L'Âcole des filles. 1680 [1655]. p. 114.

9. Davis, Jennifer J. The Laws of Eighteenth-Century Sex: Thérèse Philosophe. *Fiction and Film for French Historians* (vols 1–8). https://h-france.net/fffh/classics/the-laws-of-eighteenth-century-sex-therese-philosophe.

10. Cleland, John. *Fanny Hill: Memoirs of a Woman of Pleasure.* Printed for G. Fenton in the Strand. 1749.

11. Coleridge, Ernest Hartley. Introduction to Lord Byron's Don Juan. *The Works of Lord Byron: Poetry, Volume VI.* John Murray. 1905 [1819-1824]. p. xviii.

12. William Wordsworth, quoted in Forward, Stephanie. An Introduction to Don Juan. *The British Library.* 15 May 2014 [1820].

13. Hoppenstand, Gary and Browne, Ray B (eds). *The Gothic World of Anne Rice.* Popular Press. 1996. p. 22.

26. Valley of the Dolls

1. Ovid. *Metamorphoses* (translated by Sir Samuel Garth and John Dryden). Printed by S Powell for G Risk, G Ewing and W Smith. 1727 [c. 8 AD].

2. Hoffman, E T A. The Sandman. *Tales from the German, comprising specimens from the most celebrated authors* (translated by John Oxenford and C. A. Feiling). Chapman and Hall. 1844. p. 162.

3. Jentsch, Ernst. *On the Psychology of the Uncanny* (translated by Roy Sellars). Palgrave Macmillan. 2008 [1906].

4. A Sneak Peak to the History of Sex Dolls. *Buy Sex Dolls Review: The Original Guide to Buying Sex Dolls*. 2 February 2021. https://sexdollsreviews.co/2021/02/02/a-sneak-peak-to-the-history-of-sex-dolls/.

5. Bloch, Iwan. *The Sexual Life of our Time in its Relations to Modern Civilization* (translated by M. Eden Paul). Rebman Limited. 1909 [1906]. p. 683.

6. Ferguson, Anthony. *The Sex Doll: A History*. McFarland & Company Inc. 2010. p 21.

7. David Levy, quoted in Dockterman, Elena. "It's Valentine's Day! Should you Have Sex With a Robot?". *Time*. 14 February 2017.

8. David Mills, quoted in Petersen, Paul. "Are You Really into a Real Sex Doll?" *Love is What You Want*. 24 May 2021. https://www.loveiswhatyouwant.com/are-you-really-into-a-real-sex-doll.

9. Levy, David. *Love and Sex with Robots: The Evolution of Human–Robot Relationships*. HarperCollins. 2007. p. 22.

a. Radcliffe, Ann. *On The Supernatural in Poetry*. 1826. https://repositorio.ufsc.br/bitstream/handle/123456789/208925/On%20Supernatural%20in%20Poetry%20(Ann%20Radcliffe).pdf.

b. Asimov, Isaac. *The Rest of the Robots*. Doubleday. 1964. p. xiii.

27. Ex Machina

1. Aristotle. *Poetics* (translated by S H Butcher). Macmillan and Co. 1922. [c. 335 BC]. Part 15(b).

2. Homer. *The Iliad* (translated by Samuel Butler). Longmans, Green, and Company. 1898 [c. 8th cen. BC]. Book XVIII.

3. Ronan, Colin A. *The Shorter Science and Civilization in China: An Abridgement of Joseph Needham's Original Text. Volume 1*. Cambridge University Press. 1978. p. 92.

4. Jentsch, Ernst. *On the Psychology of the Uncanny* (translated by Roy Sellars). Palgrave Macmillan 2008 [1906]. p. 10.

5. Hoffman, E T A. The Sandman. *Tales from the German, comprising specimens from the most celebrated authors* (translated by John Oxenford and C A Feiling). Chapman and Hall. 1844. p. 160.

6. Čapek, Karel. *R.U.R (Rossum's Universal Robots): A Fantastic Melodrama in Three Acts and an Epilogue* (translated by Paul Selver and Nigel Playfair). Dover Publications. 2001 [1920]. p. 34.

7. Asimov, Isaac. The Vocabulary of Science Fiction. *Isaac Asimov's Science Fiction Magazine*. September 1979.

8. Dick, Philip K. *Do Androids Dream of Electric Sheep?* Ballantine Books. 1982 [1968]. p. 14.

9. Harmon, Amy. Making Friends with a Robot Named Bina48. *New York Times*. 4 July 2010.

10. Turing, Alan M. Computing Machinery and Intelligence. *Mind*, vol. 49. 1950.

28. The Body Electric

1–2. George Foster, Executed at Newgate, 18th of January, 1803, for the Murder of his Wife and Child, by drowning them in the Paddington Canal; with a Curious Account of Galvanic Experiments on his Body. *The Newgate Calendar*. 1780. https://www.exclassics.com/newgate/ng464.htm.

3. Giovani Aldini, quoted in *Dr. Pembroke's Clinic: Live medical theater, horror, historical writings, and everything in between* (website). https://medicinemacabre.com/2017/12/18/electrifying-medicine-pt-4-memory-loss.

4. Fessenden, Thomas Green. *Terrible Tractoration, and Other Poems*. Russell, Shattuck & Co. 1836. p. 85.

5. Wilkinson, Charles. *Elements of Galvanism, in Theory and Practice*. Murray. 1804. p. 298.

6. Godwin, William. *Memoirs of the Author of a Vindication of the Rights of Woman*. Henry S. King & Co. 1876 [1798]. p. 276.

7. Marshall, Florence J Thomas. *The Life and Letters of Mary Wollstonecraft Shelley (Volume II)*. Richard Bentley & Son. 1889.

8–10. Shelley, Mary Wollstonecraft (Godwin). *Frankenstein; or, the Modern Prometheus*. Ulverscroft. 2014 [1818]. pp. 88, 158-160.

11–12. Marshall, Florence J Thomas. *The Life and Letters of Mary Wollstonecraft Shelley (Volume II)*. Richard Bentley & Son. 1889.

CR:

er

NOTES

29. Head Hunters
1. Khan, Ali S. Preparedness 101: Zombie Apocalypse. *Center for Disease Control and Prevention*. 16 May 2011. https://blogs.cdc.gov/publichealthmatters/2011/05/preparedness-101-zombie-apocalypse.
2. Seabrook, William. *The Magic Island*. Literary Guild of America. 1929. p. 93.
3. Twitchell, James. *Dreadful Pleasures: An Anatomy of Modern Horror*. Oxford University Press. 1985. p. 267.
4. *The Epic of Gilgamesh* (translated by Maureen Gallery Kovacs). Stanford University Press. 1989. p. 54.

30. Fear Itself
1. Wohleber, Curt. The Man Who Can Scare Stephen King. *American Heritage*, vol. 46, no. 8. 1995.
2–3. Everts, R Alain. *Howard Phillips Lovecraft and Sex: or The Sex Life of a Gentleman*. https://www.hplovecraft.com/study/articles/hpl-sex.aspx.
4. Lovecraft, H P. *The Call of Cthulhu*. Penguin Books. 1999 [1928]. p. 139.
5. Lovecraft, H P. *Supernatural Horror in Literature*. Wermod and Wermod Publishing Group. 2013 [1927]. p. 1.
6. Radcliffe, Ann. *On The Supernatural in Poetry*. 1826. https://repositorio.ufsc.br/bitstream/handle/123456789/208925/On%20Supernatural%20in%20Poetry%20(Ann%20Radcliffe).pdf.
7. *King James Bible*, Deuteronomy, 10:17.
8. Poe, Edgar Allan. *The Masque of the Red Death*. 1842. https://www.ibiblio.org/ebooks/Poe/Red_Death.pdf.
9. Hobson Quinn, Arthur. *Edgar Allan Poe: A Critical Biography*. Cooper Square Publishers. 1969. p. 638.
10. Poe's Burial and Grave. *New York Times*. February 26, 1893.
11. Hobson Quinn, Arthur. *Edgar Allan Poe: A Critical Biography*. Cooper Square Publishers. 1969. p. 643.
12. Poe, Edgar Allen. The Philosophy of Composition. *Graham Magazine*, vol. XXVIII, no. 4. April 1846.
13. Poe, Edgar Allen. Letter to George W. Eveleth. 4 January 1848. (LTR-259). https://www.eapoe.org/works/letters/p4801040.htm.
14. King, Stephen. *Danse Macabre*. Everest House. 1981. p. 144.
15. Revonsuo, Antti. The Reinterpretation of Dreams: An Evolutionary Hypothesis of the Function of Dreaming. *Behavioral and Brain Sciences*, vol. 23, no. 6. 2000.

31. Best of all Possible Worlds
1. Orwell, George. *1984*. Arcturus. 2015 [1949]. p. 254.
2. Ibid., p. 44.
3. Ibid., p. 11.
4. Ray Bradbury, quoted in Fishburn, Matthew. *Burning Books*. Palgrave MacMillan. 2008. p. 8.
5. Jameson, Frederick. The Politics of Utopia. *New Left Review*, vol. 25. 2004. p. 35.
6. Ibid., p. 39.
7. John Stewart Mill, in *Hansard Commons 1517/1*. 12 March 1868.
8. Zamyatin, Yevgeny. *A Soviet Heretic: Essays* (translated and edited by Mirra Ginsburg). University of Chicago Press. 1970. p. 57.
9. Zamyatin, Yevgeny. Letter to Stalin. June 1931. http://soviethistory.msu.edu/1929-2/proletarian-writers/proletarian-writers-texts/zamiatins-letter-to-stalin.
10. Gottfried Wilhelm Leibniz, quoted in Pojman, Louis P. and Rea, Michael (eds). *Philosophy of Religion: An Anthology*. Wadsworth Publishing. 1998. p. 173.
11. Huxley, Aldous. *Brave New World*. Vintage. 2007 [1932]. p. 159.
12. Orwell, George. Freedom and Happiness (Review of 'We' by Yevgeny Zamyatin). *Tribune*. 4 January 1946.
13. Orwell, George. *1984*. Arcturus. 2015 [1949]. p. 65.
14. Ibid., p. 273.
15–16. Ibid., p. 317.
17. Huxley, Aldous. *Brave New World*. Vintage. 2007 [1932]. p. 31.
18. Ibid., p. 218.

269

19. Zamyatin, Yevgeny. *WE* (translated by Gregory Zilboorg). Monadnock Valley Press. 1924 [1921]. https://monadnock.net/zamyatin/we.html.
20. Bradbury, Ray. *Fahrenheit 451*. Simon & Schuster. 2012 [1953]. p. 56.
21. Zamyatin, Yevgeny. *A Soviet Heretic: Essays* (translated and edited by Mirra Ginsburg). University of Chicago Press. 1970. p. 131.
22. Studio 360. A 17th-Century Alleged Witch Inspired Margaret Atwood's "The Handmaid's Tale". *The World*. 13 May 2017. https://theworld.org/stories/2017-05-13/17th-century-alleged-witch-inspired-margaret-atwoods-handmaids-tale.
23. Atwood, Margaret. *The Handmaid's Tale*. McClelland and Stewart, Houghton Mifflin Harcourt. 1986. p. 275.
24. Elgin, Suzette Haden. *Native Tongue*. DAW Books. 1984. p. 7.
25. Cixous, Helene. The Laugh of the Medusa (translated by Keith Cohen and Paula Cohen). *Signs*, vol. 1, no. 4. 1976.
26. Huxley, Aldous. *Brave New World*. Vintage. 2007 [1932]. p. 47.
27. Orwell, George. *1984*. Arcturus. 2015 [1949]. p. 273.
28. Bradbury, Ray. *Fahrenheit 451*. Simon & Schuster. 2012 [1953]. p. 92.
29. Jameson, Frederick. The Politics of Utopia. *New Left Review*, vol. 25. 2004. p. 53.
30. Zamyatin, Yevgeny. *WE* (translated by Gregory Zilboorg). Monadnock Valley Press. 1924 [1921]. https://monadnock.net/zamyatin/we.html.
31. Atwood, Margaret. *The Handmaid's Tale*. McClelland and Stewart, Houghton Mifflin Harcourt. 1986. p. 93.
32. Orwell, George. *1984*. Arcturus. 2015 [1949]. p. 273.
33. Atwood, Margaret. *The Handmaid's Tale*. McClelland and Stewart, Houghton Mifflin Harcourt. 1986. p. 295.
34. Bulgakov, Michail. *The Master and Margarita*. Penguin Books. 2016 [1966]. p. 358.
a. Borges, Jorge Luis. The Wall and the Books (translated by Gaither Stewart). https://southerncrossreview.org/54/borges-muralla.htm.

INDEX